SACRED MARRIAGE

WHAT IF GOD DESIGNED MARRIAGE TO MAKE US HOLY MORE THAN TO MAKE US HAPPY?

GARY THOMAS

ZONDERVAN

Sacred Marriage

This title is also available as a Zondervan ebook. Visit www.zondervan.com/ebooks.

This title is also available in a Zondervan audio edition. Visit www.zondervan.fm.

Requests for information should be addressed to:

Zondervan, *3900 Sparks Dr., Grand Rapids, Michigan 49546*

Library of Congress Cataloging-in-Publication Data

Thomas, Gary, 1961-
Sacred Marriage : what if God designed marriage to make us holy more than to make us happy / Gary Thomas.
p. cm.
Includes bibliographical references.
ISBN 978-0-310-33737-9
1. Spouses—Religious life. 2. Marriage—Religious aspects—Christianity. 3. Spiritual life—Christianity. I. Title.
BV4596.M3 T46 2004
248.4-dc 23 99-053471

Published in association with Yates & Yates, www.yates2.com.

Cover design: James Hall
Cover photography or illustration: Ksenia Palimski / Shutterstock®
Interior design: Matthew Van Zomeren

Printed in the United States of America
Printed June 2015

PRAISE FOR *SACRED MARRIAGE*

A classic! *Sacred Marriage* lifts the first institution God created back to its noble stature. Every person contemplating marriage and every married couple should read this book.

Dr. Dennis Rainey, president of FamilyLife

Sacred Marriage is one of the best marriage books we've ever read—it's a classic. Every couple who prizes their faith and their relationship needs to read this incredible book.

Drs. Les and Leslie Parrott,
authors of Saving Your Marriage Before It Starts

Thoughtful, deep, and truly impactful. I recommend *Sacred Marriage* to engaged couples, those who have been married for decades, and everyone in-between. The heart of this book will speak to every person who wants to see God alive and at work in their marriage.

Kevin G. Harney, author of Empowered by His Presence
and the Organic Outreach series *(KevinGHarney.com)*

Much of Jesus' teaching challenges our paradigm—to find our life, we must lose it; the greatest among us is the servant; and so on. In that same spirit, Gary Thomas challenges our paradigm of marriage. *Sacred Marriage* has inspired many to consider that marriage is more about holiness than happiness. May millions more in generations to come embrace this life-giving message!

Dr. Juli Slattery, clinical psychologist
and president of Authentic Intimacy

I have personally been blessed and helped by the words in this book that will breathe hope in any relationship.

Gregory Jantz, PhD, founder of The Center: A Place of Hope

Also by Gary Thomas

Authentic Faith

Devotions for a Sacred Marriage

Devotions for Sacred Parenting

Every Body Matters

The Glorious Pursuit

Holy Available (previously titled *The Beautiful Fight*)

A Lifelong Love

Not the End but the Road

Pure Pleasure

Sacred Influence

Sacred Marriage

Sacred Parenting

Sacred Pathways

The Sacred Search

Simply Sacred

Thirsting for God (previously titled *Seeking the Face of God*)

For Lisa

CONTENTS

Chapter 1

THE GREATEST CHALLENGE IN THE WORLD

A Call to Holiness More Than Happiness

> By all means marry. If you get a good wife, you'll become happy. If you get a bad one, you'll become a philosopher.
>
> *Socrates*

I'm going to cut him open.

Historians aren't sure who the first physician was who followed through on this thought, but the practice revolutionized medicine. The willingness to cut into a corpse, peel back the skin, pull a scalp off a skull, cut through the bone, and actually remove, examine, and chart the organs that lay within was a crucial first step in finding out how the human body really works.

For thousands of years, physicians had speculated on what went on inside a human body, but there was a reluctance and even an abhorrence to actually dissect a cadaver. Some men refrained out of religious conviction; others just couldn't get over the eeriness of cutting away a human rib cage. While an occasional brave soul ventured inside a dead body, it wasn't until the Renaissance period (roughly the fourteenth to sixteenth centuries) that European doctors routinely started to cut people open.

And when they did, former misconceptions collapsed. In the sixteenth century, Andreas Vesalius was granted a ready supply of criminals' corpses, allowing him to definitively contradict assumptions about the human anatomy that had been unquestioned for a thousand years or more. Vesalius's anatomical charts became invaluable, but he couldn't have drawn the charts unless he was first willing to make the cuts.

I want to do a similar thing in this book—with a spiritual twist. We're going to cut open numerous marriages, dissect them, find out what's really going on, and then explore how we can gain spiritual meaning, depth, and growth from the challenges that lie within. We're not after simple answers—three steps to more intimate communication, six steps to a more exciting love life—because this isn't a book that seeks to tell you how to have a happier marriage. This is a book that looks at how we can use the challenges, joys, struggles, and celebrations of marriage to draw closer to God and to grow in Christian character.

We're after what Francis de Sales wrote about in the seventeenth century. Because de Sales was a gifted spiritual director, people often corresponded with him about their spiritual concerns. One woman wrote in great distress, torn because she wanted to get married while a friend was encouraging her to remain single, insisting it would be "more holy" for her to care for her father and then devote herself as a celibate to God after her father died.

De Sales put the troubled young woman at ease, telling her that, far from being a compromise, in one sense, marriage might be the toughest ministry she could ever undertake. "The state of marriage is one that requires more virtue and constancy than any other," he wrote. "It is a perpetual exercise of mortification

... In spite of the bitter nature of its juice, you may be able to draw and make the honey of a holy life."[1]

Notice that de Sales talks about the occasionally "bitter nature" of marriage's "juice." To spiritually benefit from marriage, we have to be honest. We have to look at our disappointments, own up to our ugly attitudes, and confront our selfishness. We also have to rid ourselves of the notion that the difficulties of marriage can be overcome if we simply pray harder or learn a few simple principles. Most of us have discovered that these "simple steps" work only on a superficial level. Why is this? Because there's a deeper question that needs to be addressed beyond how we can "improve" our marriage: What if God didn't design marriage to be "easier"? What if God had an end in mind that went beyond our happiness, our comfort, and our desire to be infatuated and happy, as if the world were a perfect place?

THIS BOOK LOOKS AT HOW WE CAN USE THE CHALLENGES, JOYS, STRUGGLES, AND CELEBRATIONS OF MARRIAGE TO DRAW CLOSER TO GOD AND TO GROW IN CHRISTIAN CHARACTER.

What if God designed marriage to make us holy more than to make us happy? What if, as de Sales hints, we are to accept the "bitter juice" because out of it we may learn to draw the resources we need with which to make "the honey of a holy life"?

This isn't to suggest that happiness and holiness are contradictory. On the contrary, I believe we'll live the happiest, most joy-filled lives when we walk in obedience. John Wesley once boldly proclaimed that it is not possible for a man to be happy who is not also holy, and the way he explains it makes much sense. Who can be truly "happy" while filled with anger, rage, and malice? Who can be happy while nursing resentment or envy? Who can be honestly happy while caught in the sticky compulsion of an insatiable lust or incessant materialism? The glutton may enjoy his food, but he does not enjoy his condition.

So we're not anti-happiness; that would be silly. The problem I'm trying to address is that a "happy marriage" (defined romantically and in terms of pleasant feelings) is too often the endgame of most marriage books (even Christian marriage books). This is a false promise. You won't find happiness at the end of a road named selfishness.

This is a book that looks and points *beyond* marriage. Spiritual growth is the main theme; marriage is simply the context. Just as celibates use abstinence and religious hermits use isolation, so we can use marriage for the same purpose—to grow in our service, obedience, character, pursuit, and love of God.

For centuries, Christian spirituality was virtually synonymous with celibate spirituality; that is, even married people thought we had to become like monks and nuns to grow in the Lord. We'd have to do the same spiritual exercises, best performed by single people (long periods of prayer that don't allow for child rearing or marital discussion, seasons of fasting that make preparing meals difficult for a family, times of quiet meditation that seem impossible when kids of any age are in the house), rather than seeing how God could use our marriages to help us grow in character, in prayer, in worship, and in service. Rather than develop a spirituality in which marriage serves our pursuit of holiness, the church focused on how closely married people could mimic "single spirituality" without neglecting their family. The family thus became an obstacle to overcome rather than a platform to spiritual growth.

The reason the marriage relationship is often seen as a selfish one is because our motivations for marrying often *are* selfish. But my desire is to reclaim marriage as one of the most selfless states a Christian can enter. This book sees marriage the way medieval writers saw the monastery: as a setting full of opportunities to foster spiritual growth and service to God.

You've probably already realized there was a purpose for your marriage that went beyond happiness. You might not have chosen the word *holiness* to express it, but you understood there was a transcendent truth beyond the superficial romance depicted in popular culture. We're going to explore that purpose. We're going to cut open many marriages, find out where the commitment rubs, explore where the poisoned attitudes hide, search out where we are forced to confront our weakness and sin, and learn how to grow through the process.

We'll also look at what Scripture, church history, and the Christian classics can tell us. You'll find that the classics are amazingly relevant and that the past influences the present far more than many people think.

The ultimate purpose of this book is not to make you love your spouse more—although I think that will happen along the way; it's to equip you to love your God more and to help you reflect the character of his Son more precisely. At the very least, you'll have a new appreciation for the person with whom you have embarked on this journey.

I also pray it will help you to love your marriage more, appreciate your marriage more, and inspire you to become even more engaged in your relationship with your spouse. When you realize something is "sacred," far from making it boring, it gives birth to a new reverence, a take-your-breath-away realization that something you may have been taking for granted is far more profound, far more life-giving and life-transforming, than you may ever have realized.

THE ULTIMATE PURPOSE OF THIS BOOK IS NOT TO MAKE YOU LOVE YOUR SPOUSE MORE; IT'S TO EQUIP YOU TO LOVE YOUR GOD MORE.

I *love* marriage, and I love *my* marriage. I love the fun parts, the easy parts, and the pleasurable parts, but also the difficult parts—the parts that frustrate me but help me understand myself and my spouse on a deeper level; the parts that are painful but that crucify the aspects of me that I hate; the parts that force me to my knees and teach me that I need to learn to love with God's love instead of just trying harder. Marriage has led me to deeper levels of understanding, more pronounced worship, and a sense of fellowship that I never knew existed.

"Sacred" isn't my brand; it's my way of life. And applying it to my marriage has transformed every one of my days. I believe it can do the same for you.

Chapter 2

ROMANTICISM'S RUSE

How Marriage Points Us to True Fulfillment

> Like everything which is not the involuntary result of fleeting emotion but the creation of time and will, any marriage, happy or unhappy, is infinitely more interesting than any romance, however passionate.
>
> *W. H. Auden*

While holiness as a goal of marriage may sound like a radically different view of marriage, the very concept of "romantic love," which is celebrated in movies, songs, and novels, was virtually unknown to the ancients. There were exceptions—one need merely read Song of Songs, for instance—but taken as a whole, the concept that marriage should involve passion and fulfillment and excitement is a relatively recent development on the scale of human history, making its popular entry toward the end of the eleventh century.[1]

This is not to suggest that romance itself or the desire for more romance is necessarily bad; after all, God created the romantic component of our brain chemistry, and good marriages work hard to preserve a sense of romance. But the idea that a marriage can survive on romance alone, or that romantic feelings are more important than any other consideration when choosing a spouse, has wrecked many a marital ship.

Romanticism received a major boost by means of the eighteenth-century Romantic poets—Wordsworth, Coleridge, and Blake—followed by their successors in literature, Byron, Shelley, and Keats. These poets passionately argued that it was a crime against oneself to marry for any reason other than "love" (which was defined largely by feeling and emotion), and the lives of many of them were parodies of irresponsibility and tragedy.

For example, one of the writers who embraced this romantic notion with fervor was the sensuous novelist D. H. Lawrence, whose motto was "With *should* and *ought* I shall have nothing to do!" Lawrence fell in love with Frieda Weekley, a married woman, and sought to woo Frieda away from her husband, as his "love" demanded he do. As part of his less-than-noble designs, Lawrence sent Frieda a note, proclaiming that she was the most wonderful woman in all of England.

Being married with three children and having already suffered a couple of affairs, Mrs. Weekley saw through Lawrence's emotion and coolly replied that it was obvious to her he had not met many Englishwomen.[2]

In her startling and insightful essay on marriage written in the 1940s (titled, interestingly enough, "The Necessary Enemy"), twentieth-century writer Katherine Anne Porter bemoaned how "Romantic Love crept into the marriage bed, very stealthily, by centuries, bringing its absurd notions about love as eternal springtime and marriage as a personal adventure meant to provide personal happiness."[3] The reality of the human condition is such that, according to Porter (and I agree), we must "salvage our fragments of happiness" out of life's inevitable sufferings.[4]

Porter carefully explores the heights and depths of marriage, making the following observations about a young bride:

> This very contemporary young woman finds herself facing the oldest and ugliest dilemma of marriage. She is dismayed, horrified, full of guilt and forebodings because she is finding out little by little that she is capable of hating her husband, whom she loves faithfully. She can hate him at times as fiercely and mysteriously, indeed in terribly much the same way, as often she hated her parents, her brothers and sisters, whom she loves, when she was a child ... She thought she had outgrown all this, but here it was again, an element in her own nature she could not control, or feared she could not. She would have to hide from her husband, if she could, the same spot in her feelings she had hidden from her parents, and for the same no doubt disreputable, selfish reason: she wants to keep his love.[5]

With only a romantic view of marriage to fall back on, Porter warns, a young woman may lose her "peace of mind. She is afraid her marriage is going to fail because ... at times she feels a painful hostility toward her husband, and cannot admit its reality because such an admission would damage in her own eyes her view of what love should be."[6]

Romantic love has no elasticity to it. It can never be stretched; it simply shatters. Mature love, the kind demanded of a good marriage, *must* stretch, as the sinful human condition is such that all of us bear conflicting emotions. "Her hatred is real as her love is real," Porter explains of the young wife.[7] This is the reality of the human heart, the inevitability of two sinful people pledging to live together, with all their faults, for the rest of their lives.

ROMANTIC LOVE HAS NO ELASTICITY TO IT. IT CAN NEVER BE STRETCHED; IT SIMPLY SHATTERS.

A wedding calls us to our highest and best—in fact, to almost impossible—ideals. It's the way we *want* to live. But marriage reminds us of the daily reality of living as sinful human beings in a radically broken world. We aspire after love but far too often descend into hate and apathy.

Any mature, spiritually sensitive view of marriage must be built on the foundation of mature love rather than romanticism. But this immediately casts us into a countercultural pursuit.

In his classic work *The Screwtape Letters*, C. S. Lewis satirically ridicules our culture's obsession with romanticism. The demon Screwtape, a mentor to the demon Wormwood, gloats:

> Humans who have not the gift of [sexual abstinence] can be deterred from seeking marriage as a solution because they do not find themselves "in love," and, thanks to us, the idea of marrying with any other motive seems to them low and cynical. Yes, they think that. They regard the intention of loyalty to a partnership for mutual help, for the preservation of chastity, and for the transmission of life, as something lower than a storm of emotion.[8]

I think most of us who have been married for any substantial length of time realize that the romantic roller coaster of courtship eventually evens out to the terrain of a Midwest interstate—long, flat stretches with an occasional overpass. When this happens, couples respond in different ways. Many will end their relationship and try to re-create the passionate romance with someone else. Other couples will descend into a sort of marital guerrilla warfare as each partner blames the other for personal dissatisfaction or lack of excitement. Some couples decide to simply "get along." Still others may opt to pursue a deeper meaning, a spiritual truth hidden in the enforced intimacy of the marital situation.

WE CAN RUN FROM THE CHALLENGES OF MARRIAGE, OR WE CAN ADMIT THAT EVERY MARRIAGE PRESENTS THESE CHALLENGES AND ASKS US TO ADDRESS THEM HEAD-ON.

We can run from the challenges of marriage—as doctors did from the human body, refusing to cut open the cadavers and really look at what was going on—or we can admit that every marriage presents these challenges and asks us to address them head-on. If we find that the same kinds of challenges face every marriage, we might assume God designed a purpose in this challenge that transcends something as illusory as happiness.

This book looks for that purpose and meaning and asks this question: How can we discover in the challenges of marriage the opportunities to learn more about God, grow in our understanding of him, and learn to love him more?

Numerous married couples have opened up their lives for us in this book, so I suppose it's only fair that I should allow my own marriage to be dissected first.

AN UNEXPECTED ENGAGEMENT

Lisa and I often wonder what would have happened if she had said yes.

During a free afternoon at a college campus ministry retreat when we were still dating, I asked Lisa to join a group of us for a round of Frisbee golf.

"No thanks," Lisa said. "I think I'll go for a walk instead."

She had recently returned from a summerlong mission trip to Mexico, and this retreat was supposed to be a time when Lisa and I could reconnect. We had known each other since junior high and had been dating for about a year, and we were getting "serious." Unknown to Lisa, I had asked my best friend, Rob Takemura, to begin praying about whether I should ask Lisa to marry me. And unknown to me, Lisa and her mother had spent a Saturday afternoon the week before looking at wedding dresses, "just in case" Lisa should ever need one.

I was somewhat frustrated that Lisa wasn't being cooperative, so I said, "Fine, I won't play Frisbee golf either."

"You can," Lisa said. "I don't mind walking alone."

"No, I'll go with you," I said.

We walked along the river, set inside a stunning valley on the outskirts of Glacier National Park, and talked for about forty-five minutes. Suddenly, I stopped skimming rocks, and virtually out of nowhere I said to Lisa, "I want to marry you."

Lisa's mouth dropped open.

"Is that a proposal?" she asked, astonished.

I shook my head yes, just as astonished as she was. Lisa came up and hugged me.

"Is that an acceptance?" I asked, and Lisa nodded in the affirmative.

"Whew," she said after a brief moment. "Imagine if I had agreed to play Frisbee."

We laughed about it and then experienced one of the most intense times emotionally I've ever known. There was a strange, almost mystical commingling of souls. Something was going on inside us, around us, and through us that superseded any physical connection. It was somehow deeper, more meaningful, and more amazing than anything we had ever experienced.

Over the next nine months, we made plans, as any engaged couple does. We talked about mission work, family, seminary, serving God—you name it. It was an intense time, and we often prayed, "Lord, wherever you want to take us, however you want to use us, we're all yours."

We never slept together until our wedding night, so our honeymoon was a rather intoxicating experience, but once the honeymoon was over, reality immediately set in like a dense Seattle fog.

Because I was planning to save up money for seminary, we spent our first few months living in a very tiny home, offered to us rent-free by a family friend. I left for work two days after we got back, and Lisa was stranded in a small community, out in the middle of nowhere, and she began to cry.

It was a sunny day, so she called me at work and asked if I could come home early so we could drive to a lake. I thought she was crazy. "I can't just leave work because the weather's nice!" I protested. "Besides, I just started this job!"

"Well, what's the use of getting married if I see you less now than when we were engaged?" she complained.

What's the use, indeed?

Fast-forward ten years. We had three small children, two of them in diapers. I was working for a Christian ministry, and we were still "just making it" financially, snuggled into a town house in northern Virginia. We were about to enter our Friday-night ritual—laundry and a rented movie.

"What do you want to watch?" I asked Lisa as I gathered my keys and headed out the door.

"Oh, how about a romantic comedy?" Lisa answered.

I cringed. The last three videos we had watched together had been romantic comedies. I couldn't bear to watch another impossibly beautiful couple "meet cute" under extremely improbable circumstances, fall in love, get in a fight, and then spend sixty minutes falling back in love again.

I sighed, looked at Lisa, and said. "I'm sorry. I just can't do it. I have to see at least one building blow up and one car crash. If I can find something that has a little romance to add to that, I'll see what I can do."

I took three steps out the door, then thought to myself, *When did "Please, God, change the world through us" suddenly become "Should we watch Arnold Schwarzenegger or Julia Roberts?"* I didn't remember any fork in the road or any flashing neon signs that pointed in that direction, but somehow, somewhere, it had happened.

WHAT WAS THIS THING CALLED MARRIAGE? HOW HAD I ENDED UP HERE? WAS THERE NO MORE PURPOSE TO IT THAN THIS?

I remembered the intensity of the night on which we had become engaged, the joyful exploration of our honeymoon, filling out a preliminary application for a mission organization, bringing our first child home—but now, ten years later, we had "evolved" into spending Friday nights watching other people fall in love according to the machinations of a Hollywood script.

That night I didn't have any answers, but taking an honest look at my situation definitely shook me awake. *What was this thing called marriage? How had I ended up here? Was there no more purpose to it than this?*

"IT IS GOOD FOR A MAN NOT TO MARRY"

I became a Christian at a very young age. In truth, I can scarcely remember a moment when God was not an active and conscious presence in my life. Because of this, I felt drawn to Jesus early on.

I was drawn to more than Jesus, however; I also remember being drawn to girls. I had a pretty big crush on a dark-haired girl *in kindergarten*! The first time I actually held hands with a girl was in fifth grade. Tina and I rolled around the skating rink, both of us blushing as the Carpenters' melodious harmonies described us well: "I'm On Top of the World." It sure felt like it!

As I grew older, both of these movements—toward Jesus and toward females—sometimes created an uneasy tension. The man I most admired, the one person on whom I wanted to model my life was a *single man*. As a big fan of the Christian classics—ancient books focused on building intimacy with God—I was fully aware of the long-standing tradition of celibacy—monks and nuns who lived out their dedication to God by pledging to abstain from marriage and sex. Because I knew their love for God was so intense, part of me wished I could embrace this; I wanted to be sold-out for Christ, and in college I struggled with the apostle Paul's words, "It is good for a man not to marry" (1 Corinthians 7:1, as found in the 1984 edition of the NIV).[9]

In fact, there is much in Christian history that has unofficially (and at times blatantly) considered married believers to be second-class Christians who compromised their integrity or were too weak to contain their sexual urges. Augustine thought he was being charitable when he wrote, referring to the intent to procreate, "Marital intercourse makes something good out of the evil of lust."[10] Scripture may be infallible, but Christian history isn't, and unfounded prejudices do exist.

There's no question that the "first pope," Peter, was married. (Jesus couldn't very well have healed Peter's mother-in-law if Peter didn't have a wife!) But there is also evidence in

Scripture (1 Timothy 5:9–12) that during the first century young widows were already taking vows of celibacy. By AD 110, celibates could take vows that mirrored marital vows. This became a little more institutionalized so that by the third century, lifelong vows of celibacy were not uncommon. By the fourth century, such vows were commemorated by a full liturgical celebration.[11]

Although Christianity was born out of Judaism, a religion in which marriage was considered a religious duty (one rabbi suggested that a man who does not marry is not fully a man),[12] it wasn't long until married believers were scarcely an afterthought during centuries of writing on spiritual theology (studying how Christian believers grow in their faith, learn to pray, and draw closer to God). Most of the Christian classics were written *by* monks and nuns *for* monks and nuns. The married could at best feebly try to simulate a single pursuit of God; the thought of pursuing God *through* marriage wasn't really given serious consideration; instead, the emphasis was largely on pursuing God *in spite of* marriage.

THERE IS MUCH IN CHRISTIAN HISTORY THAT HAS UNOFFICIALLY CONSIDERED MARRIED BELIEVERS TO BE SECOND-CLASS CHRISTIANS WHO COMPROMISED THEIR INTEGRITY OR WERE TOO WEAK TO CONTAIN THEIR SEXUAL URGES.

I carried some of this baggage into my own relationship, but early on, my eyes were opened to a different reality. I remember my brother asking me a few questions about what marriage was like. I thought for a moment and said, "If you want to be free to serve Jesus, there's no question—stay single. Marriage takes a lot of time. But if you want to become more like Jesus, I can't imagine any better thing to do than to get married. Being married forces you to face some character issues you'd never have to face otherwise." I had begun to realize I could further pursue God through marriage and not just in spite of it. Marriage didn't need to hold me back from my spiritual goals; it could actually help me reach them.

Jesus, of course, was celibate his entire life, so it's somewhat ironic to suggest that marriage is the preferred route to becoming more like him. But Jesus did live in a family, and, as Betsy Ricucci points out, that's all he had done at the time the Father proclaimed, "This is my Son, whom I love; with him I am well pleased" (Matthew 3:17). "What had Jesus done to receive such praise? Nothing but live in his own home, honoring his parents and serving his father's carpentry business. Apparently that was enough to please God."[13]

Family life is clearly not a compromise, and after you've been married for a while, you realize that the emphasis on celibacy is slightly overblown. All things considered, the sexual aspect takes up just a fraction of a married couple's time. I was the first of my group of friends to get married, and I remember one of them asking me if it was still okay to just "drop in" unannounced.

"Oh, you better call first," I said gravely, capturing his attention. "Married couples walk around naked all day long, you know."

For a second, I almost had him!

The real transforming work of marriage is the twenty-four-hours-a-day, seven-days-a-week commitment. This is the crucible that grinds and shapes us into the character of Jesus Christ. Instead of getting up at 3:00 a.m. to begin prayer in a monastery, the question becomes, "Who will wake up when the baby's diaper needs changing?"

Marriage calls us to an entirely new and selfless life. This insight occurred to me some years ago when Lisa and the kids were traveling while I stayed home and worked. For the first time ever, it seemed, I had a free Saturday. For as long as I could remember, I had awakened each weekend and talked over with Lisa what the family would do; I almost didn't know how to ask the question—what do *I* want to do? Yet that was the question I had asked myself as a single man virtually every Saturday before I was married.

ANY SITUATION THAT CALLS ME TO CONFRONT MY SELFISHNESS HAS ENORMOUS SPIRITUAL VALUE.

Any situation that calls me to confront my selfishness has enormous spiritual value, and I slowly began to understand that the real purpose of marriage may not be happiness as much as it is holiness. Not that God has anything against happiness or that happiness and holiness are mutually exclusive, but looking at marriage through the lens of holiness began to put it into an entirely new perspective for me.

"BUT SINCE SEXUAL IMMORALITY IS OCCURRING"

In this regard, I find it fascinating that just after Paul said, "It is good for a man not to have sexual relations with a woman," he follows it up with these words: "But since sexual immorality is occurring, each man should have sexual relations with his own wife, and each woman with her own husband" (1 Corinthians 7:2).

Though this passage refers to sexual relations, we can extend the principle to reveal truth beyond physical intimacy. Since there is so much immorality within us—not just lust, but selfishness, unrighteous anger, control mongering, and even hatred—we should enter into a close relationship with one other person so we can work on those issues in the light of what our marriage relationship will reveal to us about our behavior and our attitudes. In other words, not only is marriage a way for God to redeem us sexually; it is also a means by which God can redeem us in other areas of character.

I found a tremendous amount of immaturity within me that my marriage directly confronted. The key was that I had to change my view of marriage. If the purpose of marriage is simply to make me happy and enjoy an infatuation (which neuroscience suggests lasts a mere twelve to eighteen months), then I'd have to get a new marriage every two or three years. But if I really wanted to see God transform me from the inside out, I'd need to concentrate on changing *myself* rather than on changing *my spouse*. In fact, you might even say, the more difficult my spouse proved to be, the more opportunity I'd have to grow. Just as physical exercise needs to be somewhat strenuous, so relational exercise may need to be a bit vigorous to truly stress-test the heart.

I didn't decide to focus on changing myself so I could have a tension-free marriage or so I'd be happier or even more content in my marriage. Instead, I adopted the attitude that marriage is one of many life situations that helps me draw my sense of meaning, purpose, and fulfillment *from God*. Lisa can't make me happy, not in an ultimate sense. Certainly we have some great times together, and she is a wonderful wife, exceeding my dreams—but these great times are sprinkled with (and sometimes seem to get buried in) the demands, challenges, and expectations of paying the bills on time, disciplining children, earning a living, and keeping a house clean.

> IF THE PURPOSE OF MARRIAGE WAS SIMPLY TO ENJOY AN INFATUATION AND MAKE ME HAPPY, THEN I'D HAVE TO GET A NEW MARRIAGE EVERY TWO OR THREE YEARS.

I guess what I'm after is a quieter fulfillment, a deeper sense of meaning, a fuller understanding of the purpose behind this intense, one-on-one, lifelong relationship. As a man who believes his primary meaning comes from his relationship with God, I want to explore how marriage can draw me closer to God.

There's another reason to stress this: Marriage, for all of us, is temporary in the light of eternity. The truth is, my and Lisa's relationships with God will outlive our marriage. Most likely the time will come when either Lisa or I precede the other into eternity. The remaining spouse will be left alone, no longer married—perhaps even eventually married to someone else.

For the Christian, marriage is a penultimate rather than an ultimate reality. Because of this, both of us can find even more meaning by pursuing God together and by recognizing that he is the one who alone can fill the spiritual ache in our souls. We can work at making our home life more pleasant and peaceable; we can explore ways to keep sex fresh and fun; we can make superficial changes that will preserve at least the appearance of respect and politeness. But what both of us crave more than anything else is to be intimately close to the God who made us. If that relationship is right, we won't make such severe demands on our marriage, asking each other to compensate for spiritual emptiness. If what we desire most doesn't satisfy us, we will never be satisfied, even when our "desires" have been met! That's why finding our fulfillment in God is the cornerstone of a satisfied life. We can harm our marriages by asking too much of them.

Unfortunately, as a fallible human being I can't possibly appreciate Lisa the way God appreciates her. I can't even begin to understand her the way she longs to be understood. I'd get bored with myself if I was married to me, so it only makes sense that Lisa might occasionally be bored—or at least grow weary—of living with me.

One thing is sure: Lisa can't look to me to be God for her. And even when I try to love her like only God can love her, I fail every time and on every count. I give it my best, but I fall short every day.

LOOKING FOR LOVE IN ALL THE WRONG PLACES

We need to remind ourselves of the ridiculousness of looking for something from other humans that only God can provide. Our close friends have a son named Nolan. When he was just four years old, he saw me carrying some large boxes and asked me in all sincerity, "Gary, are you strongest or is God strongest?"

His dad laughed a little too hard at that one. And of course we adults think it's absurd to compare our physical strength with God's. But how many of us adults have then turned around and asked, perhaps unconsciously, "Are you going to fulfill me, or will God fulfill me?" For some reason, *that* question doesn't sound as absurd to us as the one about physical strength, but it should.

I believe that much of the dissatisfaction we experience in marriage comes from expecting too much from it. Though marriage is an amazing institution that reflects God's creative genius, when we want to get the largest portion of our life's fulfillment from our relationship with our spouse, that's asking too much. God didn't design marriage to compete with himself but to point us to himself. Yes, without a doubt there should be moments of happiness, meaning, and a general sense of fulfillment. And, of course, seeking God *together*, through our marriage, is certainly fulfilling in itself. But my wife can't be God, and I was created with a spirit that craves God. Anything less than God, and I'll feel an ache.

Now this is where it gets *really* interesting. Looked at in this light, rather than competing with or impeding our walk with God, marriage can actually point us *to* God. This is a big enough thought that it deserves a chapter all its own.

CHAPTER 3

FINDING GOD IN MARRIAGE

Marital Analogies Teach Us Truths about God

> [Marriage] is the merciless revealer, the great white searchlight turned on the darkest places of human nature.
> *Katherine Anne Porter*

For about a decade after college, I joined eight of my former classmates for an annual weekend retreat. On one particular retreat, a good friend pulled me aside and mentioned that he was considering returning home that night; he and his wife were hoping to conceive another child, and by his wife's calculations the time was right.

"Do it," I urged him. "You can be back by breakfast."

"I don't know . . . ," he said hesitantly.

"Do it," I said more strongly, and another friend weighed in with his support.

Finally, he gave in and went home. That night a child was conceived.

I look at that child now and smile, wondering if he'll ever know how close he came to not being (and how much he owes me!). There are few more dizzying realities of life than cooperating with God to produce another human being. If my friend and his wife had waited another month, perhaps they would have had a girl or a shorter boy or a boy with darker hair. It's amazing.

This aspect of the marital experience—cooperating with God to bring children into being—should be particularly meaningful for Christians (and a key reason that having difficulty conceiving can be so painful to so many couples). The picture of God as Creator is central to his authority, identity, and purpose. In fact, the Bible is framed around the fact that God is Creator. The first thing we learn about God in the book of Genesis is that he created the heavens and the earth (Genesis 1:1); the last image of the New Testament shows God creating a new heaven and a new earth. When God says, "I am making everything new!" (Revelation 21:5), the word *making* is in the present tense. It's an ongoing process. God walks into eternity creating.

A GIANT THREAD RUNS THROUGHOUT SCRIPTURE COMPARING GOD'S RELATIONSHIP TO HIS PEOPLE WITH THE HUMAN INSTITUTION OF MARRIAGE.

This is just one of several analogies that connect various aspects of marriage with our understanding of God. A giant thread runs throughout Scripture comparing God's relationship to his people with the human institution of marriage. In this chapter, we'll explore how these various analogies use the experience of marriage to teach us valuable truths about the nature of God. Through the experience of being married, we can come to know God in new ways.

DIVINE ROMANCE

The prophet Hosea leads us into a startling reality—that God views his people as a husband views his wife: "'In that day,' declares the Lord, 'you will call me "my husband"; you will no longer call me "my master." ... I will betroth you to me forever'" (Hosea 2:16, 19). Think about the difference between a husband and a master—and all that these images conjure up in your mind. God wants us to relate to him with an obedience fueled by love and intimacy, not by self-motivated fear, and with a loyalty to a divine-human relationship, not a blind adherence to "principles." A husband harbors a passion toward his wife that is absent in a master toward his slave.

How do you view God—as a master or as a husband?

Isaiah uses marital imagery to stress how God rejoices in his people: "As a bridegroom rejoices over his bride, so will your God rejoice over you" (Isaiah 62:5). We live in a world in which many people are simply too busy or too preoccupied to notice us. But God *delights* in us. We make his supernatural heart skip a beat.

At times, Jesus himself employed this marital imagery, referring to himself as the "bridegroom" (Matthew 9:15) and to the kingdom of heaven as a "wedding banquet" (Matthew 22:1–14). This picture is carried over into the culmination of earthly history, as the book of Revelation talks about "the wedding of the Lamb" in which "his bride has made herself ready" (Revelation 19:7).

The breakdown of spiritual fidelity is often depicted with marital analogies as well. Jeremiah compares idolatry with adultery: "I gave faithless Israel her certificate of divorce and sent her away because of all her adulteries" (Jeremiah 3:8). Jesus picked up on this same imagery, referring to an "adulterous" generation (Mark 8:38). In context, Jesus is not attacking human sexual foibles; he is agonizing over a spiritually unfaithful nation that is violating its divine marriage to God.

Throughout Christian history, teachers have explored the similarities between the marital union and the various mysteries of faith that also involve a union: Besides the Trinity there is the joining of divinity and humanity in the person of Jesus Christ; the Eucharist, in which the bread and the wine are joined to signify the body and blood of Christ; Christ's union with his church; and other similar analogies.

Ruminating on these analogies is not merely amusing wordplay. For Christians seeking to gain spiritual insight from their marriage, these analogies provide the necessary ingredients for serious, contemplative reflection. The reason God became flesh was so that we might know him. Correspondingly, God did not create marriage just to give us a pleasant means of repopulating the world and providing a steady societal institution for the benefit of humanity; he planted marriage among humans as another signpost pointing to his own eternal, spiritual existence.

GOD PLANTED MARRIAGE AMONG HUMANS AS ANOTHER SIGNPOST POINTING TO HIS OWN ETERNAL, SPIRITUAL EXISTENCE.

As humans with finite minds, we need the power of symbolism in order to gain understanding. By means of the simple relationship of a man and a woman, the symbol of marriage can call up virtually infinite meaning. This will happen only when we use our marriage to *explore* God. If we are consumed with highlighting where our spouses are falling short, we will miss the divine mysteries of marriage and the lessons it has to teach us.

In the next section, we're going to accent one particular analogy to showcase how these life-pictures can bring together our marriage and our faith and also teach us about the purpose of marriage. While future chapters may seem more "practical," it's important to briefly explore the doctrine behind Christian marriage and what makes the marriages of believers different from the marriages of unbelievers. This difference is showcased in the preeminent marital analogy of Christ and his church.

RECONCILIATION

There's an old rabbinical story about how the spot was chosen for God's holy temple. Two brothers worked a common field and a common mill. Each night they divided whatever grain they had produced and took their own portion home.

One brother was single, and the other was married with a large family. The single brother decided that his married brother, with all those kids, certainly needed more grain than he did, so at night he secretly crept over to his brother's granary and gave him an extra portion. The married brother realized that his single brother didn't have any children to care for him in his old age. Concerned about his brother's future, he got up each night and secretly deposited some grain into his single brother's granary.

One night they met halfway between the two granaries, and each brother realized what the other was doing. They embraced, and as the story goes, God witnessed what happened and said, "This is a holy place—a place of love—and it is here that my temple shall be built." The holy place is that spot where God is made known to his people, "the place where human beings discover each other in love."[1]

Marriage can be that holy place, the site of a relationship that proclaims God's love to this world. Notice what makes this story so moving: two individuals who have greater empathy for the difficulties in each other's situation rather than in their own. Selfish marriage is the opposite: each partner feels their own pain more intensely and their spouse's pain callously.

For all their ambivalence about whether marriage is an inferior state, the early church fathers at least recognized that the analogy of reconciliation is the highest aim of marriage, pointing as a sign to the union of Christ with his church. Paul explores this theme in his letter to the Ephesians (5:22–33).

One of these early thinkers, Augustine (AD 354–430), suggested three benefits of marriage: offspring, faith (fidelity), and sacrament. Of the three benefits, he clearly points to the latter (sacrament) as the greatest. This is because it is possible to be married without either offspring or faith, but it is not possible to be (still) married without indissolubility, which is what a sacrament points toward. As long as a couple is married, they continue to display—however imperfectly—the ongoing commitment between Christ and his church. Thus, simply "sticking it out" becomes vitally important.

Centuries after Augustine, Anglican Reformers responded to these three blessings with three "causes." An early (1549) prayer book suggests that marriage is for procreation, a remedy against sexual sin, and mutual comfort.[2] This last element unfortunately replaced the sacramental aspect of marriage (namely, showcasing Christ and his church) with something much more pedestrian (namely, relational comfort).

Knowing *why* we are married and should stay married is crucial. The key question is this: Will we approach marriage from a God-centered view or a self-centered view? In a self-centered view, we will maintain our marriage as long as our earthly comforts, desires, and expectations are met. In a God-centered view, we preserve our marriage because it brings glory to God and points a sinful world to a reconciling Creator.

More than seeing marriage as a mutual comfort, we must see it as a word picture of the most important news humans have ever received—that there is a divine relationship between God and his people. Paul explicitly makes this analogy in his letter to the Ephesians. You've probably read these words (or heard these words quoted) dozens, if not hundreds, of times: "Husbands, love your wives, just as Christ loved the church and gave himself up for her to make her holy, cleansing her by the washing with water through the word, and to present her to himself as a radiant church, without stain or wrinkle or any other blemish, but holy and blameless" (Ephesians 5:25–27).

WE PRESERVE OUR MARRIAGE BECAUSE IT BRINGS GLORY TO GOD AND POINTS A SINFUL WORLD TO A RECONCILING CREATOR.

Though theologically I am on the side of the Protestants, I must declare to my early Anglican brothers that I believe it is unfortunate and sad when something as profound as living out an analogy of Christ and his church is reduced to experiencing this relationship as merely something that will help us avoid sexual sin, keep the world populated, and provide a cure for loneliness.

In fact, both the Old and New Testaments use marriage as a central analogy—the union between God and Israel (Old

Testament) and the union between Christ and his church (the New Testament). Understanding the depth of these analogies is crucial, as they will help us determine the very foundation on which a truly Christian marriage is based. If I believe the primary purpose of marriage is to model God's love for his church, I will enter this relationship and maintain it with an entirely new motivation, one hinted at by Paul in his second letter to the Corinthians: "So we make it our goal to please him" (2 Corinthians 5:9). The goal of my marriage will be to please God.

WHAT MAKES GOD HAPPY?

Paul answers a lot of questions for us when he writes, "We make it our goal to please him." Ask ten people on the street what their goal in life is, and you'll get an amazing variety of answers.

For the Christian, Paul couldn't be clearer: his "consuming ambition, the motive force behind all he does,"[3] is *to please God*. But Paul doesn't just say pleasing God is *his* "consuming ambition"; he assumes it will be *ours* as well: "*We* make it our goal to please him."

When something is the motive force behind all we do, it drives every decision we make. And Paul is crystal clear: The first question we should ask ourselves is, "Will this be pleasing to Jesus Christ?"

The first purpose in marriage—beyond happiness, sexual expression, the bearing of children, companionship, mutual care and provision, or anything else—is to please God. The challenge, of course, is that it is utterly *selfless* living; rather than asking, "What will make me happy?" we are told that we must ask, "What will make God happy?" And just in case we don't grasp it immediately, Paul underscores it a few verses later: "Those who live should no longer live for themselves but for him who died for them and was raised again" (2 Corinthians 5:15).

I have no other choice as a Christian. I owe it to Jesus Christ to live for him, to make him my consuming passion and the driving force in my life. To do this, I have to die to my own desires daily. I have to crucify the urge that measures every action and decision around what is best for me. Paul is eloquent about this fact: "We always carry around in our body the death of Jesus, so that the life of Jesus may also be revealed in our body" (2 Corinthians 4:10).

Just as Jesus went to the cross, so I must go to the cross, always considering myself as carrying around "the death of Jesus" so that his new life—his motivations, his purposes, his favor—might dominate in everything I do.

This reality calls me to look at my spouse through Christian eyes: "From now on we regard no one from a worldly point of view" (2 Corinthians 5:16). The reason is clear: "If anyone is in Christ, the new creation has come: The old has gone, the new is here!" (verse 17). Part of this new identity is a new ministry, one that is given to *every Christian*, as it is inherent in the person of Jesus Christ: "All this is from God, who reconciled us to himself through Christ and gave us the ministry of reconciliation" (verse 18).

Think about this. The very nature of Christ's work was a reconciling work, bringing us together again with God. Our response is to become reconcilers ourselves. C. K. Barrett defines reconciliation as "to end a relation of enmity, and to substitute for it one of peace and goodwill."[4]

THE VERY NATURE OF CHRIST'S WORK WAS A RECONCILING WORK, BRINGING US TOGETHER AGAIN WITH GOD. OUR RESPONSE IS TO BECOME RECONCILERS OURSELVES.

Clearly Paul is talking about carrying the message of salvation. But we cannot discuss with any integrity the ending of "a relation of enmity" and the dawning of "peace and goodwill" if our marriages are marked by divorce, fighting, and animosity. Everything I am to say and do in my life is to be supportive of this gospel ministry of reconciliation, and this commitment begins by displaying reconciliation in my personal relationships, especially in my marriage.

If my marriage contradicts my message, I have sabotaged the goal of my life, which is to be pleasing to Christ and to faithfully fulfill the ministry of reconciliation, proclaiming to the world the good news that we can be reconciled to God through Jesus Christ. If my "driving force" is as Paul says it should be, I will work to construct a marriage that enhances this ministry of reconciliation—a marriage that, in fact, incarnates this truth by putting flesh on it, building a relationship that models forgiveness, selfless love, and sacrifice.

The last picture I want to give the world is that I have decided to stop loving someone and that I refuse to serve this person anymore or that I have failed to fulfill a promise I made many years before. We can't carry a message well if we don't live it first.

How can I tell my children that God's promise of reconciliation is secure when they see that my own promise doesn't mean a thing? They *may* get over it, but in that case I will have presented a roadblock rather than a stepping-stone to the gospel.

What happens with most divorces is that at least one party, and possibly both, has ceased to put the gospel first in their lives. They no longer live by Paul's guiding principle ("I make it my goal to please him"). The Bible is clear in its teaching. God says, "I hate divorce" (Malachi 2:16, NIV, 1984 ed.). If the goal of a couple is to please God, many will not seek a divorce (but some might still be forced to). I know there are exceptions. Paul allows divorce when the other spouse isn't a believer and abandons the believer; Jesus considers marital unfaithfulness as possible grounds for divorce. Certainly, exceptions are to be assumed—at least in the realm of separation—if you or your kids are in danger of violence; but most of the cases of divorce among Christians do not involve such situations. They are far more likely to involve two Christians whose priorities in life have become distorted.

The *last* thing I want to do is further hurt those faithful believers who feel their lives have been scarred because a former spouse forced them into divorce, even though they fought with all their might to keep their marriage together. I don't judge you; I grieve for what you've gone through. But the *first* thing I want to do is challenge any believer who approaches divorce with a view of "God will forgive me; it's best just to start over rather than work through the hurt."

One of the reasons I am determined to keep my marriage together is not because doing so will make me happier (although I believe it will); not because I want my kids to have a secure home (although I do desire that); not because it would tear me up to see my wife have to "start over" (although it would). The first reason I keep my marriage together is because it is my Christian duty. If my life is based on proclaiming God's message to the world, I don't want to do anything that would challenge that message. And how can I proclaim reconciliation when I seek dissolution?

This analogy of reconciliation does more than merely provide the purpose for our marriage; it also helps us live out this purpose, even when lightning strikes.

WHEN LIGHTNING STRIKES

There is something mesmerizing about standing beneath a tree that is seven hundred years old. "What was happening here when this tree first started growing?" my daughter asked as we hiked the western slope of the North Cascades in the state of Washington.

"Not much," I laughed, stunned by the realization that this tree was nearly two hundred years old when Martin Luther was born.

One of the reasons the trees on the western slope of the Cascades survive so long is quite simple: The Washington forests are so wet that lightning strikes cause relatively few fires. Whereas the traditional forest, if left alone, might face a lightning-initiated fire every fifty or sixty years, in this part of the Cascades it would be about once every two hundred years. Lightning strikes still come, but they're not as devastating, so trees have had a much longer time to take root and grow.

I think that's a good picture of a marriage that is based on the ministry of reconciliation. Strong Christian marriages will still be struck by lightning—sexual temptations, communication problems, frustrations, unrealized expectations—but if the marriages are heavily watered with an unwavering commitment to please God above everything else, the conditions won't be ripe for a devastating fire to follow the lightning strike.

If I'm married only for happiness, and my happiness wanes for whatever reason, one little spark will burn the entire forest of my relationship. But if my aim is to proclaim and model God's ministry of reconciliation, my endurance will be fireproof.

Practicing the spiritual discipline of marriage means I put my relationship with God first. Just sticking it out is a victory in and of itself and creates a certain glory. In a society where relationships are discarded with a frightening regularity, Christians can command attention simply by staying married. And when asked why, we can offer the platform of God's message of reconciliation, followed by an invitation: "Would you like to hear more about the good news of reconciliation?"

IF I'M MARRIED ONLY FOR HAPPINESS, AND MY HAPPINESS WANES FOR WHATEVER REASON, ONE LITTLE SPARK WILL BURN THE ENTIRE FOREST OF MY RELATIONSHIP.

In this sense, our marriages can be platforms for evangelism. They can draw people into a truth that points beyond this world into the next. Everyone wants a great marriage; how many more might be attracted to Christianity if they saw, lived out in front of them, the choice fruits of Christians who have found satisfaction in their relationships by putting God first?

Years ago, Paul Simon wrote a bestselling song proclaiming "Fifty Ways to Leave Your Lover." A Christian needs just one reason to stay with his or her "lover": the analogy of Christ and his church.

Chapter 4

LEARNING TO LOVE

How Marriage Teaches Us to Love

> Marriage requires a radical commitment to love our spouses as they are, while longing for them to become what they are not yet. Every marriage moves either toward enhancing one another's glory or toward degrading each other.
>
> *Dan Allender and Tremper Longman III*

> If you treat a man as he is, he will stay as he is. But if you treat him as if he were what he ought to be and could be, he will become the bigger and better man.
>
> *Johann Wolfgang von Goethe*

If you were a male believer around the time of Moses and Joshua, your job was to fight. As the Israelites entered the Promised Land, they were sometimes chastised for their cowardice and lethargy and refusal to go into battle: "How long will you wait before you begin to take possession of the land that the Lord, the God of your ancestors, has given you?" (Joshua 18:3).

For a long time, "Go into battle" was the rallying cry from God.

Jesus came with a new challenge—a far more difficult one. Someone once asked him what the greatest commandment was, and Jesus replied that there were two (Matthew 22:34–40). It wasn't enough to love God with all your heart, soul, mind, and strength. If you really wanted to please God, Jesus said, you must love others.

Marriage can be the gym in which our capacity to experience and express God's love is strengthened and further developed. To get there, we have to realize that human love and divine love aren't two separate oceans but rather one body of water with many tributaries. We show our love for God in part by loving our spouses well. And we love our spouses by loving God.

When "love" is properly defined, we can never love somebody "too much." Our problem is that typically we love God too little. The answer is not to dim our love for any human in particular; it's to expand our heart's response to our Divine Joy.

Marriage creates a climate where this love is put to the greatest test. The problem is that this kind of love must be *acquired*. Katherine Anne Porter writes, "Love must be learned, and learned again and again; there is no end to it. Hate needs no instruction, but waits only to be provoked."[1]

Love is not a natural response that gushes out of us unbidden. Infatuation does that—at the beginning of a relationship at least—but hate is always ready to naturally spring forth, like the "Old Faithful" geyser at Yellowstone National Park. Christian love, on the other hand, must be chased after, aspired to, and practiced.

The popular culture completely misunderstands this principle. One of the cruelest and most self-condemning remarks I've ever heard is the one that men often use when they leave their wives for another woman: "The truth is, I've never loved you." This is meant to be an attack on the wife—saying, in effect, "The truth is, I've never found you *lovable*." But put in a Christian context, it's a confession of the man's utter failure to be a Christian. If he hasn't loved his wife, it is not his wife's fault, but *his*. Jesus calls us to love even the unlovable—even our enemies!—so a man who says "I've never loved you" is a man who is saying essentially this: "I've never acted like a Christian."

CHRISTIAN LOVE MUST BE CHASED AFTER, ASPIRED TO, AND PRACTICED.

When we love well, we please God. This shouldn't be hard to figure out. The best way for someone to get into my good graces is to be kind to my children. All Christians are God's children; by loving others, we bring enormous pleasure to our heavenly Father.

When Jesus tells us in Luke 6:32–36 to love even our enemies and those who are "ungrateful and wicked," he is teaching us that Christian love is displayed in loving the most difficult ones to love, not the easiest or most deserving. Later in Luke (chapter 14) Jesus returns to this theme, telling us that when we hold a banquet, we shouldn't invite our friends because they might invite us back and thus repay us for our hospitality. Instead, Jesus said that we should invite the lame, the paralyzed, the poor, the blind—those who can't pay us back.

That's what's so difficult about Jesus' call to love others. On one level, it's easy to love God, because God doesn't smell. God doesn't have bad breath. God doesn't reward kindness with evil. God doesn't make berating comments. Loving God is *easy*, in this sense. But Jesus really let us have it when he attached our love for God to our love for other people.

In the marriage context, we have absolutely no excuse. God lets us *choose* whom we're going to love. Because we get the choice and then find it difficult to carry out the love in practice, what grounds do we have to ever stop loving? God doesn't command us to get married; he offers it to us as an opportunity. Once we enter the marriage relationship, we cannot love God without loving our spouse as well.

Divorce pursued unilaterally (without its being legally enforced on us) for "nonbiblical" reasons represents our inability to hold to Jesus' command. It's giving up on what Jesus calls us to do. If I can't love my wife, how can I love my annoying coworker? How can I love the drug addict or the alcoholic? Yes, this spouse might be difficult to love at times, but that's what marriage is for—*to teach us how to love.*

Allow your marriage relationship to stretch your love and to enlarge your capacity for love—to teach you to be a Christian. Use marriage as a practice court where you learn to accept another person and serve him or her.

HOLY HAPPINESS

Although young men in Israel were called to serve God by fighting in wars, God did make one exception. It's buried in the book of Deuteronomy: "If a man has recently married, he must not be sent to war or have any other duty laid on him. For one year he is to be free to stay at home and bring happiness to the wife he has married" (24:5).

In all my seminarian theology, I left little room for the thought that God would want me to devote myself to making my wife happy. My wife was there to join me as I evangelized, studied Scripture, taught younger believers, did "the work of the ministry." The thought that God wants me to serve him by concentrating on making my wife happy was extraordinary. Although verse 5 of Deuteronomy 24 addresses just the first year of marriage, it's reasonable to assume that every spouse should spend some time thinking about how to make their spouse happy—and celebrating the profound reality that making their spouse happy pleases God. On a very practical level, a husband who plots how to make his wife laugh every now and then is serving God. A wife who plans an unforgettable sexual experience for her husband is serving God. A husband who makes sacrifices so his wife can get the recreational time she needs is loving God.

When Jesus said, "Love the Lord your God ... love your neighbor," he opened up the vistas of love and removed the walls that encase us. He made divine love and "religion" much bigger than we realize.

This is a prophetic word to today's society. There are legions of books published every year that teach us how to care for ourselves. As our society becomes increasingly fractured, there is a virtual obsession with looking out for ourselves, standing up for ourselves, and bettering ourselves. This emphasis on meeting our own needs can become ridiculous. You need only consider the book I once saw advertised that was titled, *Sex for One: The Joy of Self-Loving.*

WHEN JESUS SAID, "LOVE THE LORD YOUR GOD . . . LOVE YOUR NEIGHBOR," HE OPENED UP THE VISTAS OF LOVE AND REMOVED THE WALLS THAT ENCASE US.

While people in our society have become experts in self-care, we seemingly have lost the art of caring for others. *Sacrifice* has taken on such negative connotations that people fear being a codependent more than they fear being perceived as selfish.

And yet Scripture says, in effect, "Make your wife happy. Sacrifice yourself daily. You'll find your life only when you first lose it."

A campus pastor named Brady Bobbink decided to take Scripture's admonitions about love seriously. Brady married relatively late in life. He had become well-known as a speaker on discipleship and single living, and he was in high demand, with plenty of opportunities to serve God through his gift of teaching.

When Brady asked Shirley to become his wife, life changed dramatically. Shirley had two children from a previous marriage, and it wasn't long before Shirley and Brady began to pray about having a child of their own.

"What would it mean for me to love my wife in this situation?" Brady asked himself. In prayer, Brady made a pledge: If Shirley had another baby, for the first year he wouldn't accept any outside speaking engagements other than the ones his current position required him to take. Shirley subsequently became pregnant and gave birth to their first boy, Micah.

Months later, Brady received a lucrative opportunity to speak in Singapore. Brady is a student of history and loves to travel. The chance to go to the Far East was a once-in-a-lifetime opportunity, plus it would give him the chance to teach Christians from another culture.

He excitedly told Shirley about this great opportunity, then remembered his pledge midway through his conversation, and said out loud, "I can't go."

Shirley tried to release Brady from his pledge. "Honey, I'll be fine," she said.

It would have been easy for Brady to play religious games here. "I certainly could have justified it on a noble idea," he admitted, "preaching to another culture, but if that had really been my passion, I would have moved there and taken my wife and kids with me."

Some might think Brady was passing up an opportunity to please God by taking his gospel message to another nation, but Brady realized he could please God by loving his wife in a season in which she needed extra help and attention. To stay home and care for his wife in her need was every bit as much "Christian service" as leaving his hometown to preach the gospel when he was single.

"To fail to love my wife and kids rightly in the name of loving other people rightly is a sham," Brady insists.

JOHN BARGER: LEARNING TO LOVE

Dr. John Barger gave an extraordinary address to a gathering of men on December 12, 1987. The address included his testimony of how he had walked the road from being a domineering husband to a serving one. The crux of the message, however, wasn't just that husbands can do better. We all know that. What truly inspired me about his words was Dr. Barger's message that by learning to love his wife, he got a better grip on how he could love his God.

Dr. Barger's story begins with his confession of the way in which many men view women. Some of his thoughts are less common now than in the 1980s, so for the more sensitive men reading this, please don't take offense. Shadows of a male chauvinism certainly do still exist, so let's allow God to search our hearts accordingly.

> It's easy to scorn women, and most men do. We see women as physically weak, easy to intimidate ... emotional, illogical, and often petty. Or we see them as temptresses; in desire we idolize them and parade them across the pages of magazines, yet we scorn and hate them for their commanding sexual power over us. Male scorn for women affects every aspect of our lives: our relations with our mothers, our girlfriends, [our female coworkers], our wives, our children, the church, and even God himself.
>
> I do not speak here merely of *your* scorn of women; I speak of *mine* as well ... I swaggered through marriage for many years, ruling my wife Susan and my seven children with an iron hand while citing Scripture as justification for my privileges and authority. After all, Scripture explicitly commands wives to obey their husbands.
>
> Years of dominating my wife and children left them habitually resentful and fearful of me, yet unwilling to challenge me because of the fury it might provoke ... I alienated Susan and the children, and lost their love. Home was not a pleasant place to be—for them or for me. By 1983, Susan would have left me if it weren't for the children, and even that bond was losing its force.
>
> Then a number of dramatic events occurred, which wrought a profound change in my moral, psychological, and spiritual life.[2]

The first of these "dramatic events" was when Dr. Barger watched his wife endure a difficult delivery. Susan's placenta tore loose, and she started hemorrhaging. The baby was stillborn. Dr. Barger describes further what happened:

> At two in the morning in a stark, bright hospital delivery room, I held in my left hand my tiny lifeless son and stared in disbelief at his death ... I had the power to make [my family's] lives worse by raging against my baby's death and my wife's

lack of love, or to make their lives better by learning to love them properly. *I had to choose*. And it was a clear choice, presented in an instant as I stared at my tiny, helpless, stillborn infant cradled in my hand. In that critical instant, with God's grace, I chose the arduous, undramatic, discouraging path of trying to be good.

I don't have time ... to tell you of all the afflictions we endured in the next four years: sick children, my mother's sudden death, my losing my job as a teacher, three more miscarriages, and finally a secret sorrow that pierced both of us to the very core of our beings.

In the midst of these many afflictions, I found that the only way I could learn to love, and to cease being a cause of pain, was to suffer, endure, and strive every minute to repudiate my anger, my resentment, my scorn, my jealousy, my lust, my pride, and my dozens of other vices.

I began holding my tongue.

I started admitting my faults and apologizing for them.

I quit defending myself when I was judged too harshly—for the important thing was not to be right (or to be well-thought-of) but to love.

As I had made myself the center of my attention for too many years already, I said little about my own labors and sorrows; I sought to know Susan's and to help her to bear them.

And, frankly, once I started listening to Susan—once I began really hearing her and drawing her out—I was startled at how many and how deep were her wounds and her sorrows ... Most were not sorrows unique to Susan. They were the sorrows that all feel: sorrows that arise from the particular physiology of women and from their vocation as mothers, which gives them heavy duties and responsibilities ... sorrows that arise from loving their husbands and children intensely, but not being able to keep harm from those they love; sorrows that arise from the fact that in our society even the most chaste of women are regularly threatened by the lustful stares, remarks, and advances of men ...

Women ... suffer these wounds far more often and with a greater intensity than most of us men ever realize. And unless we ask them, women generally do not speak to us of these

> sorrows—perhaps because we men so often dismiss their troubles as insignificant...
>
> Can men ... withdraw the sword of sorrow that pierces every woman's heart? I don't think so. Their problems are generally not the kind that have a solution, but rather form the very fabric of their daily existence...
>
> One of my friends, when confronted at the end of his long workday with his wife's complaints about the noise, the troubles, and the unending housework, snapped back at her in exasperation, "Well, do you want me to stay home and do the housework while you go off to the office?" You understand his point. He couldn't solve her problems. What did she want him to do?
>
> I'll tell you. She wanted him to listen, to understand, and to sympathize. She wanted him to let her know that despite her problems, her exhaustion, her dishevelment, he loved her—to let her know that it caused him sorrow that she was suffering and that if it were possible, he would change it for her.

Dr. Barger's earnest efforts at renewing his love for his wife and reaching a new plane of understanding worked. It took three years of "patience, listening, and growing in Susan's trust," spending "literally hundreds of hours talking," but eventually Susan's anger dissipated, overcoming her cynicism, which in turn "softened her and gentled her."

Living in a renewed marriage, life became unusually sweet. John and Susan believed they were "on the verge of a long and happy marriage" when tragedy struck again.

Susan was diagnosed with terminal cancer.

An eight-month battle ensued, and Dr. Barger was challenged to express his new love in very concrete ways. Caring for a seriously ill person is extremely difficult work, but John welcomed it as an opportunity "to show her how much I really loved her."

Even though Susan was given the best care, the cancer won out, and she died. She breathed her last breath surrounded by her family and dearest friends and holding the hand of her beloved husband.

Dr. Barger looked back on their lives together with bittersweet feelings. The hurt was encased in their renewal—now that they had become best friends, now that he had learned the deeper meaning found in truly loving rather than in dominating, he had to say good-bye. But the sweetness was in remembering an unusual love, knowing he had experienced something most of us yearn for but don't find—true, soul-deep companionship.

THE SWEETNESS WAS IN REMEMBERING AN UNUSUAL LOVE, KNOWING HE HAD EXPERIENCED SOMETHING MOST OF US YEARN FOR BUT DON'T FIND—TRUE, SOUL-DEEP COMPANIONSHIP.

In his reflections, Dr. Barger discussed how this experience with his wife reflected on his relationship with God:

> Consider the virtues I have recommended as necessary to a deep relation with your wife: patience, listening, humility, service, and faithful, tender love. I hope it is not heretical for me to claim that in his dealings with us, God acts in many ways like a woman.
>
> Women are capable of and sometimes commit magnificent acts that manifest incredible power and awaken in us men a profound awe, if not fear and trembling. Yet when they love, they love quietly; they speak, as it were, in whispers, and we have to listen carefully, attentively, to hear their words of love and to know them.
>
> Isn't God also this way?
>
> Doesn't he intervene in most of our lives in whispers, which we miss if we fail to recollect ourselves and pay careful attention—if we do not constantly strive to hear those whispers of divine love? The virtues necessary in truly loving a woman and having that love returned—the virtues of listening, patience, humility, service, and faithful love—are the very virtues necessary for us to love God and to feel his love returned. As we cannot lord it over women if we are to know them and grow intimate with them, so we cannot lord it over God if we are to know him and grow intimate with him.

> We cannot successfully demand the love of a woman or the love of God. We have to wait. And just as a woman's heart is melted when she encounters in us weakness accompanied by our humble admission of it, so God's heart is melted, and he is most tender and gracious to us when he encounters in us weakness accompanied by our humble admission of it.

While this story targets males, I suspect the same principle is true for women. That terrifyingly difficult man to love just may be your gateway to learning how to love God. This is a biblical truth. The beloved disciple John lays it out bluntly:

> Whoever claims to love God yet hates a brother or sister is a liar. For whoever does not love their brother and sister, whom they have seen, cannot love God, whom they have not seen. And he has given us this command: Anyone who loves God must also love their brother and sister. *1 John 4:20–21*

This man or this woman seems so different from you, I know. That's why it seems so difficult to love him or her. When you think on one level, she thinks on another. When you're certain this perspective matters most, he brings in another angle entirely. And you ask yourself, "How can I possibly love someone who is so different from me?"

MARRIAGE IS DESIGNED TO CALL US OUT OF OURSELVES AS WE LEARN TO LOVE THE "DIFFERENT."

And yet consider, if loving someone who is so different from you is impossibly difficult, how can you possibly love God? He is spirit, and you are encased in flesh and bones. He is eternal, and you are trapped in time. He is all holy, perfect, sinless, and you—like me—are steeped in sin.

It is far less of a leap for a man to love a woman or for a woman to love a man than it is for either of us to love God.

But I think it's more than that. I think marriage is designed to call us out of ourselves as we learn to love the "different." Put together in the closest situation imaginable—living side by side, sleeping in the same room, even on occasion sharing our bodies with each other—we are forced to respect and appreciate someone who is radically different.

We need to be called out of ourselves because, in truth, we are incomplete. God made us to find our fulfillment in him—the Totally Other. Marriage shows us that we are not all there is; it calls us to give way to another, but also to find joy, happiness, and even ecstasy in another.

There are no lessons to be learned when a husband dominates his wife. There are no inspiring examples to emulate when a wife manipulates a husband. But love unlocks the spiritual secrets of the universe. Love blows open eternity and showers its raindrops on us.

Christianity involves believing certain things, to be sure, but its herald, its hallmark, its glory, is not in merely ascribing to certain intellectual truths. The beauty of Christianity is in learning to love, and few life situations test that as radically as does a marriage.

Yes, at times it may seem difficult to love your spouse. But if you truly want to love God, look right now at the ring on your left hand, commit yourself to exploring anew what that ring represents, and love passionately, crazily, and enduringly the fleshly person who put it there.

It just may be one of the most spiritual things you can do.

Chapter 5

HOLY HONOR

Marriage Teaches Us to Respect Others

> We are all in the gutter, but some of us are looking at the stars.
> *Oscar Wilde*

> We must never be naive enough to think of marriage as a safe harbor from the fall ... The deepest struggles of life will occur in the most primary relationship affected by the fall: marriage.
> *Dan Allender and Tremper Longman III*

I work all day," Brian lamented to me, "and then come home, help fix dinner, play with the kids, clean up the dishes, put the kids to bed, and *bang!*—it's nine thirty, and I'm dead tired."

"What's your wife doing all this time?" I asked.

"She's on the Internet, spending all her time in one of those chat groups."

"Seriously?"

"Oh, yeah. She spends hours every day talking to people on the computer. She talks to them more than to me or the kids. It's disgusting."

Just a couple of hours later, Brian was changing a diaper on his newborn when Cheryl began launching into how Brian was ruining their marriage by running up debt, never playing with the kids, failing to take spiritual leadership, and never helping around the house.

My wife was startled. She had known Brian since high school and had always thought of him as the type of father who would be very involved with his kids and rather frugal in financial matters.

It was stunning to hear two such wildly divergent accounts of the same marriage. Throughout the rest of the day, Brian and Cheryl were caustic in their comments; they had become adversaries, not allies, relishing opportunities to put each other down.

"Yeah, Gary, *get him*," Cheryl said, as I played a hand of cards that put Brian's point total in jeopardy. This wasn't the good-natured ribbing of genuine affection; it was malicious glee at an enemy's fall.

Francis de Sales, the seventeenth-century author of the classic *Introduction to a Devout Life* wrote something in a letter that is simple but powerful: "Have contempt for contempt." Both Brian and Cheryl were so full of their contempt for each other that they spent all their time ruminating on each other's failures. Clearly one (and, more likely, both) were either lying about the situation at home or had a seriously skewed perception of what was really going on in their marriage.

WE ARE OBSESSED WITH BEING RESPECTED, BUT RARELY CONSIDER OUR OWN OBLIGATION TO RESPECT OTHERS.

This chapter deals with the discipline of showing respect, particularly to your spouse. The sad truth is that comparatively few Christians think of giving respect as a command or a spiritual discipline. We are obsessed with being respected, but rarely consider our own obligation to respect others.

Scripture has much to say about this. We are commanded to respect our parents (Leviticus 19:3), the elderly (Leviticus 19:32), God (Malachi 1:6), our spouse (Ephesians 5:33; 1 Peter 3:7), and, in fact, *everyone*: "Show proper respect to everyone" (1 Peter 2:17).

All of us have a core desire to be respected. When this desire isn't met, we are tempted to lapse into a self-defeating response. Rather than work to build our own life so that respect is granted to us, we work to tear down our spouse in a desperate attempt to convince ourselves that their lack of respect is meaningless. Spiritually, this becomes a vicious and debilitating cycle that is extremely difficult to break. Respect begets respect. And disrespect begets disrespect.

God has a solution that, if we adopt it, will revolutionize our relationships. While many people fight to receive respect, Christian marriage calls us to focus our efforts on giving respect. We are called to honor someone even when we know only too well their deepest character flaws. We are called to stretch ourselves, to find out how we can learn to respect this person with whom we've become so familiar. And in this exploration, we are urged to "have contempt for contempt."

THE EXPLORED RIVER

I have some vivid memories of the first week of our marriage. One such memory is that of looking through our medicine cabinet and picking up this metal thing that looked like scissors with an attached jaw. "What in the world is this?" I asked.

"That's to curl my eyelashes," my wife answered.

"You really do that?" I asked.

"Of course I do," she said.

I was stunned. Nobody had ever told me this. It had never occurred to me that straight eyelashes were a sign of lax hygiene.

"So what do you women say when you walk through the mall," I asked, " 'Oh, look at that woman; she forgot to curl her eyelashes—and she's out in public'?"

"Don't be silly," my wife said, yanking the eyelash curler from my hand.

Young marriage can be full of such revelations. You think that everybody keeps the garbage under the left side of the kitchen sink—until you find out that your wife's family kept it on the porch.

"But it doesn't go there," you protest.

"Why not?" your new wife asks.

"Because my mom never put it there!"

It took me years to accept the fact that Lisa likes to keep certain medicines in the spice cabinet. If you ask me, there is something inherently wrong with storing Pepto-Bismol next to the vanilla flavoring and the salt. But that's how her family did it.

After time, however, these interesting little mysteries become all too familiar—and that's when contempt can begin to seep in.

Mark Twain tells the sobering tale about deeply exploring the Mississippi River he loved very much. After virtually memorizing the river's bends, twists, and turns and navigating its waters with rapt admiration, he was chagrined to wake up one day and find that the river had lost much of its poetry. The mystery of that mighty waterway had been replaced with a boring predictability. He had literally loved his love out of that river.

Every marriage goes through this stage. An enrapturing love quiets down to a predictable routine. The mystery is replaced with an almost comical familiarity—the wife knows exactly how the husband will sit on the couch; the husband knows exactly how his wife will answer the phone.

The wife of a couple we know decided to get her husband some golf clubs for his birthday. She went to a store and told the owner, "Here's the money for a set of clubs. My husband and I will come in here tomorrow night. He'll look over these clubs, then walk over to talk to me about it, then go back to the clubs and touch the ones he decides are the best option. At that point, I want you to walk up to him and say, 'Your wife already paid for these yesterday. Happy birthday.' "

The clerk was surprised and a little suspicious, but he agreed to the plan.

The next day, our friend took her husband to a restaurant next door to the golf shop. After dinner, the husband (as predicted) pointed to the shop and said, "You mind if we just stop in there?"

"Not at all," the wife said.

The husband walked through the shop and settled on two sets of clubs. He then walked back to his wife and conferred with her about them, then returned to the clubs and touched the set he thought would be best. The owner came up and went through his spiel.

When love becomes this familiar, is it possible to love our love out of a person?

As our partners and their weaknesses become more familiar to us, respect often becomes harder to give. But this failure to show respect is more a sign of spiritual immaturity than it is an inevitable pathway of marriage. Consider Paul as he wrote to the Corinthians. Even though he was addressing a church full of quarrelers (1 Corinthians 1:11), unlearned and simple people (1:26), "worldly" infants (3:1–3), arrogant egocentrics (4:18), a man sleeping with his father's wife (5:1), greedy people suing fellow believers (6:1), and childish thinkers (14:20), he still honors them by saying, "I always thank my God for you" (1:4). He knew them well enough to be familiar with all their faults, yet he continued to be thankful for them. Why? The key is found in the second half of verse 4: "I always thank my God for you *because of his grace given you in Christ Jesus*" (emphasis added).

We can be thankful for our fellow sinners when we spend more time looking for "evidences of grace" than we do finding fault. If my wife is more aware of where she falls short in my eyes than she is of how I am witnessing evidences of God's grace in her journey of progressive sanctification, then I am a legalistic husband, akin to a Pharisee. Giving respect is an obligation, not a favor; it is an act of maturity, birthed in a profound understanding of God's good grace.

CHALLENGING OUR PREJUDICES

I walked in the door one night, and Lisa immediately handed me the phone. "Gail is freaking out," she said, "and James needs to talk to you."

I took the phone, and James got right to it.

"Gail says I'm repressing her. She thinks I don't respect her and that I belittle her."

"Really?" I said.

"Yeah. And now she wants me to go see her counselor, but I don't feel right about that."

"Why not?" I asked.

"Well, Gail's counselor is a woman, and I'm just not sure, well, you know, that I would trust her."

"Let me get this straight," I replied. "Gail doesn't think you respect her as a woman. You don't think that's true, but you don't want to go to this counselor because she's a woman and you're not sure you trust her?"

There was a long silence.

I knew this challenge would come up eventually. The first time I saw Gail, I knew why James had chosen her. James was raised a "man's man," and he was looking for a "man's woman." We talked, in fact, about the women he had dated. I didn't see any women who could have challenged him, who would push him, threaten him, or compete with him in any way. I saw women who had probably been browbeaten by their fathers and so were perfectly content to go along with a husband who wanted a pretty, thin, and preferably blonde wife attached to his right arm who knew how to smile, talk, laugh, make love, and take care of babies.

Gail wanted a real relationship. She had outgrown being just an adornment, and James was facing a crisis. It wasn't, however, a crisis—as James initially thought—of Gail "freaking out"; it was a crisis of James being forced to confront his prejudicial attitudes toward women in general and toward Gail in particular.

Jesus purposely confronted similar attitudes that lay hidden within the disciples. He blatantly broke with rabbinical tradition to speak with the woman at the well (John 4). Not only was it unheard-of for a rabbi to be alone with a woman, but to discuss theology was virtually unthinkable. One rabbi, when it was suggested to him that women be taught the Law for particular circumstances, replied, "If any man gives his daughter a knowledge of the Law, it is as though he taught her lechery."[1]

That's why, when referring to the disciples' reaction upon finding Jesus talking to the woman at the well (John 4:27), the word *surprised* is used to translate the Greek word *thaumazo*, which carries the sense of amazement and incredulity: "How could this be happening?" "Am I really seeing what I think I'm seeing?"

No doubt, much of the disciples' wonderment arose from their exposure to their blatantly antiwoman culture. Women in Palestine at the time of Jesus were subject to numerous rejections. They weren't counted among those who would make up the minimum number of ten required for a service to take place in a synagogue; their witness had no validity in law courts; they weren't considered fit for education (the Talmud reads, "The words of the Torah will be destroyed in the fire sooner than be taught to women"); and they were often segregated from the rest of society and shut up in their houses. The disparagement of women is seen in a boldly derogatory prayer often uttered by ancient Jewish men: "Praised be God that he has not created me a Gentile; praised be God that he has not created me a woman; praised be God that he has not created me an ignorant person."

JESUS CONFRONTED THESE ATTITUDES ABOUT WOMEN, LIFTING UP WOMEN AND INCLUDING THEM IN HIS INNER CIRCLE OF CONFIDANTES.

In bold moves and with courageous words, Jesus confronted these attitudes about women, lifting up women and including them in his inner circle of confidantes and supporters (see Luke 8:1–3). He valued women and wanted them to be around him—yet there was never even a whisper or hint of scandal, because Jesus acted with genuine love and purity.

It wasn't until my friend James was married that he was able to confront the misogynistic views he held about women. He had to hear his own wife say, "You don't respect me because I'm a woman," and he had to be ensnared by his own words, "She's a woman, and I'm just not sure I trust her," before he could see his sinful attitude.

THE DIFFERENCE

Many of the marital problems we face are not problems between individual couples—Jim and Susan, Mark and Diane, or Rob and Jill. They are the problems between men, generally, and women, generally. They are problems that arise because we are either too lazy or too selfish to get to know our spouse well enough to understand how different from us they really are.

I had to learn this the hard way. I'll spare you all the gory details, but getting to Raleigh, North Carolina, from Bellingham, Washington, one particular time involved five hours of driving, four airports, three rental car reservations, two very tired travelers, and one absolutely crazy taxi driver.

I was traveling with my oldest daughter, who was ten years old at the time, planning to drop her off at a friend's house in northern Virginia while I traveled south to Raleigh. Due to a canceled flight, I dropped Allison off after 11:00 p.m. and then drove until about 1:00 a.m., when weariness forced me to stop.

I got up early the next morning and completed the drive into Raleigh, where I was scheduled to address a large crowd that evening. Before the meeting, I had to complete a phone interview, send some galleys to a publisher by overnight mail, and return a few phone calls—all this while trying to squeeze in some time to go over my speech.

Just an hour or so before I had to be in the hotel ballroom, I checked in with my wife. After just a few sentences, she was in tears—something about a computer program not working right, and would we have to spend money to buy a new computer? I was doing my best to get spiritually prepped for the talk. Following an exhausting trip, I felt I needed some focused time to be prepared, and I resented Lisa's tears, particularly at that very moment. I remember thinking, *Can't she just be a little stronger when I'm on the road? I don't need this.*

I tried to pray through my frustration, but I remained rather agitated. *Great!* I thought. *What a disposition to have just before I face all those people!* I tried not to blame my wife for making me like this, but I was having less than 100 percent success.

A guy who travels just needs someone who's stronger at home, I kept saying to myself, then repented, then found myself repeating the statement with even more vigor.

Two weeks later, I read a remarkable personal-experience piece in *The Washington Post Magazine*. Liza Mundy wrote about participating in an editorial meeting and being horrified when she found herself starting to cry. She was hot, bothered, and tired—nothing extraordinary, but it all combined to make her want to cry. She writes, "Suddenly the heat had moved to my face and tears were springing to my eyes and I was blinking and blinking, hoping to drive them back. Only of course that was futile, because, as a friend later put it so beautifully, at this point in a crying-in-the-office experience, 'You're no longer crying because of what they're saying. You're crying because you're crying.'"

Then, a paragraph or so later, Mundy wrote something that astonished me: "'Pay no attention to these tears; they are meaningless. I'm thinking quite clearly; this conversation isn't upsetting me nearly as much as it seems. I'm just fatigued and a little bit stressed and feeling hot!' was what I wanted to say. Because I knew, like most women perhaps, that sometimes tears are no more significant than sweating."

As a man, I equate tears with near devastation. For me to cry in an office would require a major tragedy. And that's when I understood that perhaps tears mean something entirely different for me than they do for Lisa. I see tears and think she's falling apart; she experiences tears and thinks she's merely sweating.

If for some reason Lisa and I split up and I married someone else I thought was stronger emotionally, I might very well find myself in the same situation. Something that bothered me about Lisa may actually be true about most women. It was a man-woman thing, not a Gary-Lisa thing.

Months later, I watched as Lisa fought back tears on a Good Friday. Our youngest daughter, Kelsey, had put a shirt in the laundry with glitter on it, so it hadn't come clean and she wouldn't be able to wear it to church, as planned. Lisa's eyes grew wide — I've seen this so many times over the years — and she started blinking so she wouldn't cry.

I'm standing in the doorway. *What a thing to cry about*, I thought. *Glitter on a shirt? Big deal!*

And then I applied the discipline of respect: *Gary, stop it! Tears mean something different to her. Don't judge your wife.*

I kept my mouth shut; her tears quickly subsided; and we went to church without a big fuss.

Notice the process here: I had to learn to better understand Lisa before I could truly respect her, and I had to respect her before I could fully love her. You have to understand before you can respect, and you have to respect before you can fully love. This is a tremendously spiritually therapeutic process, an emptying of myself so I can grow more in my love for others.

AN ATTITUDE OF JUDGMENT DOESN'T BREAK ME; IT PUFFS ME UP.

An attitude of judgment doesn't break me; it puffs me up. It fills me with arrogance. When I learn to give respect, I become transformed in the process.

SPIRITUAL EQUALITY

As moral entities, men and women are equal before God. This truth doesn't mean they are synonymous, or that their roles will be or should be the same. But it does mean, as Scripture teaches, that *both* male and female are made in the image of God. This is the teaching of Genesis 1:27, and it is a teaching affirmed by Paul in the New Testament when he wrote, "nor is there male and female" in Christ Jesus (Galatians 3:28).

The fact that my wife is made in the image of God calls me to a far nobler response than simply refraining from being condescending to her. Certainly, it is wildly inappropriate for me to look down on Lisa because she's a woman, but not acting with disdain toward her is a far cry from what her creation in the image of God really calls me to do, namely, to honor her.

My family once went through the National Gallery of Art, looking at some original Rembrandts, and one of my very tactile children reached out to touch the painting. My wife let loose with a harsh whisper and grabbed our child's hand before it could even reach the canvas. "This is a *Rembrandt*!" she hissed under the guard's glare. "You can't touch these!"

My wife was created by God himself. How dare I dishonor her? In fact, shouldn't it even give me pause before I reach out to touch her? She is the Creator's daughter, after all.

The difficulty with honoring our spouse is that it calls us to adopt attitudes and actions that go far beyond merely saying we won't dishonor him or her. As Betsy and Gary Ricucci point out, "Honor isn't passive, it's active. We honor our wives by demonstrating our esteem and respect: complimenting them in public; affirming their gifts, abilities, and accomplishments; and declaring our appreciation for all they do. Honor not expressed is not honor."[2]

The biggest challenge in upholding my spiritual obligation to honor my wife is that I get busy and sidetracked. I don't mean to dishonor her; I just absentmindedly neglect to actively honor her.

The reason that giving respect to my wife is a spiritual discipline as much as it is a marital one is simple: I've found that the more I honor my wife in particular, the more I honor other women in general. The reverse is true as well. The glib statement "Oh, that's just women for you" betrays a serious spiritual disease. "*Just* women" are made in the image of God. Such a comment comes dangerously close to maligning the Creator who made women *just the way they are*.

Giving respect to others brings light and life into our lives. It leads us in the end to respect the God who created all of us and shapes us as he sees fit. It is an essential discipline, and marriage provides daily opportunities to grow in this area.

BUILDING CONTEMPT FOR CONTEMPT

Let's look now at a few practical ways we can begin to build contempt for contempt in our relationships.

Adopt a Holy Double Standard

Sadly, I spent the first few years of my marriage adding up the pluses and minuses of my and my wife's various personality traits. The problem was simple: I was spending too much time on my pluses and her minuses. Then I read a passage written by John Owen, one of the greatest Puritan scholars ever: "The person who understands the evil in his own heart is the only person who is useful, fruitful, and solid in his beliefs and obedience. Others only delude themselves and thus upset families, churches, and all other relationships. In their self-pride and judgment of others, they show great inconsistency."[3]

I am told over and over in Scripture that my duty as a Christian is to become more and more like Jesus Christ.

I realized I was being deluded by my sense of self-righteousness. Instead of focusing on what Lisa could improve, I should have been on my knees, begging God to change *me*. This thought was magnified one morning when I awoke and started praying through Scripture. All of a sudden, a question startled me: *Does Lisa feel like she's married to Jesus?*

I almost laughed out loud, until I was shaken by another thought. I am told over and over in Scripture that my duty as a Christian is to become more and more like Jesus Christ. Over time, my wife *should* start to feel like there's at least a family resemblance. I realized how pitifully short I had fallen in my task of improving myself for my wife's sake.

But wait! the selfish me wanted to cry out. *What about her?* I began thinking about how my wife could improve and how if she did that, it would undoubtedly help our marriage immeasurably—but then I remembered a passage written by William Law, the eighteenth-century Anglican writer:

> No one is of the Spirit of Christ but he that has the utmost compassion for sinners. Nor is there any greater sign of your own perfection than you find yourself all love and compassion toward them that are very weak and defective. And on the other hand, you have never less reason to be pleased with yourself than when you find yourself most angry and offended at the behavior of others ... We must set ourselves against sin as we do against sickness and diseases, by showing ourselves tender and compassionate to the sick and diseased.[4]

These were hard words to take in. Essentially, Law is telling me that when my respect slips into contempt, it's because *I'm* weak, not because my wife is failing. If I were really mature, I would have the same compassion for her weaknesses as Christ does. Respect is a spiritual discipline, an obligation I owe my wife.

Fortunately, a change in my life helped me see things from a different perspective.

GAIN A NEW UNDERSTANDING

My wife and I entered a new journey in our marriage when I became self-employed. To save on overhead, we decided I would work out of our home. The only problem was that, at the time, we lived in a town house.

With three children.

In other words, I'd really be working out of our bedroom.

When other married couples found out what we were doing, many were amazed. "And you still *like* each other?" they'd ask.

In fact, working at home did wonders for our marriage. For the first time, I could see for myself what it was like to spend an entire day being Lisa. Oh, I used to see that every weekend, but what makes her life difficult isn't an occasional forty-eight-hour stretch; it's the cumulative, never-ending, day-in-and-day-out responsibility of raising and teaching kids in a homeschool environment, while also cleaning the house, planning meals, and preparing for her own Bible study. And then, when your husband comes home, you're supposed to have enough energy to act like a wife.

On the other hand, my wife saw what it was like for me to sit in front of a computer all day long. Some days I was tired; other days I was sick. Sometimes the weather outside was beautiful, but always I stayed in my chair and worked. I made the phone calls I didn't want to make but needed to make. She saw my determination and discipline. And she had a front-row seat from which to witness the pressure of meeting deadlines and accepting assignments I knew would be tough but for which there was no doubt we needed the money they would generate.

Over time, we developed a profound appreciation for what the other person was doing. Both of us now understand in a much clearer way the challenges facing each of us and why it can sometimes be so hard to act like the perfect husband or wife. We're not married in a carefree garden of Eden; we're married in the midst of many responsibilities that compete for our energy. This new understanding has ushered in a stronger empathy for each other in our weaknesses and peculiarities.

You don't have to work out of your own home to experience this empathy. Instead of focusing your energy on resentment over how sparsely your spouse understands you, expend your efforts to understand him or her. As a spiritual exercise, find out what your spouse's day is really like. Ask her. Ask him. Draw them out—what is the most difficult part of your day? When do you feel like just giving up? Are parts of your day monotonous? Is there something you constantly fear? Take time to do an inventory of your spouse's difficulties rather than of your spouse's shortcomings.

CULTIVATE GRATITUDE

Thanksgiving is a privilege. It creates a positive focus in my life, but it is also an obligation: "Give thanks to the LORD, for he is good" (Psalm 136:1). "Give thanks in all circumstances"

(1 Thessalonians 5:18). Remember how Paul gave thanks for the Corinthians (1 Corinthians 1:4).

When I am thankful for my spouse, the control that the familiarity of contempt has on me is broken. I look for new things to be thankful for. I try not to take for granted the routine things she does. I never eat at another person's house without thanking them for providing a meal; why should I not give my wife the same thanks I'd give someone else?

WHEN I AM THANKFUL FOR MY SPOUSE, THE CONTROL THAT THE FAMILIARITY OF CONTEMPT HAS ON ME IS BROKEN.

There are few things that lift my spirits more than simply hearing my wife or children say, "Thanks for working so hard to provide for us." Those nine words can lift a hundred pounds of pressure off my back.

Contempt is conceived with expectations; respect is conceived with expressions of gratitude. We can choose which one we will obsess over—expectations, or thanksgivings. That choice will result in a birth—and the child will be named either contempt or respect.

REMEMBER THE EFFECTS OF THE FALL

We need to understand how profoundly broken this world is. Sin has radically scarred our existence. As a result of humanity's fall, I will labor with difficulty and angst (Genesis 3:17–19). Lisa will mother our children and enter relationships with mixed motives and frustrated aims (Genesis 3:16).

Even an unusually good marriage is unable to completely erase the effects of sin's curse on individuals and on society. Dan Allender and Tremper Longman write, "We must never be naive enough to think of marriage as a safe harbor from the fall ... The deepest struggles of life will occur in the most primary relationship affected by the fall: marriage."[5]

The problem is that even though we can't go back to the idyllic existence prior to the fall, we were created with an understanding of what the pre-fall days were like; in other words, we know what relationships *should be* like, but we are incapable of making them perfectly in tune with that ideal: "Our souls are wired for what we will never enjoy until Eden is restored in the new heaven and earth. We are built with a distant memory of Eden."[6]

This calls me to extend gentleness and tolerance toward my wife. I want her to become all that Jesus calls her to become, and I hope with all my heart that I will be a positive factor in her pursuit of that aim (and vice versa). But she will never fully get there this side of heaven, so I must love and accept her in the reality of living in a sin-stained world.

Accepting the fallenness of this world—with its bitter disappointments, physical limitations, and myriad demands—helps me to understand how difficult life is for Lisa, which helps me in turn to have contempt for contempt.

In the days when I still worked outside the home, I remember occasions when Lisa and I would preplan a romantic evening. Flush with morning's zest, we'd plan a "hot" night. Romance would fly. For a few brief moments, we would make the earth melt away and enjoy the blessed fruits of conjugal intimacy.

Then I'd go to work, throughout the day occasionally thinking about what marital pleasures awaited me in just a few hours. When I came home, however, I not infrequently was met at the door by a wife who wanted nothing more than a solitary bath and an early start on a good night's sleep.

"But if you still want to, you know, I can go along with it," she might say.

That's not fair! I used to think. *I don't want just a willing wife. I want an eager one!*

But now I see the process—the kitchen floor that has enough cereal on it to feed a family of mice for three winters; the pressure of getting the homeschooling lessons done, while lunches need to be made and clothes need to be washed and ballet and soccer practice need to be accounted for; and . . .

For an increasing number of marriages in which both spouses work outside the home, imagine how it must feel when you're having to make trade-offs all day long, such as meeting a deadline or making a soccer game, and then feel like you have to make the same kind of trade-offs in the evening—read a story to the kids, or get in bed early enough to have sex? Life just wears us down.

I finally realized it was nothing personal, but sometimes wives just get tired. That's just the way it works in a fallen world. Lisa didn't want to get tired. But she's made of flesh and blood—and what else could I expect?

Let me repeat this: You will never find a spouse who is not affected in some way by the reality of the fall. James 3:2 teaches that "we *all* stumble in *many* ways" (emphasis added). A different spouse will stumble in different ways, but still, according to Scripture, *in many ways*. Which means, if you can't respect *this* spouse because she is prone to certain weaknesses, you will never be able to respect *any* spouse.

LOOKING OUT FOR EACH OTHER

Several years ago, returning from a trip, I stepped inside the house and felt like I had walked every one of the four hundred miles I had just driven. I had spoken six times in four days and had driven through four different states to get where I needed to go. I pulled into the driveway thinking, *I'm so tired. All I really want to do is watch a football game.* And as I walked into the house, Lisa was thinking, *Good, he's finally home! I've had the kids to myself all weekend, and they're driving me crazy.*

This is the stuff that five-star marriage fights are made of. These are the situations that feel like they are specifically cooked up in hell.

And then, to my astonishment, I discovered that Lisa and I had matured. I tried to play with the kids as best I could. I had brought them some flavored popcorn, and we talked at the kitchen table as they ate—yet I noticed how Lisa was being graciously sensitive to how tired I must be.

"You've got to be exhausted," she said. "Let me take care of the kids tonight."

But hearing her say that made me *want* to take care of the kids. I realized that even though she had a valid reason to pass the nighttime duties to me, she was being hard on herself and easy on me—and that made me want to be hard on myself and easy on her. When there is mutual respect in marriage, selflessness becomes contagious.

Lisa and I don't always act this way, by any means, but it's wonderful when we do. I think we're led to this approach by the apostle Paul, who confessed that he was "the worst of sinners" (1 Timothy 1:16). I don't think there's a better recipe in the Bible to help us become better spouses. If we assume our spouse has the hardest road to travel and we miss the mark most frequently—and then act accordingly—we'll find a mix that's just about right.

Contempt is born when we fixate on our spouse's weaknesses. Every spouse has these sore points. If you want to find them, without a doubt you will. If you want to obsess about them, they'll grow—but *you* won't!

WHEN THERE IS MUTUAL RESPECT IN MARRIAGE, SELFLESSNESS BECOMES CONTAGIOUS.

Jesus provides a remedy that is stunning in its simplicity yet foreboding in its difficulty. He tells us to take the plank out of our own eye before we try to remove the speck from our neighbor's eye (Matthew 7:3–5).

If you're thinking, *But my spouse is the one who has the plank*, allow me to let you in on a secret: You're exactly the type of person Jesus is talking to. You're the one he wants to challenge with these words. Jesus isn't helping us resolve legal matters here; he's urging us to adopt humble spirits. He wants us to cast off the contempt—to have contempt for the contempt—and learn the spiritual secret of respect.

Consider the type of people Jesus loved in the days he walked on earth—Judas (the betrayer), the woman at the well (a sexual libertine), Zacchaeus (the conniving financial cheat), and many others like them. In spite of the fact that Jesus was without sin and these people were very much steeped in sin,

Jesus still honored them. He washed Judas's feet; he spent time talking respectfully to the woman at the well; he went to Zacchaeus's house for dinner. Jesus, the only perfect human being to live on this earth, moved toward sinful people; he asks us to do the same, beginning with the one closest to us—our spouse.

Build contempt for contempt. Give honor to those who deserve it—beginning with your spouse.

CHAPTER 6

THE SOUL'S EMBRACE

Good Marriage Can Foster Good Prayer

A magnificent marriage begins not with knowing one another but with knowing God.

Gary and Betsy Ricucci

Just a few months after we were married, as a favor to some friends, Lisa and I agreed to swap beds with another couple. They had a waterbed and wanted to move into an upper apartment where waterbeds weren't allowed. Because we lived in a basement apartment, the weight of the waterbed didn't matter, and Lisa and I decided to give our friends a break.

It was an act of charity we soon lived to regret.

Most difficult for me was the fact that throughout all my years of singleness, I enjoyed sleeping alone. Somewhat to my dismay, I learned that Lisa is a cuddler. It took me months to learn how to sleep with someone touching me.

With the waterbed, it got even worse. When one of us moved, it was like trying to sleep on storm-infested waters. I hated it. To make matters more complicated, Lisa had a tendency to drift toward my side of the bed, pushing me over farther and farther. One night, I woke up with my cheek mashed against the wooden frame of the bed.

This is ridiculous, I thought, so I got out of bed and went over to the other side, slipping in next to Lisa so I'd have three-fourths of the bed free. You can guess what happened. I awoke early the next morning with my face smashed against the other side.

"This bed has *got* to go," I insisted.

Just as difficult as learning to sleep as a married man was learning to pray as a married man. Overnight everything had changed. My usual rituals and spiritual habits just didn't seem to fit my life anymore. I had to find new ones.

THE IMPORTANCE OF MARRIAGE TO PRAYER

I took my prayer life seriously, with good reason. The words of Jesus and his disciples, not to mention two thousand years of Christian tradition, bear witness to the same reality: prayer is essential to the Christian life. There is no faith without prayer. To be a strong Christian, we must be strong pray-ers.

Paul urges us to pray continually (1 Thessalonians 5:17). This puts prayer on a far higher plane than mere intercession. It marks prayer as the heart of our devotion, the constant awareness of God's presence, our consistent submission to his will, and our frequent expressions of adoration and praise.

John Henry Newman, a nineteenth-century English scholar and churchman, wrote, "Prayer is to the spiritual life what the beating of the pulse and the drawing of the breath are to the life of the body."[1] Martin Luther insisted, "As it is the business of tailors to make clothes and of cobblers to mend shoes, so it is the business of Christians to pray." J. C. Ryle observed, "Prayer is the very life-breath of true Christianity." A modern-day writer, Terry Glaspey, sums it up well when he writes, "Prayer is a work to which we must commit ourselves if we are to make sense of our lives in the light of eternity."

I like that last phrase—prayer is how we make sense of our lives in the light of eternity. Prayer helps us to regain the proper priorities, discern biblical wisdom, and make right judgments. Without prayer, Glaspey might say, we live as temporal people with temporal values. Prayer pushes eternity back into our lives, making God ever more relevant to the way we live our lives.

Prayer pushes eternity back into our lives, making God ever more relevant to the way we live our lives.

The Christian who fails to pray will fail to grow as she should and will be trapped in a perpetual spiritual adolescence.

When you understand the centrality of prayer in Christian spirituality, few verses are more astounding than 1 Peter 3:7: "Husbands, in the same way be considerate as you live with your wives, and treat them with respect as the weaker partner and as heirs with you of the gracious gift of life, so that nothing will hinder your prayers."

When Peter says that men must be considerate of their wives and treat them with respect *so that nothing will hinder their prayers*, he's directly connecting our attitude toward and treatment of our wives with the fundamental Christian discipline of prayer. In other words, men, when we got married, a condition was placed on our prayer lives, and that condition is tied directly to how we view and treat our wives.

In fact, much Christian teaching has gotten it exactly backward. We're told that we should improve our prayer lives if we want to have stronger marriages. But Peter tells us we should improve our marriages so we can have stronger prayer lives. Instead of prayer being the tool that will refine my marriage, Peter tells me that marriage is the tool that will refine my prayers!

Once I became a father, this made perfect sense to me. It came the day I realized that Lisa isn't just my wife; she's also God's daughter—and I was to treat her accordingly. If you want to get on my good side, just be good to one of my kids. Conversely, if you really want to make me angry, pick on one of my kids. When I realized I am married to *God's daughter*—and that you, women, are married to God's son—everything about how I viewed marriage changed. God feels about my wife—his daughter—in an even holier and more passionate way than I feel about my own daughters. Suddenly, my marriage was no longer about just me and one other person; it was very much a relationship with a passionately interested third partner. I realized one of my primary forms of worship throughout the rest of my life would be honoring God by taking care of a woman who would always be, in God's divine mind, "God's little girl."

Women, of course the same is true for you. If you have sons, you are very well aware that they are not perfect, that in fact they "stumble in many ways" (James 3:2). But does that mean you don't want them to be loved by their future or current wives? Does that mean you think your future (or current) daughter-in-law has the right to withhold her love because your son isn't perfect? Not at all! From the point of view of a mother, you are likely particularly grateful that a woman loves your imperfect son in spite of his imperfections. God looks at your husband through a parent's eyes. He knows you might be frustrated with the man you married. But he also is passionately committed to the welfare of that man, who happens to be his son.

We often reflect on the fatherhood of God, which is a foundational Christian doctrine. But if we want to change our marriages, let's spend some time thinking about God as Father-*in-Law*—because when you marry a believer, that's what he becomes!

When I fail to respect my wife—when I demean her or am condescending toward her or mistreat her in any way—I am courting trouble with the heavenly Father, who feels passionately about my spouse's welfare, a spouse who just happens to be his precious child.

This puts Peter's words in an entirely different context. If a young man pledged to give me 10 percent of his income, weekly praise, and even wrote songs about me but the rest of the time I knew he was making one of my daughters miserable through abuse or neglect, I'd have nothing to say to him except, "Hey, start treating my daughter better, and then we can talk. If you truly respect me, you'll start treating her much better." That would be the first and last thing I'd want to discuss until the situation changed. It makes total sense to me that if I don't treat Lisa well, respecting her as God's daughter, with all the privileges such a high standing involves, my prayer life will come to a complete standstill.

WHEN I FAIL TO RESPECT MY WIFE, I AM COURTING TROUBLE WITH THE HEAVENLY FATHER.

EMPTY ACCOMPLISHMENTS

This sober teaching should serve as a stern warning in an evangelical world that tends to value accomplishers—people who get things done—above people of high character. The danger is that spouses often pay the biggest price for some of these accomplishments, and true spirituality can easily suffer as a result.

Bill McCartney became famous almost overnight in Christian circles during the early 1990s. He was a highly successful college football coach and was running Promise Keepers—the hottest ministry of the decade. Yet during this time, his wife, Lyndi, was lonely and hurting. She says she was in "an emotional deep-freeze," her depression becoming so great that she lost eighty pounds.[2] McCartney was too preoccupied with his football team and—ironically enough—with the Promise Keepers' ministry to notice.

As McCartney's star rose, Lyndi said something truly gripping. "I just felt like I was getting smaller and smaller and smaller." In his book titled *Sold Out*, McCartney reflects, "It may sound unbelievable, but while Promise Keepers was spiritually inspiring to my core, my hard-charging approach to the ministry was distracting me from being, in the truest sense, a promise keeper to my own family."

To McCartney's credit, once he realized what was happening, he took the drastic step of retiring from coaching football—an amazing sacrifice that his wife took to heart—and the McCartneys were able to put their marriage back together.

Making God's daughter feel smaller so we can feel larger in the eyes of the world is a good way to make our heavenly Father-in-Law very angry. Ever notice, men, how Jesus left the crowd to minister to the individual, while we rationalize leaving the individual—particularly our spouse—to curry favor with the crowd? The same temptation, of course, is true for women in ministry. It is a lie to suggest we can excuse ignoring God's daughter *or* son in the name of worshiping him.

In marriage, I am no longer free to pursue whatever I want; my wife—supported by her standing as God's daughter—has a prior claim on my energy, thoughts, and affection. Worship-based service to God invites and encourages others as we serve; it doesn't diminish them. Biblical truth finds its basis in community and in serving the community—and this community starts with the marital relationship. If a man or woman is unrelentingly ambitious, willing to ignore or to sacrifice a spouse as they pursue their own agenda, they will almost undoubtedly be unrelentingly ambitious toward others as well, bringing them on board to serve *their* purposes, not to engage them in mutual kingdom service. And their prayer life—the lifeblood of eternally significant work—will become a sham.

If, for instance, a man views his wife solely as someone to earn part of the family income while still doing most of the work at home, provide him with sexual satisfaction, and keep the home running while he serves God or pursues his dreams—in other words, using her up to make his life better and more effective, he will also likely browbeat others to fall in line regardless of whether or not that specific role is suited for them. If a woman essentially abandons her family to ambitiously serve God, she will likely display the same lack of compassion and empathy for others as she does for her own family, who feel her absence keenly. I've seen these personalities. Whether in men or women, an underlying ruthlessness, a demanding spirit, and a stark self-absorption develop and permeate every task and relationship as the person seeks to manipulate others into joining their "ministry" rather than seeking to launch people into God's. There is a veneer of religiosity, but a polluted, foul-smelling spirit reveals itself as soon as you get underneath the surface.

WE HAVE VALUED THE WRONG ACTIVITIES WHEN WE LOOK ONLY AT A PERSON'S OUTWARD ACCOMPLISHMENTS.

We have valued the wrong activities when we look only at a person's outward accomplishments. *Our relationships — especially our marriages — are an integral part of our ministry.* If we truly want to provide a genuine witness to the world and serve God's kingdom with integrity, we would do well to take Ron Sider's words to heart: "Think of the impact if the first thing radical feminists thought of when the conversation turned to evangelical men was that they had the best reputation for keeping their marriage vows and serving their wives in the costly fashion of Jesus at the cross."[3]

So, men, ask yourself, "Do I respect my wife?" If prayer has been a problem area for you, this could be the first place to look for some answers to why you've been having difficulties. And then follow this thought with another question you can ask your wife: "Am I considerate of you?" Allow her, even encourage her, to be honest. Let her tell you what it feels like when her son hears you say, "That's just like a woman for you!" and then notices a sharper tone in her son's voice the next time he speaks to her. Allow her to open up about how she feels when she wants to slow down a little, maybe sleep a little more, and be pampered, but the man she is married to is concerned only with relaxing in front of a video game after work. If you want to be really bold, ask her how considerate you are when you're making love.

If you want to grow toward God, you must build a stronger prayer life. If you're married, to attain a stronger prayer life you must learn to respect your spouse and be considerate. (If it feels like I'm picking on the men, remember that it's the men Peter is addressing.)

SEX AND PRAYER

In Paul's first letter to the Corinthians, we find another biblical passage in which marriage and prayer are linked. This one deals specifically with sex. Speaking to husbands and wives, Paul challenges or at least questions the ascetic practice of abstaining from sexual relations within marriage.[4] Paul sees this abstention as dangerous, and he makes this practical suggestion: "Do not deprive each other except perhaps by mutual consent and for a time, so that you may devote yourselves to prayer" (1 Corinthians 7:5).

Some interpreters in the past have understood this verse as implying that *sex* can distract us from prayer. Another possible reading is that *abstinence within marriage* can distract us from prayer. How so?

A married man or woman facing keen sexual frustration might find it difficult to pray simply because his or her thoughts are failing to focus on the eternal. In a healthy individual, sexual desire can be satiated; sleeping with your spouse can leave your heart, mind, and soul free for a time to vigorously pursue God in prayer without distraction. In essence, Paul is suggesting, "Use marriage the way God intended it. Meet your sexual needs by making love to your spouse. Then your mind and soul will be more open to prayer."

Paul is a practical pastor. He recognizes that the sex drive is a biological reality. By engaging in sexual relations within a permanent, lifelong relationship, a major temptation and distraction are removed, and our souls are placed at rest.

While it may sound bizarre, Paul is telling Christian husbands and wives they can serve their partner and at the same time create the climate for an enriching prayer life by serving each other sexually. Our evangelical culture may have difficulty embracing this explanation. I've certainly never read a book on prayer that included the step, "If you're married, have sex on a regular basis," but it seems clear this is what Paul intends here!

> BY ENGAGING IN SEXUAL RELATIONS WITHIN A PERMANENT, LIFELONG RELATIONSHIP, A MAJOR TEMPTATION AND DISTRACTION ARE REMOVED, AND OUR SOULS ARE PLACED AT REST.

We can give ourselves unabashedly and enthusiastically to our spouses and still give ourselves unreservedly to God. We can express sexual desires in a marital context and still be passionate about prayer. The two go together. Even stronger than that, the two complement each other. Not only are our sexual desires and spiritual needs not necessarily competitive; they can become mutually supportive.

PRAYER AND DISSENSION

Another aspect of marriage that greatly affects our prayer lives is unresolved disputes. While Jesus doesn't specifically address marriage in the context in which he makes this statement, clearly his counsel fits the marriage relationship: "If you are offering your gift at the altar and there remember that your brother or sister has something against you, leave your gift there in front of the altar. First go and be reconciled to them; then come and offer your gift" (Matthew 5:23–24).

Here is a picture of someone approaching God in prayer. As she kneels, she remembers that things aren't right between her and somebody else. Before she continues praying, her energies should be directed—as far as it depends on her (Romans 12:18)—on reconciling with that other person—who could, of course, be her spouse. God hates dissension (Proverbs 6:19) and treasures unity (Psalm 133:1).

Marriage can force us to become stronger people because if we want to maintain a strong prayer life as married partners, we must learn how to forgive. We must become expert reconcilers. Friction will inevitably develop. Anger will surely heat up on occasion. Therefore, we must learn to deal with conflict as mature Christians—or risk blowing off our prayer life in the process.

Marriage virtually forces us into the intense act of reconciliation. It's easy to get along with people if you never get close to them. I could undoubtedly allow a certain immaturity to remain in my life as a single man, choosing not to deal with my selfishness and judgmental spirit. While I'm not proud of this, I can think of one or two people with whom it has been very difficult for me to get along. I've chosen to handle this by not going deeper in a relationship with them. I'm not obligated to be in a relationship with everybody, so there's nothing inherently wrong with simply sidestepping people who raise your blood pressure.

That option is obliterated in marriage. My wife and I live together every day. We are going to disagree about some things, and I am unquestionably obligated to maintain my intimacy with her. When we face unrealized expectations, disappoint each other, or even maliciously wound each other, will we allow dissension—which God hates—to predominate, or will we do the necessary relational work to press on to unity?

> MARRIAGE CAN FORCE US TO BECOME STRONGER PEOPLE BECAUSE IF WE WANT TO MAINTAIN A STRONG PRAYER LIFE AS MARRIED PARTNERS, WE MUST LEARN HOW TO FORGIVE.

If you want an unimpeded prayer life, you must see the question that concludes the last paragraph as a rhetorical one. Jesus makes it absolutely clear that you must choose unity if you want to maintain a vital prayer relationship with God. Dissension is a major prayer killer. Looked at from this perspective, the institution of marriage is designed to force us to become reconcilers. That's the only way we'll survive spiritually.

In this, ironically, marriage points us away from our spouse and toward God. What do I mean by this? Listen to the wisdom of James, one of the pillars of the New Testament church: "What causes fights and quarrels among you? Don't they come from your desires that battle within you? You desire but do not have ... You quarrel and fight. You do not have because you do not ask God" (James 4:1–2).

Many marital disputes result precisely from this: "You desire but do not have." James says we don't get it because we're looking *in the wrong place*. Instead of placing demands on your spouse, look to God to have your needs met. That way you can approach your spouse in a spirit of servanthood.

Those of us who have been married for a while tend to forget the "single ruse"—the tendency on the part of some (certainly not all) single young people to think that what they really need is to find "the one." Once their life mate is found, they assume that everything else will fall into place. Their loneliness, their insecurity, their worries about their own significance—all this and more will somehow mystically melt away in the fire of marital passion.

And for a very short season this may appear to be the case. Infatuation can be an intoxicating drug that temporarily covers up any number of inner weaknesses.

But marriage is a spotlight showing us that our search for another human being to "complete" us is misguided. When disillusionment breaks through, we have one of two choices: dump our spouse and become infatuated with somebody new, or seek to understand the message behind the disillusionment—that we should seek our significance, meaning, and purpose in our Creator rather than in another human being.

Approached in the right way, marriage can cause us to reevaluate our dependency on other humans for our spiritual nourishment, and direct us to nurture our relationship with God instead. No human being can love us the way we long to be loved; it is just not possible for another human to reach and alleviate the spiritual ache that God has placed in all of us.

Marriage does us a great favor in exposing this truth, but it presents a corresponding danger—getting entangled in dissension. For the sake of prayer, it is essential that we live in unity. For the sake of unity, our passions and desires must be God-directed.

What I'm suggesting is that we connect our marriages with our faith in such a way that our experience in each feeds the other. By learning to respect others, meet each other's sexual needs, overcome dissension, and use the analogies of marriage to foster more creative prayer, we can build and maintain active, growing, and meaningful prayer lives while at the same time developing stronger marriages.

Chapter 7

THE CLEANSING OF MARRIAGE

How Marriage Exposes Our Sin

> Marriage is the greatest test in the world ... but now I welcome the test instead of dreading it. It is much more than a test of sweetness of temper, as people sometimes think; it is a test of the whole character and affects every action.
>
> *T. S. Eliot*

> Marriage is the operation by which a woman's vanity and a man's egotism are extracted without anesthetic.
>
> *Helen Rowland*

> One of the best wedding gifts God gave you was a full-length mirror called your spouse. Had there been a card attached, it would have said, "Here's to helping you discover what you're really like!"
>
> *Gary and Betsy Ricucci*

Admittedly, it wasn't your typical date. A former high school girlfriend was visiting me at college—she was attending Moody Bible Institute at the time—so we decided to spend a Saturday visiting a monastery in British Columbia.

We were greeted warmly by a priest. Over his shoulder, I noticed an extremely young monk—barely out of his teens, if that—approach us. He saw the young woman I was with and immediately dropped his eyes, passing us with his head bowed.

I was passionate about God in college, and I knew this man must be passionate too, given the path he had chosen. Yet his simple act of averting his eyes spoke loudly about the different ways we were pursuing the Almighty. I spent the entire day in the company of a female companion, while this young monk couldn't allow an inadvertent glance to become a five-second look. The experience certainly gave me pause—enough of one that I can still picture his young face, the angle of his bowed head, the quick shuffle of his feet as he walked away.

As someone who has great respect and love for Christian tradition, I can't deny that, historically, Christian spirituality has been infatuated with celibacy. "After all," many teachers have said, "Jesus Christ himself was celibate. What other argument do we need?" There has been an undeniable prejudice that to become *truly* holy, to earnestly pursue sanctity, one must embrace the single life.

THERE HAS BEEN AN UNDENIABLE PREJUDICE THAT TO BECOME TRULY HOLY, TO EARNESTLY PURSUE SANCTITY, ONE MUST EMBRACE THE SINGLE LIFE.

The three of us who met that day at the monastery were all in pursuit of holiness, but all of us would take a radically different path. The young man continued living as a celibate monk. I became a married full-time writer and teacher, living in the United States. My former girlfriend married and then became a missionary to Egypt. Marriage didn't eclipse my concern for holiness (at Regent College, my master's thesis was on the doctrine of sanctification), but did it involve a compromise?

Here's the crux: the young man in the monastery entered celibacy consciously as a path toward holiness. Is it possible to enter marriage consciously as a path toward holiness? If so, how?

THE SANCTIFICATION OF MARRIAGE

Although many early church leaders viewed most sexual activity (except for that intended solely for procreation) as suspect at best and mortally sinful at worst, they didn't (interestingly enough) necessarily consider a life of celibacy to be more difficult than a life of marriage. In fact, some of the ancients realized that the marital life could be even tougher than the celibate life.

Centuries ago, Pseudo-Athanasius quoted a female teacher named Syncletica as saying, "Therefore we will not seduce ourselves with the thought that people who are in the world are carefree. For perhaps in comparison they toil much more than we do. In general for women the hatred in the world is great; for they bear children difficultly and in danger, and they endure nourishing babies with milk, and they are ill with them when their children are ill; and they survive these things, without having a result for their labor."[1]

Ambrose had similar thoughts: "Let us compare ... the advantages of married women with that which awaits virgins ... She marries and weeps. How many vows does she make with tears? She conceives, and her fruitfulness brings her trouble before offspring ... Why speak of the troubles of nursing, training, and marrying? These are the miseries of those who are fortunate. A mother has heirs, but it increases her sorrows."[2]

One night during the earlier years of our marriage, I woke up astonished at my wife's endurance. We had two children at the time. It was a stressful season for me, and my wife had gone out of her way to schedule a romantic evening to ease my mind. Later that night, however, our children became ill. One of them was still nursing, and the other insisted on being cared for by Lisa.

Lisa was exhausted. She had been up late with me, and now she was suffering a hungry nursing baby's desperate sucks for breast milk that wasn't there. When the baby was put down, Lisa had to hold a feverishly hot toddler in her lap, stroking her hair, putting a damp cloth on her forehead.

I saw my wife giving virtually every inch of her body in selfless service, and the thought hit me: "She's a saint!" That night, being a celibate nun would have sounded like a dream vacation to Lisa. How could anyone suggest she had compromised her growth in holiness by entering a life situation that called for such heroic selflessness?

In fact, if celibacy (emotional or situational) is entered into selfishly, it can destroy us every bit as much as unbridled sensuality. C. S. Lewis writes the following about our heart: "If you want to make sure of keeping it intact, you must give your heart to no one, not even to an animal. Wrap it carefully round with hobbies and little luxuries; avoid all entanglements; lock it up safe in the casket or coffin of your selfishness. But in that casket—safe, dark, motionless, airless—it will change. It will not be broken; it will become unbreakable, impenetrable, irredeemable."[3]

It probably won't be a productive conversation to argue either celibacy or marriage as the preferred pathway to holiness. Christians have walked both paths successfully. The important thing is to view the challenges of our particular life situation as a platform for growth. Athletes who truly want to improve their performance don't look for the easiest workouts; they look for the ones that will challenge them the most. Marriage certainly has its challenges, but when these are faced head-on, our marriages can nurture our devotional lives in enriching ways. One of the ways is by unmasking our sin and our hurtful attitudes and thus leading us into a spirit of humility.

UNVEILED FACES

Paul writes in Ephesians 5:25, "Husbands, love your wives, just as Christ loved the church." He goes on to say that Christ gave himself up for the church that he might "make her holy" and cleanse her, so that the church would be "without stain or wrinkle or any other blemish" (verses 26–27).

A husband who truly loves his wife will want to see her grow in Christlike purity. A wife who truly loves her husband will want to see him grow in godliness. Out of true love, both will put growth in godliness above affluence, public opinion, or personal ease.

What marriage has done for me is hold up a mirror to my sin. It forces me to face myself honestly and consider my character flaws, selfishness, and anti-Christian attitudes, encouraging me to be sanctified and cleansed and to grow in godliness.

MARRIAGE FORCES ME TO FACE MYSELF HONESTLY AND CONSIDER MY CHARACTER FLAWS, SELFISHNESS, AND ANTI-CHRISTIAN ATTITUDES, ENCOURAGING ME TO GROW IN GODLINESS.

Kathleen and Thomas Hart write, "Sometimes what is hard to take in the first years of marriage is not what we find out about our partner, but what we find out about ourselves. As one young woman who had been married about a year said, 'I always thought of myself as a patient and forgiving person. Then I began to wonder if that was just because I had never before gotten close to anyone. In marriage, when John and I began ... dealing with differences, I saw how small and unforgiving I could be. I discovered a hardness in me I had never experienced before.'"[4]

I experienced this same phenomenon. In ninth grade I was voted "most polite kid" for the annual yearbook. I have always thought of myself as reasonably patient and charitable—that is, until I got married and discovered how passionately annoyed I can become when I grab empty ice cube trays from the freezer.

When I grew up, my family lived by a simple rule: If you take out an ice cube, you refill the tray before you put it back in. Now I'll pull out a tray and find nothing more than half an ice cube—which I call an ice *chip*.

It was amazing how much such a small detail irritated me and how difficult it was for me to express its "importance" to Lisa.

One night, she was speaking romantically to me, and I saw my opportunity. "Gary," she said, "I'm going to love you forever."

"I don't need you to love me forever," I said. "I just need you to love me for seven seconds."

"What are you talking about?" she asked.

"Well, I timed how long it takes to fill an ice cube tray and discovered it's just seven sec— "

"Oh, Gary, are we back to that again?"

It finally dawned on me one day that if it takes Lisa just seven seconds to fill an ice cube tray, that's all it takes me as well. Was I really so selfish that I was willing to let seven seconds' worth of inconvenience become a serious issue in my marriage? Was my capacity to show charity really that limited?

Indeed it was. (We have since been told, many times now, that refrigerators can come with something called an "ice maker," but we lived on a tight budget in those days, with bottom-of-the-line appliances.)

Being so close to someone—which marriage necessitates—may be the greatest spiritual challenge in the world. There is no "resting," because I am under virtual twenty-four-hour surveillance. Not that Lisa makes it seem like that—it's just that I'm aware of it. Every movie I download is done so with the understanding that I will watch it with Lisa next to me. Every hour I take off for recreation is an hour that Lisa will know about. Where I eat lunch (and what), how I'm doing on a particular diet—my appetites and lusts and desires are all in full view of Lisa.

This presupposes, of course, that I'm willing to be confronted with my sin—that I'm willing to ask Lisa, "Where do you see unholiness in my life? I want to know about it. I want to change it."

This takes tremendous courage, which I often lack. It means I'm willing to hear what displeases Lisa about me, as well as to refuse to become paralyzed by the fear that she will love me less or leave me because the sin in me is being exposed.

I don't naturally gravitate toward the honesty and openness that leads to change. My natural sin-bent is to hide and erect a glittering image. Dan Allender and Tremper Longman describe the dichotomy in forceful words: "Man was meant to be a bold creative artist who plunges into the unformed mystery of life and shapes it to a greater vision of beauty. At the fall he became a cowardly, violent protector of nothing more than himself. Intimacy and openness were replaced by hiding and hatred."[5]

Marriage, they add, is "the relationship where depravity is best exposed and where our dignity is best lived out."[6] Just go back in time to the days of Adam and Eve. The first marriage was the context for the first sin. And the first obvious result of the fall was a breakdown in marital intimacy. Neither Adam nor Eve welcomed the fact that their weaknesses were now as obvious as a little girl's first attempt at makeup. All of a sudden they felt kind of funny about being naked. And they started blaming each other.

Do you hide from your spouse? Or do you utilize the spotlight of marriage to grow in grace? Some of us need this spotlight to understand how truly sinful we are.

Howard Hendricks told about a time he had just completed a sermon and an eager young man came up to him and called him a "great man." On the drive home, Hendricks turned to his wife and said, "*A great man*. How many great men do you know?"

"One fewer than you think," she answered.

As a spiritual exercise, few things are more profitable than this kind of spiritual examination. François Fénelon, a seventeenth-century Christian, wrote that "all the saints are convinced that sincere humility is the foundation of all virtues,"[7] an opinion shared by the Anglican writer William Law: "[Humility] is so essential to the right state of our souls that there is no pretending to a reasonable or pious life without it. We may as well think to see without eyes or live without breath as to live in the spirit of religion without the spirit of humility."[8]

And what is humility? Fénelon tells us it is "a certain honesty, and childlike willingness to acknowledge our faults, to recover from them, and to submit to the advice of experienced people; these will be solid useful virtues, adapted to your sanctification."[9]

Is your desire to be accepted by your spouse stronger than your desire to become more like Christ? Do you value words of affirmation over and above words of inspiration? It doesn't have to be either-or, of course, but often we feel the lack of unconditional acceptance keenly and resent redemptive correction. If there's no encouragement, we probably won't hear the words of challenge, but when there are *only* words of encouragement, it might mean we have stopped seeking *first* his righteousness (Matthew 6:33) and started seeking first something much less.

I believe it is possible to enter marriage with a view to being cleansed spiritually, if, that is, we do so with a willingness to embrace marriage as a spiritual discipline. To do this, we must not enter marriage predominantly to be fulfilled, emotionally satisfied, or romantically charged, but rather to become more like Jesus Christ. We must embrace the reality of having our flaws exposed to our partner and thereby having them exposed to us as well. Sin never seems quite as shocking when it is known only to us; when we see how it looks or sounds to another, it is magnified ten times over. The celibate can hide frustration by removing themselves from the situation, but the married man or woman has no true refuge. It is hard to hide when you share the same bed.

WE MUST NOT ENTER MARRIAGE PREDOMINANTLY TO BE FULFILLED, EMOTIONALLY SATISFIED, OR ROMANTICALLY CHARGED, BUT RATHER TO BECOME MORE LIKE JESUS CHRIST.

THE DATING DANCE

I have a theory: Behind virtually every case of marital dissatisfaction lies unrepented sin. Couples don't fall out of love so much as they fall out of repentance. Sin, wrong attitudes, and personal failures that are not dealt with slowly erode the relationship, assaulting and eventually erasing the once lofty promises made in the throes of an earlier (and less polluted) passion.

All of us enter marriage with sinful attitudes. When these

attitudes surface, the temptation will be to hide them or even to run to another relationship where the attitudes won't be so well-known. But Christian marriage presumes a certain degree of self-disclosure. When I gave my hand in marriage, I committed to allow myself to be known by Lisa—and that means she'll see me as I am—with my faults, my prejudices, my fears, and my weaknesses.

This reality can be terrifying to contemplate. Dating is largely a dance in which you always try to put your best face forward—hardly a good preparation for the inevitable self-disclosure implied in marriage. In fact, I wouldn't be surprised if many marriages end in divorce largely because one or both partners are running from their own revealed weaknesses as much as they are running from something they can't tolerate in their spouse.

May I suggest an alternative to running? Use the revelation of your sin as a means to grow in the foundational Christian virtue of humility, leading to confession and transformation. Then go the next step and adopt the positive virtue that corresponds to the sin you are renouncing. If you've used women in the past, practice serving your wife. If you've been quick to ridicule your husband, practice giving him encouragement and praise. Humility can restore and bless your marriage, as well as grow you into a person who is more like Jesus.

View marriage as an entryway into sanctification—as a relationship that will reveal your sinful behaviors and attitudes and give you the opportunity to address them before the Lord. But here's the challenge: Don't give in to the temptation to resent your partner as your own weaknesses are revealed. Don't run from what you are hearing about yourself, or push your spouse away because of it—accept it and use it to grow. Correspondingly, give them the freedom and acceptance they need in order to face their own weaknesses as well. In this way, we can use marriage as a spiritual mirror, designed for our sanctification and growth in holiness.

WE CAN USE MARRIAGE AS A SPIRITUAL MIRROR, DESIGNED FOR OUR SANCTIFICATION AND GROWTH IN HOLINESS.

RECEIVING ANOTHER'S SIN

This way of viewing marriage points to another important principle—not just having *my* sin exposed, but reflecting on how I treat my wife when *her* sin is exposed. Do I use this knowledge to crush her, humiliate her, or gain power over her, or do I use it to gently and lovingly lead her into living out the character of Jesus Christ?

Possessing the knowledge of someone's sin is a powerful and dangerous thing. On several occasions, men have shared with me their frustration with their difficulty in forgiving their wives for having an affair. Their natural tendency is to throw the affair back in their wives' faces. It's a vicious grasp for power. As soon as their wives point out something that needs to be changed in their lives, their natural inclination is to say, "Oh, does this mean you're going to run back to Jim if I don't change?" Or, "Well, I might lose my temper, but at least I know how to control myself sexually!"

The men usually hate saying these words as much as the wives hate hearing them. They are cruel and vindictive comments, but sometimes we are cruel and vindictive husbands.

"Do you ever tell your wife how much you hate it when you say these things?" I asked one man.

"Yeah, but she still hates hearing them, even though she knows I hate saying them."

In order for this discipline to work, we will have to link it with the discipline of forgiveness (discussed in chapter 10). This discipline of having our own sin exposed and being a spotlight for our spouse is a difficult one to master. It takes tremendous courage, and it takes what will seem (particularly to men) like an almost melodramatic gentleness. The marital relationship shouldn't be a grilling experience but rather a nurturing one—encouraging one another on the pathway of sanctification: "Therefore encourage one another and build each other up" (1 Thessalonians 5:11).

Let's look at a couple of real-life examples of how having the sin revealed in our lives can help us grow by demonstrating our true motivations.

THE SIN BEHIND DISSATISFACTION

Greg looked at his wife, Sharon (not their real names), and tried not to show what he was really feeling. They were celebrating their eighth anniversary by going out for dinner, and Greg was, well, bored. An avid computer geek, Greg felt chagrined that he would much rather be talking about computers with a colleague than trying to find something to say to his wife.

Sharon's choice for the dinner setting was a funky antique store/restaurant. Greg collects old metal advertisement signs, and he had to fight the urge to get up and browse in the antique shop. This was his wedding anniversary, he reminded himself; he should want to share it with his wife and not wander off alone seeking his own satisfaction.

But Greg believed his wife's world had shrunk to an almost unbearable degree. She had little to say beyond giving a tedious, play-by-play account of the day's events. "And then, right after I mopped the floor, I went up to take a shower—and guess what? Rebecca dropped her entire bowl of applesauce and didn't clean it up. Peter walked right through the mess and started making applesauce footprints all over the house! And I had just cleaned the floors!"

Greg nodded, struggling mightily against his internal thoughts. He felt bad because he knew his wife wanted something he wasn't sure he could give her—she wanted someone to be interested in these domestic challenges, and frankly, keeping floors clean wasn't all that interesting to Greg. Greg has a fertile mind. He loves figuring out computer glitches ("It's like a digital crossword puzzle," he explains), and his wife's seemingly endless anecdotes of messes and hassles put him to sleep.

"But, Greg," I suggested when we talked a few days later, "this is how you serve your wife—by listening to her world. Do you think Jesus' mind was excited by washing the disciples' feet and listening to their foolish arguments over and over again? Besides, these are your kids. Of course Sharon's going to think you're interested in what happens to them throughout the day."

Greg reluctantly nodded his head. "I guess. But ..." His

pause told me we were about to get to the crux of the matter. "Well, there's this woman I work with. We're able to talk code—something Sharon has absolutely no interest in—and when we figure out problems together, there's nothing else like it. I feel so close to her."

There was another long pause. "Sharon and I have nothing in common anymore."

Right then and there the selfish lie was exposed. "Nothing in common?" I asked. "What about Peter and Rebecca?"

"Well, maybe the children."

"And having conceived them together and caring for them together—including cleaning up after them—counts less in your book than connecting a bunch of numbers in order to write computer code with this other woman? Is that what you're saying? Do your children mean so little to you that you find them less engaging than creating a new program that will be obsolete in eighteen months?"

"Ouch," Greg said, blowing out a long breath. "I guess I hadn't thought of it that way."

Greg wanted to rewrite his reality so his thoughts wouldn't sound as evil as they really were. The truth was, he *did* value writing computer code over spending time with his family—but instead of admitting and reevaluating that attitude, he blamed everything on his wife: "Sharon's boring," "Sharon doesn't understand me," "We've grown apart." These accusations were much more comfortable for him than admitting, "I'm selfish, and I'm having serious priority problems—even to the point of mentally risking an affair."

Marian is as disappointed in her husband as a woman could be. According to her, he's not involved with his kids as much as he should be. He doesn't go to church as often as she does. He doesn't hold her hand like he used to. In the course of our conversation, however, Marian vaguely alluded to several addictions of her own—an addiction to food that resulted in her having gained more than seventy-five pounds since they had been married. A prior sexual addiction that still made it difficult for her to pursue her husband sexually. A biting tongue paired with a quick, clever mind that could cut people apart in seconds. Added to all this was a propensity to become seriously depressed a couple of times a year.

Here's the thing: Marian's frustrations with her husband are understandable and real. But she had an excuse for every one of *her* failings, and passionate bitterness toward every one of her husband's. She wasn't using marriage as a mirror; she was using it as a weapon. I don't want to sound more important than I am, but I don't have a lot of time to see a lot of people. She had forty-five minutes with me, and we could have talked about how God was helping her with many of her issues, but *her* "stuff" was the last thing she wanted to talk about; Marian is convinced her marriage will get better only when everyone agrees with her that her husband is just a really bad guy. She is more concerned that everyone agrees that her husband is a bad guy than she is with her becoming a godlier woman. I'm a pastor, not a therapist, which means there isn't much I can do if someone approaches me with a hard heart.

If we approach marriage in the right manner and are willing to look honestly at our deepest motivations and our own failings, marriage can be like a photograph. Looking at pictures isn't always pleasant. I remember the time we looked at photographs we had picked up at the store, and I realized for the first time how much weight I had put on. "Whoa—where did that chin come from?" The natural inclination is to blame the camera angle, but the truth is, those fifteen pounds were showing from *every* angle!

The same thing happens with our sin in marriage. We resent the revealed truth, and we are tempted to take it out on our spouse—the camera, so to speak. What if Greg were to reexamine his motivation and his lack of interest in what happens at home while he's away, instead of overlooking his sin by blaming his wife for "being boring"? What if Marian were to ask herself what it was like for her husband to be married to a woman who reveled in food more than sex, who had the wit and intellect to tear him down verbally whenever she was feeling mean, and who all but checked out on her family a couple of times a year as she battled depression?

In my book *The Glorious Pursuit*, I reflect on a truth that applies here. A mature Christian finds his or her fulfillment in living faithfully before God—that is, in being a mature person, not in being around a particular person. Much of our marital dissatisfaction stems from self-hatred. We don't like what we've done or become. We've let selfish and sinful attitudes poison our thoughts and lead us into shameful behaviors, and suddenly all we want is out.

A MATURE CHRISTIAN FINDS HIS OR HER FULFILLMENT IN LIVING FAITHFULLY BEFORE GOD.

The mature response, however, is not to *leave* a sinner (our spouse); it's to *change* a sinner (ourselves).

Whenever marital dissatisfaction rears its head in my marriage—as it does in virtually every marriage—I simply check my focus. The times I am happiest and most fulfilled in my marriage are the times I am intent on drawing meaning and fulfillment from becoming a better husband rather than from demanding a better wife.

I don't know why this works. I don't know how you can be unsatisfied in your marriage and then offer yourself to God to bring about change in your life and suddenly find yourself more than satisfied with the same spouse. I don't know why this works; I only know it does work. It takes time, and by time I mean maybe years. But if your heart is driven by the desire to draw near to Jesus, you find joy by becoming like Jesus. You'll never find that joy by doing something that offends Jesus—such as instigating a divorce or an affair.

In the nineteenth century, Marie d'Agoult left her children to follow after the most famous pianist of her day, Hungarian composer and virtuoso Franz Liszt. After the ardor of her infatuation cooled and the reality of missing her children set in, Marie is said to have made this observation: "When one has smashed everything around oneself, one has also smashed oneself."

Sin will lead to self-destruction if we allow it to. The same sin that confronts two different people can lead one to a greater understanding, and therefore to greater maturity and growth, at the same time it leads another into a cycle of denial, deception, and spiritual destruction.

The choice is ours. Sin is a reality in this fallen world. How we respond to it will determine whether our marriages become a casualty statistic or a crown of success.

CHAPTER 8

SACRED HISTORY

Building the Spiritual Discipline of Perseverance

> It is very hard to be entirely faithful, even to things, ideas, above all, persons one loves. There is no such thing as perfect faithfulness any more than there is perfect love or perfect beauty. But it is fun trying.
>
> *Katherine Anne Porter*

> May the Lord direct your hearts into God's love and Christ's perseverance. *2 Thessalonians 3:5*

Marti entered marriage with an enormous burden—a previously failed relationship (not marital) that had included sexual activity and a gut-wrenching breakup. As a result, she struggled with feelings of insecurity, even after she and her husband were married. She just couldn't get over the perception that "conflict leads to breakup, and breakup leads to intense pain."

After several years of marriage, Marti and her husband started fighting over financial problems. Weeks of vigorous discussion and occasional bouts of yelling ensued, but no conclusions were drawn. The dispute became so acute that the marital relationship started showing the strain. There was little joy—just angst and frustration.

Marti subconsciously slipped back into feelings that were born out of her earlier failed relationship. Because she still hurt over the dissolution of that bond, she experienced acute anxiety over whether her marriage could survive this challenge. In her past, unresolved issues meant an inevitable breakup, so she secretly began mourning a relationship that had not yet died.

Then one night, after yet another vigorous and ultimately unresolved discussion, Marti's husband did something so wonderfully prophetic and profound that Marti will never forget it as long as she lives. You could see the joy of her husband's tender care reflected in her eyes as she told the story: "He wrapped his arms around me and said, 'Marti, you need to know that no matter what we decide or don't decide, I'm never going to quit on this marriage. Even if we have to live with this tension for the rest of our lives, I will never leave you.' "

Marti burst into tears as she shared this story. Even though there was nearly constant contention in her marriage, she didn't want this relationship to end, and now her husband had promised it wouldn't.

WE PROCLAIM THE PROPHETIC GRACE OF MARRIAGE WHEN WE UNDERSTAND THE SACREDNESS OF BUILDING A HISTORY TOGETHER.

Marti and her husband embraced the sacredness of their history together; they both found great meaning in the simple fact that the marriage would survive. Suddenly, the original problem seemed less significant than the overall fact that their history together was secure.

We proclaim the prophetic grace of marriage when we understand the sacredness of building a history together. Sharing an infatuation is fun, but it passes almost as soon as it arrives. It's a fading reality. Building a sacred history together can be hard work but it grows through the years instead of fades. To enjoy a truly sacred marriage, we have to move from sharing an intense infatuation to building a sacred history. What makes this history sacred is that it shadows another relationship that has preceded our own.

THE GOD OF ABRAHAM

A well-known theologian was once asked to give the best piece of evidence for the existence of God. Without hesitating, he said, "The Jew."

Throughout a tumultuous history, the Jewish people have sometimes hung by the slenderest of threads as yet another tyrant or enemy sought their extinction. Yet for centuries, they have survived.

There is a theological reality embedded in this history. The God of the Old Testament is unique in that he attached himself to a people. For thousands of years, loyal adherents worshiped the god of the hills, the god of the valley, or the god of the sea, but the idea that there was a God of Abraham, Isaac, and Jacob—a God of people—this was something new.

Even more stunning was the direct line of this relationship—from Adam and Eve to Abraham and Sarah, from Abraham and Sarah to David and Bathsheba, from David and Bathsheba to Mary and Joseph. There was a sacredness to this history. Meaning was derived from the fact that God had been with the fathers, grandfathers, and great-grandfathers, and with their fathers and grandfathers before them.

This relationship between God and his people was anything but easy. There were periods of great joy and celebration (witness the love affair of God and his people when Solomon dedicated the temple); seasons of frustration and anger (when God allowed foreign tyrants to conquer); times of infidelity and apostasy (when Israel chased after other gods); and excruciating seasons of silence (including a four-hundred-year stretch of time between the Old and New Testaments).

Now take these examples and break them down, thinking of them in a smaller context. There were times of great joy and celebration, frustration and anger, infidelity and apostasy; and there were excruciating seasons of silence. Sound like any relationship you know? Isn't it stunning how closely God's relationship with Israel mirrors the relationship of a husband and wife?

Looking at marriage through this lens will help us appreciate *all* aspects of marriage, not just the fun parts. Of course we'd all like to live in perpetual joy and celebration, and we are grateful when marriage offers many such seasons. And though frustration, anger, infidelity, and silence aren't anything any of us are usually seeking more of, the truth is, there are lessons to be learned as we walk through these times. They won't be fun seasons, but they can be profitable seasons that help us experientially identify with God and his relationship with Israel. Has your marriage had periods of great joy and celebration? God can relate to and rejoice with you. Have you experienced the heartbreaking betrayal of unfaithfulness? Or the frustration of mournful silence? If so, you are not alone, and you have been given the raw materials with which to build a more intimate relationship with God.

One characteristic holds the history of God and Israel together—*perseverance*. When Israel turned her back on God, God didn't turn his back on Israel. He may have stepped back for a time, but the overall commitment remained steadfast.

I particularly relate to the four hundred years of silence between the Old and New Testaments. So often it isn't that our marriages are either good or bad; they just are. We get tired of the routine, and our souls occasionally grow numb toward each other.

Kathleen and Thomas Hart describe it this way: "Marriage is a long walk two people take together. Sometimes the terrain is very interesting, sometimes rather dull. At times the walk is arduous, for both persons or for one. Sometimes the conversation is lively; at other times, there is not much to say. The travelers do not know exactly where they are going, nor when they will arrive."[1]

Adding to this sometimes numbing effect of sameness is the fact that this walk is longer for us than it was for our ancestors. In previous centuries, many marriages were cut short because women frequently died during childbirth and things like antibiotics and cancer cures weren't even thought of, much less invented. Thomas Cranmer, the famous archbishop of Canterbury from 1533–1553, lost his wife in the first year of his marriage. Jeremy Taylor (1613–1667), an English bishop and writer (*The Rule and Exercises of Holy Living* and *The Rule and Exercises of Holy Dying*) lost his wife after less than thirteen years of marriage. John Calvin's wife (of whom he spoke with passionate affection and gratitude in remembrance) didn't make it to their tenth wedding anniversary, and John Donne's wife, Anne, died just sixteen years after they were married.[2]

Men didn't live as long as they do today either. As recently as 1870, a woman couldn't count on her husband still being alive when their youngest child left home. In 1911, the average length of marriage was twenty-eight years; by 1967, it had risen to forty-two years.

MARRIAGE HELPS US TO DEVELOP THE CHARACTER OF GOD HIMSELF AS WE STICK WITH OUR SPOUSES THROUGH GOOD TIMES AND BAD.

With medical advances and increasing life expectancy, many of us can realistically look forward to celebrating a sixtieth or even seventieth wedding anniversary. This phenomenon of being married for six or seven decades can pay rich dividends for our spiritual life and growth. Marriage helps us to develop the character of God himself as we stick with our spouses through good times and bad. Every wedding gives birth to a new history, a new beginning. The spiritual meaning of marriage is found in maintaining that history together.

NEUROPLASTICITY

The fact that we have the potential to be married longer today gives us opportunities some of our ancestors didn't get to enjoy. One of the surprises for me in studying the seasons of marriage is how slowly true intimacy grows. In fact, some experts suggest it takes from nine to fourteen years for a couple to truly "create and form its being."[3] This is because of what neurologists — those who study the brain — call "neuroplasticity." Neuroplasticity means that our brains are literally — i.e., physiologically — shaped by our experience, choices, and actions. Repeated actions create neurological "grooves" that eventually become automatic. That's what gives rise to addictions and to muscle memory, for example. When you learn a new golf swing or the skills to play a new instrument, you have to think about what to do. After practicing, it becomes automatic. How many times have you driven home from work or church, pulled into your driveway, and realized you didn't make a single conscious decision the entire time you drove home? It was like you were on automatic pilot. That's neuroplasticity in action.

Which means, when we first get married, our brains are stuck in "singleness" *grooves*. We don't think of ourselves as part of a couple, but as one individual trying to relate to another. In fact, the journey from "me" to "we" is about a decade to a decade and a half; it takes that long for our brains to make the shift from thinking thoughts of singleness to embracing our new identity as one half of a couple.

All of this means that when couples break up after just six or seven years, they haven't even begun to experience what being married is really like. It's sort of like climbing halfway up a mountain but never getting to see the sights; you're in the middle of the task and your soul is consumed with the struggle, but it's much too soon to experience the full rewards. You don't even know what it would really be like to have your brain "shaped" around your spouse's brain (all of this is a gross oversimplification, but I think it makes the point). Evaluating your marriage so soon is like trying to eat a cake that's half-baked. Becoming one — in the deepest, most intimate sense — takes time. It's a journey that never really ends, but it takes at least the span of a decade for the sense of intimacy to really display itself in the marriage relationship.

On the flip side, if you abort your marriage, say, seven years in and remarry someone else, you will have to spend several years "untangling" your brain from your prior marriage before you can fully give yourself to the new marriage. It is common for a partner in a second marriage to watch their spouse overreact to a seemingly small trigger. What's going on is that the spouse is patterned by the previous relationship, perhaps even unconsciously thinking, *I know where this goes. She says this, I say that, and then we go there.* They've jumped five steps forward out of prior mental conditioning. The new spouse needs to be patient and say, "You're fighting with someone else. That's not where I was going at all." This is part of what makes second (and later) marriages so difficult. You're not just marrying a new person; you're neurologically trying to unmarry the previous spouse.

BECOMING ONE—IN THE DEEPEST, MOST INTIMATE SENSE—TAKES TIME. IT TAKES AT LEAST THE SPAN OF A DECADE FOR THE SENSE OF INTIMACY TO REALLY DISPLAY ITSELF IN THE MARRIAGE RELATIONSHIP.

The payoff is that after several decades together, our brains will have formed around each other, providing a certain comfort and intimacy that newlywed couples can't possibly experience. Now married almost thirty years, Lisa and I are a part of each other in a way we couldn't have been twenty years ago, or even fifteen years ago when I first wrote this book. I treasure this aspect of marriage. You'll miss it if you have passed through several "serial" marriages, as our brains simply aren't designed by God to walk that path.

THE SPIRITUAL DISCIPLINE OF PERSEVERANCE

What's so fascinating about all of this is that what we need to develop to enjoy an intimate marriage—commitment, tenacity, perseverance—is exactly what Scripture says we need to develop as faithful servants of God. This isn't a coincidence. It makes sense that God would design the fundamental human relationship—that between a husband and wife—as a relationship that complements our spiritual walk. The stronger we grow as spouses, persevering and pressing further into our marriage, the more we'll develop the very character traits we need to become mature believers. Growing in our marriages, then, can build up our faith, even as growing in our faith will build our marriages. It's a wonderful circle of spiritual life!

Though perseverance is woven through every major book in the New Testament, it's not appreciated as much today as it was by the biblical writers. Jesus heralded this trait in his famous parable of the sower—which could more accurately be called the parable of the soils, because that is what the teaching is really about. In Luke 8, Jesus warns that some will hear God's word and believe for a while, "but in the time of testing they fall away" (verse 13). Others hear but have their faith choked by "life's worries, riches and pleasures, and they do not mature" (verse 14). But those commended by Jesus are those who "hear the word, *retain it*, and *by persevering* produce a crop" (verse 15, emphasis added).

Biblical spirituality emphasizes perseverance: James tells us, "Let perseverance finish its work so that you may be mature and complete, not lacking anything" (1:4). The apostle Paul puts it this way: "To those *who by persistence* in doing good seek glory, honor and immortality, he will give eternal life. But for those who are self-seeking and who reject the truth and follow evil, there will be wrath and anger" (Romans 2:7–8, emphasis added).

Righteousness—true holiness—is seen over time in our persistence. It is relatively easy to flirt with righteousness—being occasionally courteous to other drivers (if you happen to be in a good mood), helping someone in need by opening the door for them (if you have time), throwing a few extra bucks into the offering plate (as long as you won't miss them). But this behavior is, in reality, superficial righteousness. The righteousness God seeks is a *persistent* righteousness, a commitment to continue making the right decision even when, perhaps hourly, you feel pulled in the opposite direction. Holiness is far more than an inclination toward occasional acts of kindness and charity; it is a commitment to persistently surrender to God.

Married men or women who find themselves falling in love with someone else will have to continually make a choice not to act inappropriately and to watch their tongue. A one-time decision to be faithful and true to their marriage vows likely won't kill their feelings. They may have to choose to gradually grow out of their feelings by not acting on them. In other words, if God doesn't take the feelings away, they will have to persevere in righteousness until the feelings naturally fade.

Because marriage is such a long journey, it goes through many stages. Some of these are more difficult than others. Certainly, the season of raising small children presents an enormous challenge to fostering intimacy and having fun. It's exhausting work. Two researchers, William J. Lederer and Don Jackson, note that they "have never observed a generally constant collaborative union between spouses during the period when they are raising children."[4]

Now that Lisa and I are empty nesters, we treasure even more those years when the kids were young and always at home. At the time, however, there were some exhausting days, and we had to fight for our marriage in the midst of a tight budget, high stress, and low sleep. Now that our children are young adults, we're in awe of what they've become and the journey God allowed us to be a part of. You need to know, though, that it took a toll on our marriage. In retrospect the journey of child rearing has united us and strengthened our bond. During the process, however, it sometimes threatened to divide us (or at least created some frustrating days).

Life presents us with some seasons that, quite frankly, must be endured. There are many miraculously fulfilling moments we will experience as we raise our kids, but other aspects of our lives—including solitary time together as a couple—will, of necessity, suffer. This is merely a season, and it is foolish to quit persevering during a time when all marriages have to adapt and reevaluate previous expectations to some extent.

What causes us to give up on our marriages? Although Jesus wasn't specifically addressing the marriage relationship in his parable of the soils, he covers many of the sources of our failure to persevere in marriage. Some of us give up when "the time of testing" comes (Luke 8:13). We thought marriage would be easy; when it gets hard, we bail out. Others give up when they are choked by "life's worries" (verse 14). Marriage counselors tell us that money problems have destroyed more marriages than just about anything else. There is also our selfishness and our sin—both of which are capable of polluting a once-precious affection.

What gives us the power to persist in doing good? Paul hints at the answer in the Romans 2 passage mentioned above. He notes that in our persistence we seek "glory, honor and immortality" (verse 7). Persistence doesn't make sense unless we live with a keen sense of eternity. I'll expand on this thought in the next chapter, but this truth needs to make a brief appearance here as well.

Persons struggling with infatuation for someone who is not their spouse may need to make a decision that in the short run may make them less happy and bring them less pleasure (though I would argue that the decision will, in many cases, make them more fulfilled in the long run). Christian endurance is based on the idea that there is another life, commonly known as heaven, which is eternal and for which this world is a preparation. The coming world is so glorious and weighted with so much honor that it is worth making sacrifices now to receive glory, honor, and immortality then.

PERSISTENCE DOESN'T MAKE SENSE UNLESS WE LIVE WITH A KEEN SENSE OF ETERNITY.

Around which world is your life centered? Your marriage will ultimately reveal the answer to that question. If we have an eternal outlook, preparing for eternity by sticking with a difficult marriage makes much more sense than destroying a family to gain quick and easy relief. Most divorces are marked by the actions of someone running from, at most, a few difficult decades — and for this relief, people are throwing away glory and honor that last for eternity. It's a horrible trade! (I'm not speaking here to those of you whose spouses have compromised your union through abuse, affairs, and addictions.)

The holiness that will be rewarded in heaven is a *persistent* holiness. Read through the entire Bible, and I promise you that you won't find one reference to a crown in heaven that goes to the person who had the happiest life on earth. That reward just doesn't exist. Nor is there a heavenly ribbon for the Christian who felt the least amount of pain.

The priority of a sacred history is an *eternal* priority. Marriage is a beautiful and effective reminder of this reality. One of the most poetic lines in Scripture, one I wish every husband and wife would display in a prominent place in their home, is found in 2 Thessalonians 3:5: "May the Lord direct your hearts into God's love and Christ's perseverance."

God's love and *Christ's perseverance* — there's the Bible's best recipe for holiness and a successful life here on earth. Oh, that our hearts could be directed into more and more of God's love! Oh, that we could learn the patient perseverance of Christ himself!

The alternative is explained in Paul's letter to the Romans. Instead of heavenly rewards, some will receive "wrath and anger." And who are they? "Those who are self-seeking and who reject the truth and follow evil" (Romans 2:8). What is more self-seeking than to ignore what is best for your children — an intact, peaceable home — and to dump a marriage because you're tired of your spouse, even though doing so may seriously diminish your ministry of reconciliation discussed in chapter 3? I know many of you have fought, unsuccessfully, to stay married. This is not to brand you a failure, but to applaud your effort, even if it didn't succeed. If you are in the midst of such a struggle, this is a plea for you not to give up. Perseverance does pay off — in our character and in heavenly rewards, if nothing else.

AN UNCERTAIN FUTURE

One of the great dangers of breaking a marriage history is that we can't know the future. Let me explain with a true story.

My selfishness was seen at its most despicable level the day I was picked up at the airport by a woman from a group that had invited me to speak. I was directed to sit in the back of her van with her son, but as soon as the door opened, I cringed. The van was filthy. I was wearing slacks and a sports coat. I was scheduled to speak later in the day, so I was particularly wary about sitting in that seat—I was quite sure that the food bits and dirt would stick to my wool clothing like Velcro.

Not wanting to offend the woman, I tried my best to inconspicuously flick off as much of the debris as possible before I sat down, but her son behind me wasn't making my job easy, urging me to quickly find a seat.

Terrible, selfish thoughts ran through my head—*How could she let her van get like this when she knew she would be picking me up?*

Within hours, I found out that this woman was divorced—and thus living as a single mom. *That explains the dirty van*, I thought. *She has her hands full.* And I felt terrible for judging her. When you're a single parent, it's not easy to find time to vacuum out the van.

Then as we got to know each other even better, she shared that she was in the middle of a round of chemotherapy. The drugs made her so sick that she could work just one day a week—as a waitress. The next six days were spent gathering sufficient strength to go back to the restaurant and eke out another hundred dollars. She was earning next to nothing, trying to parent three kids by herself, and undergoing chemotherapy—yet she had sacrificed her time and energy and money (gas certainly isn't free!) to taxi me around town, volunteering her time for a good cause.

She was an absolute hero, and I was disgusted with myself. I had silently begrudged a dirty seat, absorbed by my own potential embarrassment at walking into a meeting room with food hanging from my clothes—something that was utterly insignificant compared to the real-life challenges this woman was facing.

After I repented and started thinking like a servant instead of a prima donna, I turned my thoughts toward her ex-husband. *How could a professing Christian man allow a woman with whom he had conceived three children go through this ordeal alone?* I felt so sorry for this woman; my heart bled for her. My next phone call to my wife was filled with the account of this sad story. "What kind of man," I sputtered, "wouldn't immediately rush to the aid of someone in this situation when he had already pledged before a church full of people to be with her in sickness and in health? How hard does a heart have to be not to be moved by the suffering of someone you once loved?"

When this husband divorced this woman, he couldn't have anticipated she would get cancer, of course, but that's why we build a *sacred* history. None of us can accurately see into the future. This woman set aside her career and hadn't developed any particular vocational skills as she raised this man's three children. She made herself vulnerable for his benefit. And after that—after he had built his career and she was still saddled with tremendous responsibility for the rearing of three children—he broke their history together and left her nearly destitute.

When you divorce your spouse, you have no idea what the future holds for him or her. The situation can and often does lead to chaos, because odds are that at least one spouse will need care in the not-too-distant future. Certainly such neglect qualifies as the "self-seeking" that Paul says naturally results in God's "wrath and anger."

Also subject to this anger are those who "reject the truth." Clearly, Paul is talking about the truth of salvation here, but another truth can be inferred from this passage as well—the truth of God's will and his laws.

Most of us know that God hates divorce because Scripture says it explicitly: " 'I hate divorce,' says the LORD God of

Israel" (Malachi 2:16, NIV, 1984 ed.). Jesus elaborated on this perspective on divorce, telling his disciples that "anyone who divorces his wife, except for sexual immorality, makes her the victim of adultery, and anyone who marries a divorced woman commits adultery" (Matthew 5:32). The only reason God made provision for divorce in the Old Testament, Jesus added elsewhere, was because he was dealing with hard hearts (Matthew 19:8–9).

This, my friends, is *truth*. To reject it, Paul warns in Romans 2, is to risk God's wrath and anger. I'm still amazed at Christian men who can leave their wives and children nearly destitute financially so they can pursue a new relationship—all the while trying to maintain the illusion that Jesus Christ is still Lord of their lives.

BUILDING A SACRED HISTORY TOGETHER TEACHES US TO BE PERSISTENT IN DOING GOOD, EVEN WHEN WE WANT TO DO SOMETHING ELSE.

Building a sacred history together teaches us to be *persistent in doing good*, even when we want to do something else. This commitment to perseverance teaches us the basic Christian discipline of self-denial. As part of this, we must reject self-seeking behavior and instead think about the future, a future that points beyond this world to the next. For those who don't believe in heaven, divorce can make a lot of sense. Once heaven becomes part of the equation, the cost of an unbiblical divorce—God's wrath and anger, jeopardizing the future by a selfish attitude—becomes much too high.

THE IDEAL

We have reached high to make a strong point. Divorce, by definition, is a failure—of love, forgiveness, and patience—or (at the very least) it is the result of poor judgment in choosing a difficult partner in the first place. But we are all failures at some point. Jesus' words are frequently severe; according to Matthew 5:28, I and virtually every other man alive must be considered an adulterer. One lustful look and *Boom!* we've fallen. One angry exclamation, "You fool!" and, according to Jesus, I'm in danger of being thrown into the fire of hell (Matthew 5:22).

Jesus makes a number of harsh, seemingly unrelenting statements pertaining to how we should live, and there isn't a man or woman alive who hasn't broken some of those commands. But look at the life of Jesus, and you see tremendous mercy. The adulterous woman isn't condemned; she's simply told to turn her back on her life of sin (see John 8:11). Jesus once said that if we put our hand to the plow and look back, we're not fit for the kingdom of God (Luke 9:62), but he willingly and lovingly took Peter back after Peter had disowned him three times (Mark 14:66–72).

If you're reading this after you've gone through a divorce, you serve no one—least of all God—by becoming fixated on something you can't now undo. That's what forgiveness and grace are for—a fresh start, a new beginning. God offers grace precisely for the reason that he *wants* to forgive us. He is eager to forgive us so we can start afresh and live a new meaningful life in service to him from this point on.

I have affirmed a high ideal in part to encourage people mired in a difficult marriage to hang in there. At the risk of emptying what we've just said, however, we need to be honest. It is going too far to equate leaving our spouse with leaving our faith. There are certainly severe spiritual repercussions every time we break an oath, and one thing that makes divorce even more perilous spiritually is that the marriage vow is an oath that is broken over time. Rather than being a sin of passion—something we do but immediately regret—divorce is a considered decision, with plenty of opportunities to reconsider and reject it. This makes it, at best, a very dangerous choice spiritually.

But sometimes divorce can even be the right choice. Matthew records an exception for infidelity (Matthew 19:9). Paul articulates an exception for being married to an unbeliever who refuses to remain in the marriage (1 Corinthians 7:15).

Anyone who has been married for any length of time should

be able to understand how truly difficult marriage can be and how, even among Christians, tensions can rise so high and hurt can be so deeply embedded that reconciliation would take more energy than either partner could ever imagine possessing in ten lifetimes. In many cases, God can and will provide the energy; in some cases, people are just not willing to receive it.

Before a divorce is finalized, I will usually encourage someone to hang in there, to push on through the pain, and to try to grow in it and through it. Happiness may well be beyond them, but spiritual maturity isn't—and I value character far above any emotional disposition. An intact marriage is an ideal worth fighting for when we have heaven as a future hope, spiritual growth as a present reality, and, in many cases, children for whom our sacrifice is necessary. But that doesn't mean we should treat those whose marriages have crumbled as second-class Christians. Though Jesus was an idealist, he was, perhaps surprisingly, very much also a *realist.* He loved real people with acceptance and grace.

THOUGH JESUS WAS AN IDEALIST, HE WAS VERY MUCH ALSO A REALIST. HE LOVED REAL PEOPLE WITH ACCEPTANCE AND GRACE.

And, of course, sometimes divorce is foisted on a partner unilaterally. Such was the case with a woman I know by the name of Leslie.

BROKEN HISTORY: LESLIE

"Leslie, I'm leaving you."

Leslie backpedaled in disbelief. She never thought she would hear those words. As a young girl growing up, she imagined a white wedding dress, a happy couple, a home full of children. Her fantasies had not left room for the devastating chill these words carried, spoken by a man to whom she'd entrusted her life, her body, her deepest secrets and intimacies. And now he was telling her he couldn't stand to be around her anymore.

At the time both Leslie and Tim were committed Christians. Although they had lived together before their wedding, they had recommitted their lives to the Lord before they got married, and immediately they began growing in their faith. They attended a Bible study and regularly prayed together. In the early years of their relationship, people often commented, "Y'all have such a good marriage," and the couple would humbly respond, "It's the Lord's doing, not ours."

The first cracks appeared about six years into their marriage when Tim confessed to a one-night stand. He told Leslie he was deeply sorry and was willing to seek counseling. After a lot of tears, they were able to put the affair behind them.

Leslie had to work through some issues of trust, but the good times returned. Five years passed. Tim was being trained as a church elder, and Leslie was working full-time directing a Christian ministry. They were enduring the pain of infertility but had passed through the angst to begin the process of adoption. In fact, they had passed the first home study and now were preparing for a second. Soon, Leslie hoped, she would be a mother.

And then Leslie felt Tim slipping away. The fears seemed irrational at first—just a premonition, nothing more—but the corroborating evidence grew. The distance became acute when Leslie traveled with Tim to a national convention. She felt crushed and humiliated when Tim left her alone for long periods of time and then treated her rudely when they finally did get together. Leslie became hysterically upset, something of which she is now ashamed, causing Tim to withdraw even further.

At home, Leslie confided to a prayer partner, "If I didn't know Tim better, I'd think he was getting ready to leave me."

"That's ridiculous," her prayer partner assured her.

Tim was gone on business for a total of three weeks and scheduled to return on a Saturday afternoon. Leslie was anxious for him to be home on time. She wanted them to be ready for the second adoption home study, which was scheduled for early Monday morning.

Tim didn't return home on Saturday afternoon. Leslie put the dinner dishes away and went to bed, expecting Tim to join her later that night. She woke up, wondering if Tim would be lying beside her—but he still hadn't made it home. Leslie went to church that Sunday morning, convinced she would see Tim's car in the garage when she got back, but the garage was empty.

Her heart was beginning to sink, and then, later that evening, Leslie heard a noise coming from the garage. She opened the door and saw Tim putting his golf clubs into the trunk of the car.

"What's going on, Tim?" she asked. He had been gone for three weeks. Surely he wasn't preparing to go play golf in the morning.

And then the words came—those four soul-numbing words that blasted Leslie's world apart: "Leslie, I'm leaving you."

Leslie almost collapsed on the spot. "You can't leave me," she lamented.

"I am. I don't love you anymore. I haven't loved you for a long time."

Leslie felt hysteria taking over again, and she began to panic emotionally. "I forced myself to remain calm," she remembers, "because I knew becoming hysterical wouldn't make him stay. Besides, I didn't want him to remember me in a hysterical fit."

Then Leslie looked at Tim's hand and felt her heart stop. Tim wasn't wearing his wedding ring.

"You're not wearing your wedding ring. Does that mean you're going to start dating?"

"Yes."

Slam! His immediate, calm, almost casual reply took her breath away.

"Do you know who?" The fear started rising. Did she really want to hear this?

"Yes—but I'm not leaving you for anyone in particular. You and I just aren't right for each other. I've been living a lie all these years, and I'm tired of it."

"Tim, please, won't you stay the night? Just one night?"

"I can't."

Leslie began to feel herself losing control. She didn't become hysterical, but the tears took over, and she lost her composure. She held on until Tim drove away, and *then* she became hysterical.

The sobs that came up from within her were deep and physically painful. Finally, Leslie knelt down on a chair to pray, but there was still too much agony inside her. She simply couldn't pray on her own. Instead she stood up, stumbled over to the phone, and dialed some close friends. "Tim just left me," she whispered through her tears. "Can you come over?"

Leslie and her friends wept and prayed, prayed and wept, and wept and prayed some more. After hours of spiritual struggle, Leslie finally felt a release and some semblance of peace.

"Would you like me to spend the night?" one of her friends asked.

"No, I'll be okay," Leslie said. She's thankful now that at the time she didn't realize what really lay ahead.

TELLING THE NEWS

As Leslie prayed throughout the week following Tim's departure, she sensed that God was asking her to tell her story to the church and ask for prayer. Leslie couldn't imagine doing this; she thought she had to put on a strong face because she led a ministry. "God," she argued, "they'll think I haven't been a good wife, so how can I possibly be adequate to run the ministry center? If I'm incapable of keeping a husband, how can I keep a ministry going?"

During the church service that Sunday morning, the worship leader did something that had never been done before (and hasn't been done since). He asked the congregation to share prayer requests or praises. Leslie gulped, sighed, and stood up. Every eye in the church was fixed on her. She swallowed hard and then said, "I need the church to know that Tim left me last week."

A big, horrible gasp followed, but Leslie continued. "Tim and I really need your prayers for our marriage to be healed."

Being the weak one was devastating for Leslie, but it blew the windows open in her church with respect to other marriages that were struggling and on the brink of divorce. Leslie was thankful for that, even as she waited for her own marriage to be healed.

FALSE HOPE

What helped Leslie make it through the first few months of her separation was her confident expectation that Tim would come back. She was optimistic that once she was able to understand why Tim left and what she had done wrong, she'd be able to fix everything and her marriage would be okay. But it wasn't okay, and it wasn't going to be okay. Tim was actively dating and showing little interest in reconciliation.

Bitterness became a frequent seducer, but Leslie fought it off, in part because God had begun to reveal some of her own failings—the self-righteousness with which she had treated her husband and the way she expected so much of herself and of him, for starters.

For the first time, Leslie was able to see the chains of perfectionism that had bound her for so many years. She remembered how, before Tim left her, she had bristled inside when her pastor pointed a finger her way and said she was a sinner. Her thought was, *Where do you see sin in my life? Just tell me so I can get rid of it.*

"I saw there was no grace and no mercy in my Christian life," Leslie admits. Months went by, and then years—and then finally the day that Tim told Leslie he was marrying someone else.

SHARED SUFFERINGS

Sometimes depression would creep up on Leslie, bringing a good dose of fear with it, especially as Tim's wedding day drew near. But then—there's no other way Leslie could describe it—the Lord would take her face in his hands and say, "Leslie, look at *me.* Look at me."

As the marital breakup began to appear permanent, Leslie began to grieve anew. She berated herself at times, blaming herself, thinking that if she had only done something differently, Tim wouldn't have left.

"That's not true," she sensed God telling her. "*I* loved him perfectly, and he left me too."

Leslie wept at that thought, and she began to feel a new kinship with the Lord. Somehow she was sharing in his sufferings. They were going through this together.

Well-meaning Christian friends eventually started asking Leslie if she was dating yet. Leslie did her best to mask her shock and respond with grace. She still wore her wedding ring, and while some Christians felt that she should "just let go," the ring was a sign of a covenant Leslie had made, not just with Tim, but with God. Even though Tim had walked out of the relationship, the Lord was still there—so two out of the three parties were hanging in there.

"The wedding ring didn't represent my love for Tim anymore," Leslie says. "That old love was dead. But it represented my commitment before the Lord—the One before whom I said, 'Till death do us part.' "

Right up until the day Tim remarried, Leslie wore her wedding ring and kept praying for a reconciliation. By remaining faithful in the midst of unfaithfulness, her eyes were opened to God's presence in a new way. "The faithlessness of Israel and the faithfulness of God, as well as the faithfulness of Hosea and the faithlessness of Gomer, really spoke to me," Leslie says. "This entire experience has helped me to get to know God better. I've gained a sense of the incredible unconditional love that his covenant represents. The more I sought God's permission to take off my ring and start dating, the more he would talk to me about his covenant promise."

This, in a nutshell, is one of the key messages of this book.

Even when something as tragic as betrayal, unfaithfulness, and an unwanted divorce are foisted on us, the experience can be used for spiritual benefit. By remaining true and by respecting the sacredness of her history with Tim, even though he no longer respected that history, Leslie learned valuable spiritual lessons and drew closer to God in the process.

But Leslie was a pioneer of sorts. Most of her fellow Christians couldn't understand why she wouldn't just give up. "They could understand why someone would take back a wayward child—the whole bit about the prodigal son," she says. "But with a husband and wife, many Christians just don't see it."

But now Leslie sees God in a whole new light.

THE DIVINE HUSBAND

Leslie now says, "God is the perfect Husband. He has met my needs before I even anticipated them. I'm not just talking about big things either; he has met my small, personal needs in very intimate ways."

Two weeks before Easter—just months before Tim's wedding—Leslie was asked to speak at a church that was decorated with beautiful Easter lilies. Since the divorce, Leslie has lived on a substandard income. She believes that God wanted her to forgive Tim and not fight to make him pay for leaving her, so she lives under extremely tight budget constraints. *Buying an Easter lily*, she thought, *would be a frivolous expense*, but she found herself wistfully praying, *They sure are beautiful, Lord. I would love to have one.* It was a silent prayer, and her request was spoken to no one.

The day before Easter, Leslie went into work and saw an Easter lily on her desk. Leslie stopped, stared, and then began to weep. Though the lily was from a friend, Leslie accepted it as a gift from God, who had heard her prayer and now was buying his "wife" a flower for Easter.

"By losing my earthly husband, I've drawn closer to my heavenly one." Leslie says it emphatically: "He's my Husband, my Provider, my Sustainer." Though Leslie's relationship with God used to be based on performance, this season of hurt and pain has taught her how to receive from God.

I spoke with Leslie less than two weeks before Tim's wedding. "God can still restore my marriage," Leslie told me, "but even if he doesn't, he's still God." She paused, looking wistful. Tears welled up from the bottom of her eyes.

"This has been such a rich time for me spiritually, Gary. I wouldn't trade it for anything."

"Think about that for a second, Leslie," I asked her. "Do you really mean that?"

"I do—with all my heart. It's been so rich, so profoundly life-changing. Of course, I can't say I'm glad my marriage broke up, but I *am* glad for the fruit it has created."

Leslie has entered a new realm. She has learned the secret that regardless of what others do to us—even if they betray us in the most intimate sense—God can use that occasion to draw us closer into his heart. And then God can use it to draw others to him as well.

REGARDLESS OF WHAT OTHERS DO TO US—EVEN IF THEY BETRAY US IN THE MOST INTIMATE SENSE—GOD CAN USE THAT OCCASION TO DRAW US CLOSER INTO HIS HEART.

As a special blessing, two years after Tim left Leslie, Leslie's father called her on the phone. "I've watched what you've gone through," he said. "I've seen how you've reacted, and I want what you have."

This was a profoundly moving conversation for Leslie, for, like Tim, her father had been unfaithful to his wife (Leslie's mother), leaving Leslie to grow up with the pain of a broken home. Leslie had spent much of her adult life reaching out to her father—with a tract, a book, a sermon recording. Each time, her father broke her heart anew by saying, "I wish I could do this for you, but I just can't." Yet watching his daughter remain true to her vows moved Leslie's dad in a way that a book, tract, or sermon never could. He sensed a power in Leslie's actions that had no earthly explanation, and finally he believed. All the anguish began to melt away when Leslie knelt beside her father as he prayed to receive Jesus Christ as his Lord and Savior at the age of sixty-two.

There is an exalted truth in this conversion experience. What really happened was that by remaining faithful to an unfaithful husband, Leslie demonstrated the truth of a God who remains faithful to an unfaithful people. Her father had heard the gospel many times, but it wasn't until he saw it displayed in Leslie's life that he wanted it for himself.

Leslie is even able to smile now. "How can I not thank God?" she asked me. "Quite honestly, I'm more than willing to pray, 'God, you can have my marriage if it means the salvation of my family.' "

After hearing about her story, a man called Leslie for help. His wife had left him. He was gravitating toward bitterness and anger, but Leslie pointed him in a different direction.

"This season in your life can be so productive spiritually if you use it to allow God to break you, shape you, and remake you," she told him. "We're always looking at what our spouses have done wrong, but God wants to deal with our own hearts first."

TELL THE STORY

If we are serious about pursuing spiritual growth through marriage, we must convince ourselves to refrain from asking a spiritually dangerous question: "Did I marry the right person?" Once we have exchanged our vows, little is gained and much harm can be done by asking that question.

A far better alternative to questioning one's choice is to learn how to live with one's choice. A character in the Anne Tyler novel *A Patchwork Planet* comes to realize this too late. The book's thirty-year-old narrator had gone through a divorce and now works at an occupation that has him relating almost exclusively with elderly people. As he observes their long-standing marriages, he comes to a profound understanding:

> I was beginning to suspect that it made no difference whether they'd married the right person. Finally, you're just with who you're with. You've signed on with her, put in half a century with her, grown to know her as well as you know yourself or even better, and she's *become* the right person. Or the only person, might be more to the point. I wish someone had told me that earlier. I'd have hung on then; I swear I would. I never would have driven Natalie to leave me.[5]

To be honest, our kids sometimes laugh at how incompatible Lisa and I seem. I'm not sure either of us would be the "perfect" person for each other if we were matched by a computer. But it's a relationship that we cherish and thank God for every day. Rather than spending time wondering if we married the right person, we can take all that energy and work on creating a beautiful story of how two imperfect and seemingly incompatible people made their marriage into something amazing—creating kids, finding purpose, worshiping God, and being loyal to each other to the very end.

> HALF THE BATTLE IS JUST KEEPING OUR STORY ALIVE, REFUSING TO QUIT, BELIEVING THAT IF WE KEEP HANGING IN THERE, WE'RE GIVING GOD MORE TIME AND MORE OPPORTUNITIES TO WORK HIS GRACE INTO OUR LIVES.

Half the battle, then, is just keeping our story alive, refusing to quit, believing that if we keep hanging in there, we're giving God more time and more opportunities to work his grace into our lives. It's not easy, but it's sacred and it's strong, and it leaves a lasting legacy. I love how author Jerry Jenkins encourages us to revel in our own marital story:

> Tell your [marital] story. Tell it to your kids, your friends, your brothers and sisters, but especially to each other. The more your story is implanted in your brain, the more it serves as a hedge against the myriad forces that seek to destroy your marriage. Make your story so familiar that it becomes part of the fabric of your being. It should become a legend that is shared through the generations as you grow a family tree that

> defies all odds and boasts marriage after marriage of stability, strength, and longevity.[6]

Don't abort your history with the spouse whom God has called you to love. Don't cheapen the experience of walking hand in hand with the God who can identify with every relational struggle you face.

"May the Lord direct your hearts into God's love and Christ's perseverance."

CHAPTER 9

SACRED STRUGGLE

Embracing Difficulty in Order to Build Character

One was never married, and that's his hell; another is, and that's his plague.

Robert Burton, English clergyman

They dream in courtship, but in wedlock wake.

Alexander Pope

Because marriage, more than any other relationship, reflects God's involvement with us and bears more potential to draw our hearts to heaven, it can more readily give us a taste of hell.

Dan Allender and Tremper Longman III

There are few natural wonders more startling in their beauty than Mount Everest, the highest spot on earth. Geologists believe that the Himalayas were created by the Indian continent crashing into Eurasia. "Crashing" is a writer's hyperbole;

actually, the two continents collide with a movement of about ten centimeters per year. But slow and steady does the job. As India keeps moving inward, compressing and lifting southern Eurasia, a spectacular natural treasure continues to be created.

If there were no collision between India and Eurasia, there would be no Himalayas. Without the wrenching force of continental shifting, the world would be a poorer place aesthetically.

In the same way, the "collisions" of marriage can create relationships of beauty. Beauty is often birthed in struggle. These points of impact may not be fun — in fact, they can make us feel like we're being ripped apart — but the process can make us stronger, build our character, and deepen our faith.

Suffering is a necessary part of the Christian life, modeled by Jesus Christ himself, who suffered immeasurably in his service to God. Dietrich Bonhoeffer wrote that if we do not have something of the ascetic in us, we will find it hard to follow God.[1] And yet most of those who leave marriage and break its sacred history do so precisely because it's tough. Few people leave a marriage because it's too easy! This tendency to avoid difficulty is a grave spiritual failing that can and often does keep us in Christian infancy. The great spiritual writers warned that this life *is* difficult and that we should use the difficulty to be built up in our character.

William Law, an eighteenth-century Anglican writer, asks, "How many saints has adversity sent to Heaven? And how many poor sinners has prosperity plunged into everlasting misery?"[2] Saint John of the Cross mocks our demand to have it easy and to shun struggle: "I would not consider any spirituality worthwhile that wants to walk in sweetness and ease and run from the imitation of Christ."[3]

Jesus promised us that *everyone* will be seasoned with fire, and every sacrifice will be seasoned with salt (Mark 9:49 NKJV). The desire for ease, comfort, and stress-free living is an indirect desire to remain an "unseasoned," immature Christian. Struggle makes us stronger; it builds us up and deepens our faith.

But this result is achieved only when we face the struggle head-on, not when we run from it. Gary and Betsy Ricucci point out, "Our Lord has sovereignly ordained that our refining process take place as we go *through* difficulties, not around them. The Bible is filled with examples of those who overcame as they passed *through* the desert, the Red Sea, the fiery furnace and ultimately the cross. God doesn't protect Christians from their problems—he helps them walk victoriously *through* their problems."[4]

STRUGGLE MAKES US STRONGER; IT BUILDS US UP AND DEEPENS OUR FAITH. BUT THIS RESULT IS ACHIEVED ONLY WHEN WE FACE THE STRUGGLE HEAD-ON.

If your marriage is tough, get down on your knees and thank God that he has given you an opportunity for unparalleled spiritual growth. You have the prime potential to excel in Christian character and obedience.

APPRECIATING STRUGGLE

As a cross-country runner, my most satisfying victories were those that took every ounce of strength I possessed. Races I won easily, though less painful, were ultimately less satisfying. Struggling successfully and profitably brings a deeper joy than even trouble-free living. God created us in such a way that, in one sense, struggle keeps us interested and engaged. But to be profitable, our struggle must have *purpose*, and it must be *productive*. Two people who do nothing but fight in their marriage and make each other miserable are not engaging in a helpful spiritual exercise. It's only when we put struggle within the Christian context of character development and self-sacrifice that it becomes profitable.

Jesus portrayed struggle as the entry point into the Christian life, stressing that it would be a *daily* reality of our faith: "Whoever wants to be my disciple must deny themselves and take up their cross *daily* and follow me" (Luke 9:23, emphasis added). Though sickness and sorrow will catch up to most people eventually, to the young living in affluent countries this verse may sound melodramatic. Medicine has become so advanced that many young people can live virtually pain-free lives. We have machines to wash our clothes and do the dishes. We can wake up in Seattle and have dinner in New York that same evening.

When life starts out so easy, we can be lulled to sleep, thinking that life *should* be easy or that it will *always* be easy. Once it gets a little difficult, we tend to become consumed with trying to make our lives comfortable again—just like they used to be. Rather than embrace Jesus' words in the present, we want to recapture an easier past, but when we do this, we miss a great spiritual opportunity.

Mountain climbers often step back from a particularly difficult overhang or stretch and discuss how to surmount it. Much of the fun in the sport is encountering the challenges and figuring out a way to get around them. If mountain climbing were easy, it would lose a great deal of its appeal.

Our relationships can be looked at the same way. Instead of immediately thinking about how we can take a helicopter to the top, we might take a climber's approach and think, "This is really tough. This is a challenge, no doubt about it. How do I keep loving this person in the face of this challenge?"

WOULD I RATHER LIVE A LIFE OF COMFORT AND REMAIN IMMATURE IN CHRIST, OR AM I WILLING TO BE SEASONED WITH SUFFERING IF BY DOING SO I AM CONFORMED TO THE IMAGE OF CHRIST?

Thomas à Kempis noted that "the more the flesh is wasted by affliction, so much the more is the spirit strengthened by inward grace. And sometimes he is so comforted with desire of tribulation and adversity, for the love of conformity to the cross of Christ, that he would not wish to be without grief or tribulation."[5]

Ask yourself this question: Would I rather live a life of comfort and remain immature in Christ, or am I willing to be seasoned with suffering if by doing so I am conformed to the image of Christ?

It is unrealistic to assume that the initial pledge of marital fidelity will be an easy one to keep. The late Otto Piper, who was a professor of New Testament at Princeton Seminary, points out that "there is always an element of mistrust implied in the marriage contract."[6] The reason we promise to love each other "till death do us part" is precisely because our society knows that such a promise will be sorely tried—otherwise, the promise wouldn't be necessary! We don't make public promises that we will regularly nourish our bodies with food or buy ourselves adequate clothing.

Everyone who enters the marriage relationship will come to a point where the marriage starts to rub somewhat adversely. It is *for these times* that the promise is made. Anticipating struggle, God has ordained a remedy, holding us to our word of commitment. In this struggle we become nobler people.

SWEET SUFFERING

Without degenerating into becoming a masochist, the mature Christian recognizes and appreciates the sweet side of suffering. Teresa of Avila wrote, "Lord, how you afflict your lovers! But everything is small in comparison with what you give them afterward."[7] This is the same reality experienced by Saint John of the Cross, who wrote, "If individuals resolutely submit to the carrying of the cross, if they decidedly want to find and endure trial in all things for God, they will discover in all of them great relief and sweetness."[8]

This teaching mirrors Paul's words in 2 Corinthians 4:17: "For our light and momentary troubles are achieving for us an eternal glory that far outweighs them all."

Because we have hope for eternity, we do not become nearsighted, demanding short-term ease that would short-circuit long-term gain. Our demands for comfort and ease show us what we truly value. It is the definitive test of whether we are living for God's kingdom and service or for our own comfort and reputation.

A heavyweight champion who dodges all serious contenders to consistently fight "marshmallows" is mocked. Christians who dodge all serious struggle and consciously seek to put themselves in whatever situations and relationships are easiest are doing the same thing—they are coasting, and eventually that coasting will define them and, even worse, shape them.

If there is one thing young engaged couples need to hear, it's that *a good marriage is not something you find; it's something you work for*. It takes struggle. You must crucify your selfishness. You must at times confront and at other times confess. The practice of forgiveness is essential.

This is undeniably hard work. But eventually it pays off. Eventually, it creates a relationship of beauty, trust, and mutual support.

It helps when we view our struggles in light of what they provide for us spiritually rather than in light of what they take from us emotionally. Working through disagreements is taxing. There are a million things I'd rather do than put in the time and effort to resolve a relational hassle. If I'm in my marriage for emotional stability, I probably won't last long. But if I think it can reap spiritual benefits, I'll have plenty of reason to not just *be* married but *act* married.

Otto Piper challenges us, "If marriage ... is a disillusioning experience for many people, the reason is to be found in the passivity of their faith. People dislike the fact that the blessings of God may only be found and enjoyed when they are persistently sought (Matthew 7:7; Luke 11:9). Marriage is, therefore, both a gift and a task to be accomplished."[9]

DON'T RUN FROM THE STRUGGLES OF MARRIAGE. EMBRACE THEM. GROW IN THEM. DRAW NEARER TO GOD BECAUSE OF THEM.

Don't run from the struggles of marriage. Embrace them. Grow in them. Draw nearer to God because of them. Through them you will reflect more of the spirit of Jesus Christ. And thank God he has placed you in a situation where your spirit can be perfected.

Let's take a close look at two individuals, Abraham Lincoln and Anne Morrow Lindbergh, who struggled mightily in their marriages—but who became outstandingly influential people as a result.[10]

THE GREAT EMANCIPATOR

Mary Todd was hardly the type of woman with whom one could enjoy a quiet evening. She was, in fact, a woman of intense impulses and tremendous temper, though this, ironically enough, was some of her attraction for Abraham Lincoln. The future president called her the "first aggressively brilliant, feminine creature" who had crossed his path.

Mary's bouts of temper made retaining hired help extremely difficult; Lincoln responded by giving the girls an extra weekly dollar. After one particularly forceful eruption between Mary and a maid, Lincoln quietly patted the girl on the shoulder and said, "Stay with her, Maria. Stay with her." He had to hold on to the "help," because hiring new workers, with Mary's growing reputation, was next to impossible.

When a salesman called on the White House and was treated to Mary's fervid verbal assault, he marched right up to the Oval Office—those were different days, to be sure—and proceeded to complain to President Lincoln about how the first lady had treated him. Lincoln listened calmly, then stood and gently said, "You can endure for fifteen minutes what I have endured for fifteen years."

Lincoln suffered numerous indignities at the hand of his wife, from Mary's publicly throwing coffee in his face to her profligate spending. In those days, presidents were not as well-off as they are today, but Mary went on bizarre spending binges, during one stretch buying hundreds of pairs of gloves. On another occasion, she actually contracted with a builder to redo their house while the future president was away—without his knowledge, and certainly without his (frugal) assent. When the Lincolns lost Willie—Mary's favorite son—the ensuing grief cracked Mrs. Lincoln's already fragile psyche. It became more and more difficult for her to control her hysterics. In the turmoil of this tremendous grief (losing his son) and distraction (watching his wife fall apart), Lincoln did his best to keep a crumbling nation together.

Added to the sometimes bizarre pressure at home, Lincoln's political life was equally chaotic. His insistence on fighting the Civil War to the end made him so unpopular that a fellow politician scoffed at Lincoln's planned visit and address to Gettysburg with the words, "Let the dead bury the dead." Lincoln himself saw little hope for being reelected, writing in his journal that he fully expected to be a one-term president. Keep in mind that over 600,000 men perished in this increasingly unpopular and horrific conflict that Lincoln was determined to bring to a conclusion. Many, perhaps most, knew a son, a brother, a husband, a father, an uncle — or sometimes all of the above — who gave their life for "Lincoln's War." The people had had enough.

But Lincoln lived with this almost mystical sense that he had been chosen by God to keep the United States together and to preserve this experiment called democracy. So he fought on, changing generals, changing tactics, but staying on course, even in the face of the public's growing disgust, ridicule, and sometimes hatred.

What gives a man such tenacity? How does a man develop the character to persist in the face of widespread hatred, chaos, disappointment, and tragic defeat? How does a man keep going when his home *and* his nation seem to be falling apart?

Shortly before Lincoln left for Gettysburg, his son Tad became ill, which once again intensified Mary's hysterics as she was reminded anew of the son she had lost less than two years earlier. With all the distractions at home, Lincoln was able merely to scribble out a few notes as he left for Pennsylvania.

In this highly emotional moment, Lincoln could be forgiven for delivering his words with less-than-powerful rhetoric. One reporter described Lincoln's delivery as "a sharp, unmusical treble voice." The applause was scattered and restrained, so much so that Lincoln believed he had failed miserably. He leaned over and told a friend, "It is a flat failure, and the people are disappointed."

But the words were true and genuine, and they were moving and powerful—and as the newspapers recorded them without Lincoln's understandable gloom coloring them, the nation was inspired as never before. The Gettysburg Address is one of the most famous speeches ever delivered on American soil, and its words would eventually be carved in stone, accompanying Lincoln into history. It may be a cliché to say this, but it's still true: He shone brightest when his personal life was darkest.

The connection one can make between Lincoln's marriage and his mission is not difficult. It is easy to see how a man who might quit on a difficult marriage wouldn't have the character to hold together a crumbling nation. Lincoln was virtually obsessed with saving the Union; what better training ground than the difficult marriage that required such tenacity from him?

Not only did Lincoln's difficult marriage not deter him from achieving greatness; one might argue that it actually helped prepare him for greatness. Lincoln's character was tested and refined on a daily basis so that when the true test came, he was able to stand strong. His spiritual muscles were strengthened to the point that he didn't falter just when he needed them most. This story exposes the lie behind the thinking of the pastor who declares, "I really could have done something if I hadn't married this woman," or the wife who says to herself, "Just think what I might be if I weren't held back by such a loser." One of our greatest presidents was, without question, married to one of the most difficult first ladies, and one could make the case that this difficult and trying marriage helped create such a great leader.

INSTEAD OF HATING YOUR MARRIAGE, LEARN TO LOVE IT AS A WAY GOD CAN GROW FAITHFULNESS AND PERSEVERANCE INTO YOUR CHARACTER.

It's fitting that Abraham Lincoln should be known as the "great emancipator." *Emancipator* means "deliverer from bondage and oppression." Perhaps Lincoln's example can deliver us from the oppression of an empty pursuit of happiness. Perhaps he can help set us free from the notion that a difficult marriage will hold us back rather than prepare us for our life's work; maybe he can yet cut us loose from the chains that bind us to seek tension-free lives over lives of meaning and character. In the truth of Lincoln, learn to accept difficulty as a blessing rather than resenting it. Instead of hating your marriage, learn to love it as a way God can grow faithfulness and perseverance into your character.

THE GREAT AVIATOR

Imagine being a young, Ivy League-educated woman in the 1920s. You love books and harbor dreams of becoming a writer or a poet. Your father is a United States ambassador, and your family is well respected and well-off. You have been raised to esteem refinement, good manners, and "superior breeding."

Then through your father's door walks a man who is larger than life but who is also everything you have been taught not to respect—an adventurer rather than a scholar, a man who tinkers with engines rather than with words. He is from humble origins, but his transatlantic flight from New York to Paris has given him a fame almost unparalleled in the history of this country.

Thus begins the account of Anne Morrow Lindbergh's marriage.

Charles Lindbergh's successful flight across the Atlantic put him in a class all by himself. His fame was unparalleled. Today you can't really pick a "favorite" celebrity; the list of who's in and who's out changes every week. But Lindbergh was undoubtedly, for a time, the most popular man in America—perhaps in the world. Imagine having Wall Street close down for a parade in *your* honor—a parade that drew 4.5 million people! Lindy's popularity reached such heights that women would check into hotel rooms he had just left, so they could bathe in his bathtub and sleep in his bed. Lindbergh found he couldn't even send his shirts to the laundry—they never came back. And Lindy had a particularly difficult time balancing his checkbook, because most people refused to cash his checks; they opted instead to keep them as souvenirs.

When Anne Morrow met Charles Lindbergh, she was prepared to thoroughly dislike the famous aviator. A Smith-educated, well-bred, bookish sort of woman, Anne wasn't about to be swept off her feet by what she called "all this public-hero stuff." She wrote in her diary, "I certainly was not going to worship 'Lindy' (that odious *name*, anyway)." Her teacher derided Lindbergh, saying Charles was "really no more than a mechanic ... Had it not been for the lone eagle flight, he would now be in charge of a gasoline station on the outskirts of St. Louis."

In spite of Anne's initial resolve not to be swept off her feet by this great adventurer, much to her own consternation she did find herself smitten after she met him. Somehow the man who bore "that odious name" suddenly became "keen, intelligent, burning, thinking on all lines." Anne feverishly poured words into her journal that were more reminiscent of a lovesick adolescent than an aspiring poet: "The intensity of life, burning like a bright fire in his eyes. Life focused in him—when he in turn focuses his life, power, force on *anything*, amazing things happen."

Because of Lindy's fame, dating presented several problems. As soon as he was seen with a young woman, newspapers ran photographs and started speculating about an engagement. Early on, Lindy warned Anne, "Don't worry about *my* publicity. It's coming to me anyway. I've got to take it, but I don't want it to be embarrassing for you."

Anne learned to play along. When she wrote to her sisters, she used the code name "Robert Boyd" in place of the name Charles Lindbergh, lest her letters be intercepted and leaked to the press. As Anne got to know Charles better, she had ambivalent feelings. In one sense, he overwhelmed her, but in another sense she recognized how very different they were. The two of them, adventurer and poet, seemed like an utter and complete mismatch. She poured out her thoughts in a letter to her sister:

"As you can see, I am completely turned upside down, completely overwhelmed, completely upset. He is the biggest, most absorbing person I've ever met, and doesn't seem to touch my life anywhere, really."

Finally, they married.

TRAPPED IN FAME

Anne's joy at her wedding was tempered in part by the ridiculous lengths to which she and her new husband had to go in order to escape the public eye. To slip out of the wedding, Anne had to lie down in a borrowed car, passing the usual crowd of reporters that gathered at her parents' gate. She and Lindy then changed cars, drove to Long Island, and rowed out to a boat that had been left anchored for them in the water.

While everyone raved about how lucky Anne was to capture the world's most eligible bachelor—a perception she chafed against, as it assumed Lindy wasn't lucky to have *her*—the private young woman struggled to get used to her notoriety.

"It is difficult to believe or even to remember how little privacy we had; how hard we struggled to be alone together," she reminisced many years later. "In Mexico City, reporters waited for us at the Embassy gates, their cars and cameras set to follow us. At [my parents'] weekend house ... enterprising photographers climbed up onto nearby roofs to photograph us in our garden. Disguised, we sneaked out of back doors, went to friends' houses, changed cars, and fled into the wild country of Mexico, which was then considered dangerous because of bandits."

This flight from photographers and journalists came at a cost. As Anne herself points out, "Total isolation is not normal life any more than total public exposure. Like criminals or illicit lovers, we avoided being seen in the world together and had to forgo the everyday pleasures of walking along streets, shopping, sightseeing, eating out at restaurants, or taking part in public events."

Although Anne was an insightful person with literary

ambitions, early on in her relationship with Charles that part of her life had to be curtailed. Charles warned her to "never say anything you wouldn't want shouted from the housetops, and never write anything you would mind seeing on the front page of a newspaper."

Anne reflects, "I was convinced I must protect him and myself from intrusion into our private life, but what a sacrifice to make never to speak or write deeply or honestly! I, to whom an experience was not finished until it was written or shared in conversation. I who had said in college that the most exciting thing in life was communication ... The result was dampening for my kind of inner life. I stopped writing in my diary completely for three years, and since even letters were unsafe, I tried to write cautiously or in family language and jokes."

The "dream life" that all the papers wrote about so exuberantly had its dark side. Anne laments, "We had no private life—only public life ... We had no home; we lived in hotels, planes, or other people's homes. We traveled constantly."

This is not the life that someone "born to letters" envisions. It is not the environment or existence that a quiet, reflective poet would choose.

SET FREE WITH SORROW

In 1932, the fame took a cruel turn. The Lindberghs' eighteen-month-old child, Charles Lindbergh Jr., was taken from his crib in the Lindberghs' New Jersey home. The kidnappers left a note on the windowsill demanding a ransom in exchange for his safe return. Negotiations lasted for six weeks, after which a ransom was paid, but the child wasn't returned. Four excruciating weeks later—ten weeks in all—the ordeal came to a tragic end when the little child's dead body was found discarded in the woods, just a few miles from the Lindberghs' home.

As a father of three children, I can't imagine a more difficult experience to live through than the loss of a child. The kidnapping, the uncertainty, the waiting, then finding the body—all of this must have been devastating. It is one thing for fame to steal your poetry or your hopes for a quiet life; it is another thing altogether when fame steals and destroys your firstborn child.

Because the boy had been abandoned in the woods, animals had gotten to him; it took a while for authorities to positively identify the body. Adding severe insult to cruel injury, some photographers broke into the morgue and published photos of Anne's partially decomposed son for all to see.

This was a parent's worst nightmare, compounded fifty times. Yet, ironically enough, it was this tragedy that released Anne to write again. She had allowed the absurdity of fame to put a part of her inner core to sleep, but something in the magnitude of this tragedy brought new life, like green grass poking up in the aftermath of a devastating forest fire.

"There were other values, I was beginning to learn, more important than discretion or even privacy," Anne writes. "As I discovered the following spring, in the abyss of tragedy, I needed to return to a deeper resource. I had to write honestly. So one can say perhaps that sorrow also played its part in setting me free."

Think about this line: "Sorrow also played its part in setting me free." So often today sorrow is something that is to be avoided at all costs. Sorrow is the enemy, the persecutor, the fearful emotion. If there is sorrow in our marriage, we must leave our marriage, for how could anyone suggest I remain in an unhappy marriage? While few of us would (or even should) have the courage to willingly choose sorrow, when we find ourselves in it, if we quieted our souls—if we learned to float in sorrow rather than thrash about like a drowning emotional victim—we might find, as Anne did, that it can be used to set us free.

Anne isn't sentimental about this, just honest and vulnerable: "What I am saying is not simply the old Puritan truism that 'suffering teaches.' I do not believe that sheer suffering teaches. If suffering alone taught, all the world would be wise, since everyone suffers. To suffering must be added mourning, understanding, patience, love, openness, and the willingness to remain vulnerable."

Anne is right, of course. A difficult marriage, in and of itself, may not cause us to grow. We have to apply ourselves to understanding, love, and patience. We must commit ourselves to a pursuit of virtue within that difficult marriage. We can't control how our spouse will act or how the world will act, but we can control how we will act and how we will respond.

IF WE LEARNED TO FLOAT IN SORROW RATHER THAN THRASH ABOUT LIKE A DROWNING EMOTIONAL VICTIM, WE MIGHT FIND THAT IT CAN BE USED TO SET US FREE.

This perspective puts us in the driver's seat. No longer tossed about as a victim of sorrow, we become the architects of a new character. It is either this, or giving up control and allowing the toxic eruption of bitterness to pollute our souls.

It may sound antiquated to talk about the pursuit of virtue in today's world, but this is only because we don't fully understand what virtue truly represents. At its root, *virtue* means "strength." It's related to a word that more directly addresses this meaning: *virile*. Virtue is strength—power to do what is right; power to make the right choice; power to overcome the weakness of sin, bad choices, victimhood, and self-pity.

Years later, as Anne Lindbergh reflected on the kidnapping, she remarked that she found comfort in two teachings—one Christian and one Buddhist. "Undoubtedly," she wrote, "the long road of suffering, insight, healing, or rebirth is best illustrated in the Christian religion by the suffering, death, and resurrection of Christ."

The other story concerns a mother who approached Buddha after losing her child. Legend has it that Buddha told her that all she needed for healing was a single mustard seed from a household that had never known sorrow. You can probably guess the ending. The mother traveled from house to house and was never able to find a family without sorrow. She never received the mustard seed she was looking for, but she did receive understanding, truth, wisdom, and perspective.

The same conclusion could be made about marriage. Every marriage has sorrows. Every marriage has trials. There isn't a shared bedroom in this country where tension doesn't occasionally or perhaps frequently lift its snarling head. Many a pillow has been a solemn receptacle for soul-felt tears, cried late at night or even all throughout the day. We don't get to choose which sorrows or trials we are called to bear, only that we must endure them.

LIBERATING FORCE

Although Charles Lindbergh was famous, and by most accounts a gracious man, there were aspects of his character that brought tremendous grief to Anne. Charles's stoicism was such that he saw crying as a weakness. Accordingly, he insisted that if Anne had to cry, she do it alone, in her room. He made one exception: after the baby was found dead, he let Anne weep without rebuke.

Later in their marriage, Charles's fame spoiled into infamy. Lindbergh made half a dozen trips to Germany and vehemently opposed American entry into World War II. Soon thereafter, he was sneered at as vehemently as he had been cheered.

"Imagine," his sister-in-law wrote, "in just fifteen years he had gone from Jesus to Judas."

He was also a controlling and somewhat eccentric man. One of his daughters told a biographer, "There were only two ways of doing things — Father's way and the wrong way." When Anne told Charles she wanted a new stove, he insisted she wait until they could discuss the purchase "from personal, economic, and military standpoints." Once, as Charles prepared to leave on a trip, he made Anne cancel their children's dental appointments, fearing that war might break out with the Soviets (which could lead the enemy to poison the water supply).

These are admittedly somewhat petty concerns, but the fame, the tragedy, the way Anne and Charles were so radically different from each other—all these created enormous and serious tensions. Had Anne focused on these difficulties and let herself obsess over them, she could easily have turned bitter and withdrawn and found herself with a shrunken life. Instead of becoming an alcoholic or turning to food for comfort or taking things out on her children and ruining them, Anne chose to apply virtue to suffering and thereby enlarge her life significantly.

Out of this difficult marital situation, Anne became a woman of tremendous accomplishment—the first United States woman, in fact, to get a glider pilot's license. In spite of her preference for books and for conversation over against adventure, Anne learned to use the radio and became remarkably proficient at using Morse code.

When their second son, Jon, was young, Anne and Charles went on a North Atlantic survey flight that covered four continents and lasted just two weeks shy of six months. Anne's work as copilot and radio operator for the survey was recognized by the National Geographic Society, which in 1934 awarded her the Hubbard Gold Medal for distinction in exploration, research, and discovery. She was the first woman to receive this award.

As life slowed down, Anne was finally able to put more effort into writing. She wrote numerous books—including many bestsellers—in the 1950s and 1960s. Eugene Peterson includes Anne's *Gift from the Sea* in his selective list of books that are "spiritually formative in the Christian life," calling it "a penetrating account of a homemaker/mother/wife who goes to the seashore for a few days and finds metaphors among the seashells that connect the presence of God and the meaning of the soul in the traffic of her everyday housewife world."[11]

Her difficult marriage didn't confine her; it released her. Anne recounts, "As a married woman, I had my husband at my side and developed a new confidence. I always feel like standing up straight when he is behind me."

This is what a good, difficult marriage does. Marriage can never remove the trials—in fact, it almost always creates new ones. But even difficult marriages to difficult men can give women the strength to become the people God created them to be. (So it is as well for men married to difficult women.)

In a collection of letters and journal writings titled *Hour of Gold, Hour of Lead*, Anne talks about how "the hour of lead"—difficult, burdening times—can be "transmuted" into an "hour of gold." As long as our pain and wisdom and lessons are "locked up in the heart" or "hoarded high in barns," she wrote, they remain sterile and unfertile. To grow in the midst of difficulties, we must rip open the bags of grain and seeds and pour them out wherever we see fertile ground. This is the classic death and rebirth theme of Christianity, in which "the seed of love must be eternally resown." It is the essence of a spiritually meaningful marriage.

TO GROW IN THE MIDST OF DIFFICULTIES, WE MUST RIP OPEN THE BAGS OF GRAIN AND SEEDS AND POUR THEM OUT WHEREVER WE SEE FERTILE GROUND.

MERE TROUBLES

Some of you might be thinking, *My marriage situation is much worse than most. You don't understand my difficulties.* The hard reality is this: We often can't choose which trials we face.

When we moved back to Washington State from Virginia, I had to renew my driver's license, which involved taking a vision test. I was asked to look into a machine and read the letters. I knew I must have made a mistake when the woman said, "Please start by reading the letters in the left column."

I read them again.

"That's the middle column," she stated.

I looked back in the machine. "You mean there are three columns?" I asked.

"Is something wrong with you?" she asked.

There were so many ways in which I could answer that question that I just remained silent. In fact, I suffer from keratoconus in my left eye, which severely curtails my sight and virtually obliterates my peripheral vision. I wasn't even aware there was a third column.

The doctor who diagnosed my condition gave me a pamphlet for a support group for people with this problem, but it really doesn't bother me. Just about everyone I know has some physical malady—a bad back, severe allergies, migraine headaches, arthritis. We don't get to pick and choose which part of our body goes out of whack, but most of us will face the degeneration of something as we grow older.

I think we need the same attitude with our marriage. All of us experience certain things about our spouses that may be difficult for us to accept. I've known men who were married to alcoholics and women who were married to demanding tyrants who showed little appreciation or respect.

But here's where it gets difficult for most of us—where it causes us to forget the lessons learned through Lincoln and Lindbergh. Some may say, "Being famous doesn't sound so bad," and they wish they could exchange their troubles for Anne's. Others may think, *I wouldn't mind being married to such a contentious woman if I could be the president of the United States!*

For those of us who live relatively anonymous lives, for those couples who silently grieve over their own personal and private trials, for those who seem lost in a difficult marriage but don't particularly view their "mission" in life as meaningful—maybe they work in a factory and are wondering just what their mission in life actually is—trials seem to take on an added weight. In cases like these, our trials don't appear to us as a teacher, but more like a taskmaster, a tyrant, a brutal burden.

In the previous chapter, we touched briefly on how eternity helps us maintain a sacred history. It also helps us endure struggle. Remember Paul's words in Romans 2:7–8: "To those who by persistence in doing good seek glory, honor and immortality, he will give eternal life. But for those who are self-seeking and who reject the truth and follow evil, there will be wrath and anger."

If we live without an eternal perspective, earthly trials become larger than life. Without the hope of heaven or the sense of the importance of a growing character and refinement, there is nothing to prepare for, nothing to look forward to; it is like practicing and practicing but never getting to actually play a game. Life gets boring, tedious, and tiresome.

IF WE ARE SEEKING GLORY, HONOR, AND IMMORTALITY BEFORE GOD, THE ROAD TO GET THERE IS DAILY AND QUIET PERSISTENCE, FAITHFULNESS, AND OBEDIENCE.

If we are seeking glory, honor, and immortality before God, the road to get there is daily and quiet persistence, faithfulness, and obedience. Anonymous sufferings are actually the best kind, Jesus tells us; otherwise, others might recognize us and compliment us, and that alone will be our reward (Matthew 6:16–18).

Christianity doesn't make much sense without the reality of heaven. The great classical writers never let go of this heavenly hope. Eternity undergirded virtually every word they uttered. Paul himself said that if we have hope only for this life, "we are of all people most to be pitied" (1 Corinthians 15:19).

So what if your marriage is about more than obtaining happiness in this life? What if it's about attaining glory in the next life?

If we take our faith seriously and make our way through a difficult marriage in pursuit of witnessing God's reconciling love for a sinful world, then a difficult marriage becomes part of our exercise to prepare us for heaven. Of course, the refinement of our character won't make it into the pages of *Sports Illustrated* or *Vanity Fair*—but heaven will notice, God will notice, and eventually the promise of Jesus will come true: "The last will be first" (Matthew 20:16).

I feel sorry for Christians who try to live obedient lives without keeping heaven firmly in their sights. Meditating on the afterlife is one of the best spiritual exercises I know of. It strengthens me like few other spiritual disciplines do. *I can endure this*, I say to myself, *because it will not always be this way.*

Cynics will say I'm falling into Marx's trap. Marx, you'll recall, called religion "the opium of the people." Yet Marx had it exactly backward, at least as far as his words pertain to Christianity. Opium deadens the senses; Christianity makes them come alive. Our faith can infuse a deadened or crippled marriage with meaning, purpose, and—in what we so graciously receive from God—fulfillment. Christianity doesn't leave us in an apathetic stupor; it raises us and our relationships from the dead! It pours zest and strength and purpose into an otherwise wasted life.

God never promises to remove all our trials this side of heaven—quite the contrary!—but he does promise there is meaning in each one. Our character is being perfected; our faith is being built; our heavenly reward is being increased.

There's a scene from *Star Wars* that I'm somewhat ashamed to admit still tears me up inside. After Luke Skywalker, Princess Leia, and Han Solo save the rebel forces, they are honored as they enter a great hall. They walk down a long aisle, with everybody standing at attention, and then they climb some high steps, until the leader of the rebel forces honors them in front of everybody.

CHRISTIANITY DOESN'T LEAVE US IN AN APATHETIC STUPOR; IT RAISES US AND OUR RELATIONSHIPS FROM THE DEAD! IT POURS ZEST AND STRENGTH AND PURPOSE INTO AN OTHERWISE WASTED LIFE.

The reason I think this hits me so hard is that it shadows a heavenly truth I yearn for. Jesus never told us to erase our ambition. Jesus never said to shun all thought of rewards. He told us to turn from *earthly* ambition and to shun *earthly* rewards. He said in effect, "Put yourself last here on earth, and in heaven you'll be first." That's a trade, not a complete denial! That thirst for glory you feel in your heart is part of what makes you human. Jesus just wants us to focus it on heaven, looking for our rewards there.

Now to believe this isn't to suggest we just "hang on" until heaven comes. I've found that obedience to God creates quiet fulfillment in the present. There is a spiritual satisfaction that comes even in the midst of our trials. It is a demeanor that may not be as showy as gleeful happiness, but it is much less subject to moods and makes for much more permanent a disposition.

A difficult marriage does not pronounce a death sentence on a meaningful life. It presents several challenges, to be sure, but it also provides wonderful opportunities for spiritual growth. Look at your marriage through this lens: What am I learning? How is this causing me to grow? What is this doing for me from an eternal perspective?—and see if it doesn't lighten the load, at least somewhat. More important, contrast how your marriage draws you closer to God and shapes you in the character of Jesus Christ with how closely it draws you to the elusive state of carefree happiness. Look at your situation through the lens of eternity, the lens employed by the apostle Paul: "If we are children, then we are heirs—heirs of God and co-heirs with Christ, if indeed we share in his sufferings in order that we may also share in his glory. I consider that our present sufferings are not worth comparing with the glory that will be revealed in us (Romans 8:17–18).

Chapter 10

FALLING FORWARD

Marriage Teaches Us to Forgive

Love is a heart that moves … Love moves away from the self and toward the other.

Dan Allender and Tremper Longman III

Merely being faithful to your spouse is quite a testimony in this society. But as you go beyond that to communicate love for your spouse in a consistent, creative, and uninhibited way, the world can't help but notice. God will be honored. *Gary and Betsy Ricucci*

When a girl marries, she exchanges the attentions of all the other men of her acquaintance for the inattention of just one. *Helen Rowland*

Many years ago, a few close friends celebrated our high school graduation by hiking on Mount Rainier. Before I attempted to jump a fast-moving creek that had enough force to carry me halfway down the mountain, one of my friends advised me, "Just make sure you fall forward." The advice was well heeded. Even if I didn't make the jump, as long as I kept my momentum going forward, I wouldn't be swept downstream.

The advice has stayed with me down through the years, as I believe that Christian marriage is also about learning to fall forward. Obstacles arise, anger flares up, and weariness dulls our feelings. When this happens, the spiritually immature respond by pulling back, becoming more distant from their spouse, or even seeking to start over with somebody more exciting. Yet maturity is reached by continuing to move forward past the pain and apathy. Falls are inevitable. We can't always control whether or not we fall, but we *can* control the direction in which we fall—toward or away from our spouse.

WE CAN'T ALWAYS CONTROL WHETHER OR NOT WE FALL, BUT WE CAN CONTROL THE DIRECTION IN WHICH WE FALL—TOWARD OR AWAY FROM OUR SPOUSE.

In Hollywood language, romance is expressed as a passive activity. Usually couples will say they have "fallen in love." Or they may talk about being "swept off their feet." Adulterous couples sometimes even say, "We couldn't help ourselves; it just happened!" This passivity is as foreign to Christian love as paper is to a Kindle. Christian love is an aggressive movement and an active commitment. In reality, we *choose* where to place our affections.

Marriage and family therapist Donald Harvey writes, "Intimate *relationships*, as opposed to intimate experiences, are the result of planning. They are built. The sense of union that comes with genuine spiritual closeness will not just happen. If it is present, it is because of definite intent and follow-through on your part. You choose to invest, and do. It's not left to mere chance."[1]

It took years for me to understand I have a Christian obligation to continually move *toward* my wife. I thought that as long as I didn't attack my wife or say cruel things to her, I was a "nice" husband, but the opposite of biblical love isn't hate; it's apathy. To stop moving toward our spouse is to stop loving him or her. It's holding back from the very purpose of marriage.

THE MALE MASQUERADE

At the risk of offending some readers, I think it's necessary to point out that this is one area of spirituality that may be more difficult, generally, for men than for women. First, men tend to be less communicative, perhaps not realizing the message of disinterest this sends. It's one thing to *think* warm thoughts about your spouse; it's quite another to *express* them. Many men don't realize the damage they do simply by remaining silent.

Second, men tend to view independence as a sign of strength, maturity, and manhood. *Interdependence* is more than a long word. For men it is often a bitter pill to swallow, a sign, even, of weakness.

While this sense of independence may be culturally celebrated, it is a misunderstanding of real manhood, and it is not a biblical truth. It needs to be critiqued using the framework of the nature of God. While it is true that we must be willing and unafraid to stand alone if need be (consider Jesus on the cross), it is even more true that the movement of God is a movement toward people, even sinful people. The reason Jesus stood alone was that others could be brought near to God. In essence, he stood alone in order to gather his children to himself. His solitary act was a radical statement of the importance of community. If we desire to be remade in God's image, we will be molded in such a way that we move toward others. Men, in the same way that you are not satisfied unless your wife is at least occasionally the initiator in sex, women are not satisfied unless we are the initiators in expressing love. We need to become, in three words, *initiators of love.* If we want to be like Jesus, we need to begin *initiating love toward others*—starting with our spouses and moving on to friends, family, and coworkers.

In fact, for most men, the flight from others is an act of cowardice, not courage. A man can't handle a maturing relationship with a woman his age, so he divorces his wife and marries someone the age of his daughter in a futile attempt to preserve his power. Another man is unwilling to face the fact that his wife is not his mother, but a partner who expects to receive as well as to give, so he sulks and gives his wife the silent treatment rather than owning up to his own sense of neediness. Still other men may be unwilling to enter the give-and-take required of a complementary relationship, so they ignore their wives and throw themselves into their work, where they are always in charge and where their subordinates must bend to their will, or they disappear into their electronic devices. They may succeed in a game, but it's at the cost of failing in real life.

These are not profiles in courage; they are monuments of male shame.

When God calls me to continually move toward my wife, to initiate, he is calling me to be shaped into his very image.

EBBING EMOTIONS

One of the things that makes falling forward so difficult is the reality of conflicting emotions. Madeleine L'Engle wrote a simple poem that captures this marvelously.[2] Her words are directed toward God, but I think they apply just as well to anyone with whom we have a relationship of love:

Dear God,
I hate you.
Love, Madeleine.

Have you ever experienced this frustrating reality of being disgusted with someone while at the same time knowing you love them dearly? L'Engle is honest about her frustration with God, yet the last two words make all the difference. Even though she is exasperated with her Creator, she is pledged to move toward him. "Love, Madeleine" becomes the denominator that defines every numerator. No matter what the exasperation is about, no matter how intense the frustration, Madeleine's relationship with God is marked by that foundational love.

That's how it should be with our marriages. Even in the moments of anger, betrayal, exasperation, and hurt, we are called to pursue this person, to embrace them, and to grow toward them—to let our love redefine our feelings of disinterest, frustration, and even hatred.

THE BLOOD OF MARRIAGE

This call to fall forward puts the focus on initiating intimacy. We cheapen marriage if we reduce it to nothing more than a negative "I agree to never have sex with anyone else." Marriage points to a gift of self that goes well beyond sexual fidelity. Getting married is agreeing to grow together, into each other, to virtually commingle our souls so that we share a unique and rare bond. When we stop doing that, we have committed fraud against our partner; we made a commitment we're not willing to live up to.

GETTING MARRIED IS AGREEING TO GROW TOGETHER, TO COMMINGLE OUR SOULS SO THAT WE SHARE A UNIQUE AND RARE BOND.

This "interpenetration" can be a wonderful—and even fun—experience. Lisa and I had been married for just over a decade when we began saying the same things in some uncanny ways. During one of our son's soccer games, I went up to a friend and said, "If they gave near misses half a point, we'd be killing them."

Jill's eyes grew wide. "Did you just hear Lisa say that?"

"No."

"Lisa told me the exact same thing just ten seconds ago."

It started to happen with enough regularity that sometimes it felt almost creepy. Many married couples have experienced this same phenomenon. Our thinking and our turns of phrases have literally been so shaped by each other's presence that we have begun to resemble one person.

Such an interpenetration of being points to a reality that goes far beyond sexual exclusivity. Marriage is defined by a positive virtue. It presumes the gift of self. Kathleen and Thomas Hart write, "One can do many external deeds of love and still hold back the really precious gift, the inner self. This gift can be given only through communication."[3]

Communication is thus the blood of marriage that carries vital oxygen into the heart of our romance. At first, communication can seem glorious. In the rush of infatuation, the person standing before us seems virtually infinite in his or her mystery, beauty, insight, and ability to create the feeling of pure pleasure in us. Just a few months or perhaps years later, it is amazing how finite and earthy this "angel" has become.

Part of this is simply the humbleness of the human condition. No matter how lovely a young woman, no matter how smooth a young man, eventually the human flaws will appear. Funny noises and smells come out of all of us. It's the discovery of these banal realities that often causes us to pull back, as if the other person has tricked us.

Along with verbal communication comes physical communication—the act of touching. This includes sexual expression, but also nonsexual touch. As a rule, I can't stand having someone touch my face, but my wife can't get enough of having her face touched. It took me years to understand just how important it is for Lisa to be touched—especially when she knows that the touch is not for the purpose of leading to something else.

And while men may need to be reminded of the importance of frequent nonsexual touching, many wives have learned that if a woman is not pursuing her husband sexually, just about every other movement toward her husband may go unnoticed. She might contribute more than 50 percent to the family budget, run two marathons a year, and be voted Realtor of the Year at work and Mother of the Year at church, but if she's always the last one to arrive in the bedroom at night and the first one to leave in the morning, her husband may still define her by her denials rather than accomplishments.

There's a classic scene in an old Woody Allen movie. A husband and wife are separately questioned by a marriage counselor, and the viewer is privy to their differing responses. The counselor first asks the wife, "How often do you and your husband have sex?" The wife responds, "Almost always. Three times a week." The counselor is then shown asking the husband, "How often do you and your wife have sex?" The husband responds, "Almost never. Three times a week."

For the most part, this is a male-female thing, but it's becoming historically dated. More and more therapists admit that these previous roles are being reversed, and it's the wives who lament the relative infrequency of sexual relations. The other stereotype, of course, is the wife's desire to have conversation and the husband's preference for silence. Regardless of who wants what more often, both arenas offer an avenue for maturity where both sides can grow toward each other in selflessness.

We need to look at it this way: Interpenetration of souls is a duty incumbent on every husband and wife. Some of us naturally gravitate toward the desire for sex, and some toward verbal communication. We have a duty to meet our spouse in their need. Correspondingly, we also have a Christian duty not to demand too much of our spouse. The wife can recognize that her husband may be able to tolerate just so much conversation; the husband will need to accept the idea that daily sexual relations may be less than enticing to his wife.

This commitment toward interpenetration teaches us to surrender our own demands at the same time we strive to meet our spouse's demands. Ideally, if both spouses do this, the end result will be a marvelous and happy compromise. Usually, however, it's not nearly this easy, and one spouse begins to give far more than the other. This is the ground on which marital breakdown often begins, when one partner feels they are not receiving many benefits from all their sacrifices.

INTERPENETRATION OF SOULS IS A DUTY INCUMBENT ON EVERY HUSBAND AND WIFE.

But what if that "giving" spouse found motivation other than through their own desires? What if they viewed meeting the other partner's demands as part of their own spiritual formation? Instead of saying, "Why should I talk to her or be affectionate when she never wants to have sex?" a husband might say, "Regardless of how often we make love, out of a desire to please God and grow spiritually and internally, I'm going to make myself available for long conversations with my wife."

Typically, marriage books will describe such a scene, and then come the words, "And when the husband does that, he'll find that his wife suddenly has a new desire to join him in bed!" But this is grossly overstating the case. I'm not suggesting the husband should meet his wife's needs so his own needs can be better met. I'm suggesting he do it as a spiritual exercise. The harder it is, the more he'll profit from it. If his wife immediately repays him in a physical way, he might go to sleep with a smile on his face but, perhaps, with less spiritual training. The commitment to do this regardless of the results sets up a win-win situation; either the relationship becomes more mutual, or you gain the true virtue of selflessness—sacrifice without pay. Or maybe you receive both!

A mature husband and wife can grow leaps and bounds spiritually as they learn to compromise and move toward the other. But it is often the case that one spouse doesn't care about spiritual growth; they may be fully consumed with their own desires and sense of need. While such a situation may result in a less satisfying and less happy marriage, it can still provide the context for Christian growth. A Christian is never dependent on the response of others to grow spiritually. It's our own heart's decisions that matter.

Talking and touching are thus two of the most important ways we give ourselves to each other. The refusal to give the gift of self can sometimes be malicious. At other times, this withholding may not be done consciously. We just wake up one day and realize we have made no effort to keep moving toward our spouse physically, emotionally, and spiritually. Most of us, in fact, probably never approached the relationship of marriage with the thought that apathy is the antithesis of Christian love. As long as we're not mean, vindictive, or cruel, we may think we're fulfilling our Christian duty.

But we're not.

The truth is that I owe my wife this gift of self. When I

refuse to fall forward and begin withholding myself, I am saying in effect, "I will no longer be married to you on a spiritual level."

THE DISCIPLINE OF FELLOWSHIP

The spiritual discipline embedded in learning to fall forward can be described as "the discipline of fellowship." In addition to the more general nature of pursuit, this discipline is further nurtured through three spiritual practices: learning not to run from conflict, learning how to compromise, and learning to accept others. These practices will serve us well both in the church and in the home.

NOT RUNNING FROM CONFLICT

I've seen churches fight about the stupidest things, and I've seen long-term ministry partners tear a church apart in the process. The spiritual discipline of fellowship is not easy. Sinful people wound each other; imperfect people see reality differently; and egocentric people have a difficult time perceiving somebody else's perspective.

The problem is that *all of us* are sinful, imperfect, and egocentric!

Marriage provides the small experimental laboratory in which we can learn to engage in spiritual fellowship. Everything that happens broadly in social contexts has a mirror in marriage—disagreements, wounding words, conflict of interest, and competing dreams.

When disagreements arise, the natural tendency is to flee. Rather than work through the misunderstanding (or sin), we typically take a much more economical path—we search for another church, another job, another neighborhood, another friend, another spouse.

Marriage challenges this "flight" tendency. It encases us with a rock-hard, given-to-God promise that insists we work through the problem to arrive at some sort of resolution.

Mature adults realize that *every* relationship involves conflict, confession, and forgiveness. Unless you truly enjoy hanging around a sycophant, the absence of conflict demonstrates that either the relationship isn't important enough to fight over or that both individuals are too insecure to risk disagreement.

Conflict provides an avenue for spiritual growth. To resolve conflict, by definition we must become more engaged, not less. Just when we want to tell the other person off, we are forced to be quiet and listen to their complaint. Just when we are most eager to make ourselves understood, we must strive to understand. Just when we seek to air our grievances, we must labor to comprehend another's hurt. Just when we want to point out the fallacies and abusive behavior of someone else, we must ruthlessly evaluate our own offensive attitudes and behaviors.

It's this self-emptying act of understanding that explains how successfully negotiated conflict creates an even stronger bond in the end. "Make-up sex" has become a cliché, but there's a truth buried in there somewhere. When conflict arises and is overcome, the couple has *had* to move toward each other. They've fallen forward, sought resolution, and in the process built an urgent hunger for each other.

Glossing over disagreements and sinful attitudes and behaviors isn't fellowship; it's polite pretending. True fellowship insists that we fall forward.

Learning to successfully negotiate conflict will have a direct influence on our relationship with God, for the time will come when we feel we have a bone to pick with him too. One of the most famous fights in the Bible involved God and Jacob. The two combatants wrestled all night long, and the encounter so transformed Jacob that his name was changed to Israel ("he struggles with God"). Near the end of the confrontation, Jacob insisted that God "bless" him (Genesis 32:26). God eventually granted Jacob's request and then built an entire nation out of the descendants of this conniving, deceitful man.

Sometimes we, too, will find ourselves wrestling with God. "How could you take this child away from me?" "How could you allow Jim to lose his job, just when we need it most?" "How come you stay up there all silent and aloof?"

It is not a mark of Christian maturity to pretend we are not bothered by our heavenly Father's silence. A healthy spirituality will call us to fall forward with God no less than with our spouse. This falling forward is certainly a more appropriate response than simply writing God off and kicking him out of our lives at the first sign that he is doing something or allowing something we don't understand.

Like Jacob, wrestling with God may well result in an unforeseen blessing. We may also—as did Jacob—receive a lifelong limp, but any interaction with God will prove beneficial, provided the movement is always toward him.

COMPROMISE

The second way we practice the spiritual discipline of fellowship within marriage is by learning to compromise. Sadly the word *compromise* is seen as a dirty word by many in our society who view it as an attack on individualism—"my wants, my life, and my choices." But virtually every relationship, if it is to continue and grow, must embody compromise in some way, shape, or form. There are no two perfectly fitting people with exactly the same wants and desires, so at some point in the relationship each person must give up something or become something in order to become one. The goal in compromise is for two different people to become one. Allowing someone to have their way, for the right reasons, can be a form of saying, "I love you." It's proof that we're willing to give ground for no other reason than that we value the ongoing relationship more than we value asserting our rights, preferences, or wishes. Compromise is the cement of fellowship.

ALLOWING SOMEONE TO HAVE THEIR WAY, FOR THE RIGHT REASONS, CAN BE A FORM OF SAYING, "I LOVE YOU."

Many congregations have had to address the issue of their younger members' desire for "contemporary worship" without losing the "traditional worship" preferred by older members. Some churches have opted to go with two services; others have tried to combine liturgy and informality. Some have sold off the organ; others have built a bigger organ but occasionally leave it silent while someone plays a guitar. Churches everywhere are learning the art of compromise.

In the same way, couples must learn to compromise over the mundane (where do we celebrate the Christmas holiday?) and the profound (how many children should we have?). For such compromise to work, there must be numerous mini-funerals. We must choose to die to ourselves and to give ground, and, conversely, not to gloat when ground is given to us.

ACCEPTANCE AND LOYALTY

A third discipline of fellowship is learning to accept real people. So often, new members will attend a church and rave about the pastor's teaching, the worship leader's ability to cultivate the presence of God, and the friendliness of the other church members. And then, a year or two later, when they've heard the pastor's best stories, grown bored with the worship leader's favorite songs, and are expected to invite others to come for lunch rather than be invited themselves, it's amazing how what was once "the best church in the world" is now "a dead and dying body."

This, too, mirrors what often happens in a marriage. The man whom the wife once thought of as confident is now seen as arrogant. The wife who attracted her husband with her quiet and gentle spirit is now seen as a weak woman unworthy of respect. In the flush of infatuation, dating couples often focus on what is right about the person, and then after marriage all they begin to see is what is *wrong* about the person—even if nothing changed! After marriage, the perspective completely shifts from idealizing someone, which is imagining a perfect and untrue picture of who they are, to the sobering realization that the spouse is not the person they imagined them to be. Instead of receiving a knight in shining armor, they receive a green ogre named Shrek, a man or woman full of their own problems, imperfections, and sin. One of the most common complaints given to pastors and counselors is this: "He's not who I thought he was."

Marriage based on romanticism embraces an idealized lie (infatuation) and then divorces the reality once it presents itself. Marriage based on life in Jesus Christ invites us to divorce the lie (an idealized view of our spouse) and embrace reality (two sinful people struggling to maintain a lifelong commitment). As Evelyn and James Whitehead observe, "The challenge is not to keep on loving the person we thought we were marrying, but to love the person we did marry!"[4]

The discipline of fellowship requires us to learn the art of loyalty. Just because the church down the street has called a younger and more exciting pastor doesn't mean we should blow off years of commitment and relationships at our present church and go to hear the new "star." Just because a younger woman or a more sensitive man appears on the scene doesn't mean we skip out on the life commitment we have made.

It's all about falling forward. You meet someone you find very exciting and attractive, but you choose to put strict limits on the relationship and instead redouble your efforts to declare your commitment to your spouse. You feel hurt and wounded by your partner's selfishness, but instead of sulking and responding with the silent treatment, you take the initiative to express your feelings in a gentle and respectful way.

Ironically, falling forward leads in the end to greater marital satisfaction. Although the purpose of this book is to help us use our marriages to draw closer to God, when we do that, we often find that our marriages will improve as well, increasing our own satisfaction. Therapist Donald Harvey puts it succinctly: "Couples who place their relationship in a high-priority position have the greatest potential for achieving what they want out of the marriage. Those who do not have a lesser potential. It's as simple as that."[5]

When you entered this relationship of marriage, you committed to keep moving toward your spouse. Any step back, any pause, any retreat, is an act of fraud. Learn to move toward the person God has given to you for the purpose of teaching you how to love.

FOSTERING FORGIVENESS

What do we do when our spouse doesn't want us to fall forward—when, in fact, our spouse is pushing us away?

The Bible provides clear guidance. The father let the prodigal son go, but love demanded that the father always be ready with open arms to fall forward should the son ever return (Luke 15:11–32).

Someone else's action can't dictate our response. God sent his Son into a world that hated him. If God had waited for the world to be worthy to receive him, his Son would never have come. This truth entails yet another spiritual discipline of fellowship, in fact, one of the most difficult spiritual disciplines of all—the discipline of forgiveness.

> ONE OF MARRIAGE'S PRIMARY PURPOSES IS TO TEACH US HOW TO FORGIVE.

The more enterprising among us might attempt to use our spouse's sin as an excuse to pull back, but this is hardly a Christian response, because all of us sin against each other. In fact, I believe one of marriage's primary purposes is to teach us how to forgive. This spiritual discipline provides us with the power we need to keep falling forward in the context of a sinful world.

THE CALL TO GRACE

A stonemason in Seattle followed a wife's directions and carved a headstone for the woman's husband with these traditional words:

Rest in Peace

A few months later, the wife discovered that her husband had been unfaithful, so she returned to the stonemason and asked him to add four more words. The stonemason did as he was told, and the gravestone now reads:

Rest in Peace ...
Till We Meet Again

There's something about being sinned against by a spouse that strikes us at a deeper level than when others sin against us. A sense of betrayal is added to the sin, so that when we're wronged, we may be so offended we want to continue the dispute into the grave.

We get married for all sorts of reasons. "Because it gives us an opportunity to learn how to forgive" probably doesn't top the list of most honeymooners, but the spiritual practice of continually moving toward someone provides an excellent context in which we can practice this vital spiritual discipline. Sin in marriage (on the part of both spouses) is a daily reality, an ongoing struggle that threatens to hold us back. You will never find a spouse who is without sin. The person you decide to marry will eventually hurt you—sometimes even intentionally, making forgiveness an essential spiritual discipline.

Paul offers wonderfully helpful words in the book of Romans. He writes that "no one will be declared righteous in God's sight by the works of the law; rather, through the law we become conscious of our sin" (Romans 3:20).

Having read this verse seemingly a hundred times or more, I've been well warned, and you have too: Our spouses will never achieve a "lawful" sinlessness. It just won't happen. We will be sinned against, and we will be hurt. When that happens, we will have a choice to make: We can give in to our hurt, resentment, and bitterness, or we can grow as a Christian and learn yet another important lesson on how to forgive.

The law wasn't created by God for two spouses to hold each other to an impossible standard with which they can then beat each other over the head. A self-righteous spouse is an obnoxious spouse, even if, by the letter of the law, they're momentarily blameless and in the right. Eventually, that spouse will slip up too.

What, then, are we called to?

Paul goes on to say that "now *apart from the law* the righteousness of God has been made known" (Romans 3:21, emphasis added). It's a righteousness based on the "redemption that came by Christ Jesus" and on "faith" (Romans 3:24, 27).

Marriages invariably break down when a pious partner

impales his or her spouse on the law. None of us can live up to the law; all of us will break it. Marriage teaches us — indeed, it practically forces us — to learn to live by extending grace and forgiveness to people who have sinned against us.

If I can learn to forgive and accept my imperfect spouse, I'll be well equipped to offer forgiveness outside my marriage. Forgiveness, I'm convinced, is so unnatural an act that it takes practice to perfect it.

LOVING THE SINNER

I once spoke at a staff retreat for an Episcopal church that was held at a Roman Catholic retreat center. The chapel was small but distinguished, and I poked around a little shortly after I arrived. I saw a confessional in the back — one of those tiny rooms where people make their confessions. Curious to see what it looked like, I opened the door and was startled to find, of all things, a file cabinet.

Sometimes that's what marriage is like: Our spouse has confessed sins and weaknesses to us, and we've kept every confession in a mental file cabinet, ready to be taken out and used in our defense or in an attack. But true forgiveness is a process, not an event. It is rarely the case that we are able to forgive "one time" and the matter is settled. Far more often, we must relinquish our bitterness a dozen times or more, continually choosing to release the offender from our judgment.

This necessary ongoing fight to forgive is why forgiveness is so very hard. In his book *What's So Amazing About Grace?* Philip Yancey writes the following:

> In the heat of an argument ... we [my wife and I] were discussing my shortcomings in a rather spirited way when she said, "I think it's pretty amazing that I forgave you for some of the dastardly things you've done!" ... It [forgiveness] is no sweet platonic ideal to be dispersed in the world like air-freshener sprayed from a can. Forgiveness is achingly difficult, and long after you've forgiven, the wound — my dastardly deeds — lives on in memory. Forgiveness is an unnatural act, and my wife was protesting its blatant unfairness.[6]

The Claude Lanzmann-filmed documentary on the Holocaust titled *Shoah* records the gripping moment when a leader of the Warsaw ghetto uprising talks about the bitterness that remains in his heart: "If you could lick my heart," he says, "it would poison you."* A number of marriages are like that. The infighting and personal attacks have become so bitter that the participants have developed poisonous hearts. The tragedy, of course, is that a poisonous heart doesn't just pollute the person who licks it; it is itself an infected organ that pours toxic bile into a person's own life. Forgiveness, in this sense, is an act of self-defense, a tourniquet that stops the fatal bleeding of resentment.

Any life situation that exercises our ability to extend forgiveness is a life situation that can mold us further into the character of Jesus Christ. I know of few life situations that call us to such a regular practice of forgiveness as the relationship of marriage.

In the practice of this discipline, marriage forces us to embrace that most difficult of Christian clichés: "Hate the sin but love the sinner." This is a staggering thing to do, as every self-righteous fiber within us pushes us to transform revulsion toward sin into revulsion toward the sinner—and therefore revulsion toward our spouse. Philip Yancey encourages us to move in the direction of loving the sinner by thinking what it must have been like for Jesus. Because Jesus was morally perfect, imagine what platform Jesus had to be disgusted! "Yet," writes Yancey, "he treated notorious sinners with mercy and not judgment."[7] No one loved sinners with the depth that Jesus did.

FORGIVENESS IS AN ACT OF SELF-DEFENSE, A TOURNIQUET THAT STOPS THE FATAL BLEEDING OF RESENTMENT.

C. S. Lewis confessed that he too struggled with how to

* This is not to slam a man who suffered such brutal loss. I can fully understand his bitterness, which is what makes the giving of grace in Christ sound so revolutionary.

truly love the sinner while hating the sin. One day it suddenly became clear:

> It occurred to me that there was one man to whom I had been doing this all my life—namely myself. However much I might dislike my own cowardice or conceit or greed, I went on loving myself. There had never been the slightest difficulty about it. In fact the very reason why I hated the things was that I loved the man. Just because I loved myself, I was sorry to find that I was the sort of man who did those things.[8]

We extend this charity to ourselves, so the question begs to be asked: Why do we not extend this same charity to our spouse?

During a conference I spoke at, a woman who was very open about her own struggle with eating disorders confessed to her inability to forgive her husband for his past use of pornography. Her husband had been gracious, forgiving, and gentle as she had gained more than a hundred pounds after they were married, but she had little empathy for any man who used photographs of naked women in the same way she used food. Her hurt was understandable, but her bitterness sadly kept her from seeing the similarities between their struggles. Please understand that I'm *not* equating these two struggles, just pointing out that both of them call us to apply appropriate grace. Some men are drawn to pornography in the face of past abuse, in ways similar to how some struggle with food issues. That doesn't excuse behavior; it's just a recognition that even someone who needs grace may have difficulty extending grace.

The key to the discipline of fellowship is understanding this fundamental reality: All of us face struggles, and each one of us is currently facing a struggle that we're having less than 100 percent success overcoming. If we're married, the fact is we're also married to someone who is failing in some way.

We can respond to bitter juice by becoming bitter people, or we can use it as a spiritual discipline and transform its exercise into the honey of a holy life. In this fallen world, struggles, sin, and unfaithfulness are a given. The only question is whether our response to these struggles, sin, and unfaithfulness will draw us closer to God — or whether it will estrange us from ourselves, our Creator, and each other.

We have a choice: Will we initiate forgiveness and resolve to overcome every obstacle? Or will we run away? In other words, will we fall forward, or will we fall away?

Chapter 11

MAKE ME A SERVANT

Marriage Can Build in Us a Servant's Heart

> How great, then, is the constraint in marriage, which subjects even the stronger to the other; for by mutual constraint each is bound to serve. Nor if one wishes to refrain can he withdraw his neck from the yoke, for he is subject to the [sexual desires] of the other ... You see how plainly the servitude of marriage is defined.
>
> *Ambrose*

The essence of Christianity is found in Philippians 2, where Paul urges us to do nothing (it's these absolutist words that can make Scripture so troubling) "out of selfish ambition or vain conceit. Rather, in humility value others above yourselves, not looking to your own interests but each of you to the interests of the others" (Philippians 2:3–4). Paul escalates this teaching by calling us to emulate Christ Jesus, who, though he was "in very nature God,... made himself nothing by taking the very nature of a servant" (verses 6–7).

To be a Christian is to be a self-volunteering servant. It is not sufficient to merely voice our assent to a few choice doctrines. We are called to act in such a way that we put others above ourselves. We are expressly forbidden from exalting ourselves for the sole purpose of furthering our own comfort or fame. Otto Piper nails the marriage relationship's potential to create a servant heart in us when he describes marriage as "a reciprocal willingness of two persons to assume responsibility for each other."[1] In other words, marriage calls us to become servants of each other's welfare. It's precisely this servant call that makes marriage so beneficial spiritually—and so difficult personally. When I asked my wife to marry me, I was just twenty-two years old. My decision was based almost entirely on what I thought she would bring to the marriage. She looked good; we had fun together; she loved the Lord. And my suspicion is that her thoughts were running in the same direction: *Can this guy support our family? Do I find him attractive? Would he be a good father?*

These aren't bad questions to ask, but once the ceremony is over, if we want to enter a truly Christian marriage, we have to turn 180 degrees and ask ourselves, "How can I serve my mate?"

For much of the past century, this was a question most Christian men didn't take all that seriously. It was assumed the wife would unilaterally serve her husband in virtually all matters. Even though our culture is now moving well past this view, a few men still cling so fiercely to a sense of privilege in marriage that they've decided to go outside the United States to find what amounts to a slave bride.

A company called Cherry Blossoms feeds off the poverty of the Philippines to offer matchmaking services between older American males and young (sometimes extremely young) Filipino women. The men pay to receive a catalogue titled *Island Blossoms*, which contains photographs and brief personal sketches of available women. They then pay Cherry Blossoms another fee for the women's addresses.

The men offer the women a way out of the densely populated and muddy squatters' towns with houses as small as walk-in closets. But this "salvation" comes at a price. One man sent a two-page, single-spaced contract to a prospective bride that read, in part:

> Your primary function in life is to serve me ... Your secondary function is to be a model mother ... but never to the extent that it will conflict with proper attention to me ... You will rise approximately at 6:00 a.m. After going to the bathroom, brushing your teeth, combing your hair, cleaning your face with alcohol or Seabreeze, you will wake the children ... Each day there will be absolute order in the house by the time that I arrive ... You will clean your face no less than three times a day ... You will immediately reply VERBALLY when I speak to you ... When we make love, I expect that you do so at any and all times and with enthusiasm.[2]

Another man seemed determined to find the most desperate bride so she would be extremely agreeable sexually once she got to the States. In a letter to an interested young woman, he wrote, "There are two young ladies ... who have written that they would do ANYTHING for me ... if only I gave them a chance to be my permanent partner and, of course, the opportunity to come to the United States with me. Tell me, Vilma, how do you feel about that?... Would you do anything I ask?" He then mentions a particular sexual activity and writes, "My preference is [for a] partner [who] would be willing, able, and skillful enough to perform that activity for me, at any time."

This attitude is so offensive to the spirit of Christian marriage that it borders on being nothing but lifetime prostitution. Because the man has the money, he wants to buy the woman's services—for a lifetime instead of for a night, but buy them nonetheless. Sex is something he expects to receive, not something he plans to give. Perhaps it's not so surprising that one young Cherry Blossom bride complained that on her wedding night, "it felt like rape."

While some elements of the feminist movement have led

to some atrocious moral positions, the challenge that women are not to be treated by their husbands as unilateral servants was — dare I say it? — a prophetic one. Unfortunately, rather than hearing the call to both men and women to serve each other, all too frequently women are hearing the call to become as self-serving and self-absorbed as men. This completely misses the picture of marriage as God intended it to be — two equals, albeit different, completely and wholly serving the other person as though they are greater than themselves, thus creating not a male-female power struggle over who is more worthy, but a harmony that reflects the character of God in the Trinity and the ministry of reconciliation in the world.

A MAN'S LOVE: THE SACRIFICE BEHIND SERVICE

Although many speak of the sterility of modern seminaries, I had a completely different experience at Regent College in Vancouver, British Columbia. Its faculty challenged me in many ways, including the way in which I treated my wife.

I remember the semester I worked as a teacher's assistant for Dr. Gordon Fee. He and his wife invited a few students and their wives over for dessert. Lisa was pregnant with our first child — and showing it. Listening to Dr. Fee's lectures, I had learned a great deal about how to preach a moving sermon. Reading Dr. Fee's writings, I had had the book of 1 Corinthians opened up in new ways. But I was about to learn something about being a husband.

Lisa walked in the door, and Dr. Fee immediately jumped up. "Here," he said, "you need the softest chair."

His words were seasoned with sincerity and genuine concern. My wife was surprised at the attention, but she took the chair and sat down. I sat beside her. Dr. Fee, I noticed to my embarrassment, was still standing.

"Now," he said, "can I get you a pillow for your back?"

"No, I'm fine," Lisa said.

"How about a glass of water? Do you need something to drink?"

"That would be great," my wife answered.

Dr. Fee marched into the kitchen. He came back with a full glass. "Is the heat all right?" he asked. "Are you too cold, too hot? Do you need to raise your feet?"

Lisa was almost blushing by this time, and I was greatly humbled. I had never served my wife in the way my seminary professor was now doing. Just seeing his empathy, his dedication to making another person comfortable, and his willingness to put himself entirely at my wife's disposal was an eye-opener, to be sure. I saw the heart of a servant and realized I had a long way to go in order to grow into maturity as a husband.

It was one thing to be shown up by a seminary professor. I was even more chagrined when I found my growth as a husband exceeded by that of a professional football player.

Four-time All-Pro NFL linebacker Chris Spielman had played football for twenty-six of his thirty-three years. He is the type of guy who relishes the game, even going to rather absurd lengths to get ready for a contest. On one occasion, he slept in the nude with the air-conditioning blasting so he could be fully prepared for the brutally cold winter chill that envelops Buffalo's Rich Stadium.

He met his wife, Stefanie, in 1983 when he was just seventeen years old. They were married six years later. Stefanie is beautiful—she worked as a model before she became a full-time mother—and the two embarked on a rich marriage. Spielman played for many years with the Detroit Lions and then signed with the Buffalo Bills in 1996.

The year 1997 came with a fistful of trials. In July, just as preseason camp was getting started, a doctor spoke the grave diagnosis: *breast cancer*. Stefanie, the beautiful model, opted for a mastectomy, to be followed by six weeks of chemotherapy, a time period during which she would lose all her hair.

The Spielmans had two small children under the age of five, and Chris knew the chemo treatments would drain his wife's energy. He had a decision to make. "It was my test," Chris said in a magazine article. "It was my defining moment."[3]

In a show of solidarity, Chris shaved his head. Even more important, he quit football — not forever, but for a year — until Stefanie was back on her feet. If you're not a football fan, you may not realize the astounding sacrifice this act represented. The average career span of an NFL linebacker is less than three years. The fact that Chris took an entire season off left him with no guarantee he'd ever get back to doing what he loved so much — playing football.

"[Stefanie] always supported me 100 percent," Chris explained. "I had to offer it back."

This was a sacrifice Stefanie didn't want Chris to make. "I never cried about the cancer or how it hurt," she confessed. "I cried because of what it was doing to Chris."

Instead of watching game film and meeting with the coaches, Chris woke up early to feed the kids (he learned that his oldest hated to have any of the food on her plate touch any other food), and then he got Stefanie up an hour or so later and served her breakfast. He then did the laundry, took the kids to their gymnastics lessons, and made sure Stefanie got her medication.

Clearly, Chris had learned the meaning of sacrificial giving to his wife. Somehow he'd learned to live out what Paul urges husbands to strive toward in Ephesians 5:25 — loving their wives, just as Christ loved the church, and he explains quite explicitly how Christ loved the church: by *giving up his life for her*.

Chris told *GQ* magazine, "For ten years our entire lives had been about me. My career came first, always. Stefanie made every sacrifice in the world to support me unconditionally ... What kind of husband would I be if I didn't drop everything for Stefanie when she got sick? Did I want her *sister* to have to hold her hand while she suffered, because I wasn't there? Did I want Stefanie's *mother* to have to sit with her in the hospital while they were shooting needles into her and filling her up with those awful chemicals, or did I want to be there myself? ... This is my family. This is my responsibility. This is my home. This is my duty."[4]

The very definition of the word *sacrifice* means that sacrifice isn't sacrifice unless it costs us something; so men, it's a fair question for you to ask, "How have I loved my wife in the past two or three weeks in such a way that it has cost me something—vocationally, financially, and with my hobbies, time, or comfort?" If we can't come up with something, we're not loving like the Bible calls husbands to love in Ephesians 5:25. My friend Dr. Kevin Leman likes to point out that he has yet to meet a man who, after a long day at work, thinks to himself, "What I really need right now is a long, forty-five-minute talk with my wife." But that's precisely why a man's willingness to engage in such conversation is so beneficial to him spiritually—it costs him something. It teaches him to sacrifice.

MARRIAGE CREATES A SITUATION IN WHICH OUR DESIRE TO BE SERVED AND CODDLED CAN BE REPLACED WITH A NOBLER DESIRE TO SERVE OTHERS.

Marriage creates a situation in which our desire to be served and coddled can be replaced with a nobler desire to serve others—even to sacrifice for others. This is a call for both husbands and wives. The beauty of marriage is that it confronts our selfishness and demands our service twenty-four hours a day. When we're most tired, most worn-out, and feeling more sorry for ourselves than we ever have before, we have the opportunity to confront feelings of self-pity by getting up and serving our mate.

SCANDALOUS TEACHING

If there is a Bible verse sure to set our culture's teeth on edge, it has to be Titus 2:4. The apostle Paul says something so seemingly offensive to modern minds that I suspect if there was one verse certain elements of our society would remove from Scripture, it would be this one. Paul tells older women they should "train the young women to love their husbands" (ESV). The thought that the church should actually teach young women how to please a man, serve a man, and take care of a man borders on uttering a racial slur in our popular culture's thinking, but in context that is exactly what Paul intends. He cannot mean that women should be trained to "have feelings" for their husbands. That would be absurd. He's talking about serving them, taking care of them.

I believe God designed marriage, in part, to "pinch our feet." Both men and women need to have their pride assaulted. All of us, men and women alike, if we are to become like Christ, must, by definition, learn to become servants. And marriage gives us the opportunity to do just that. Paul's words to Titus assume that none of this is natural; you don't have to teach people to do what they already do. The assumption is that loving their husbands is an unnatural skill that wives must learn—better yet, we could describe it as a *supernatural* skill.

I once heard a man describe how his wife served him in a way that made just about every male person listening to him start salivating. This man has a job that starts early in the morning, so he's home in the middle of the afternoon. His wife knows he's a huge sports fan, so on the first day of the March Madness NCAA basketball tournament, he came home to his favorite chair in the family den and to a plate of his favorite snacks and a cup of his favorite beverage.

"You've been working so hard," his wife said. "I don't expect you to get up from this chair all weekend unless there's something you need to do for yourself. If you run out of snacks or drinks, just let me know."

Occasional acts of dramatic service like this can go such a long way—not only in cementing intimacy as a couple, but in reminding the spouse who does the giving that to know Christ is to know service; to become like Christ is to become like a servant; to follow Christ is to follow the way of service.

So many marriages are filled with resentment, but voluntary acts of service can be the quickest way to replace resentment with love. When we act in service with godly motives, resentment suffocates and dies. It is only when we see that our pride and selfishness are the greatest barriers to our joy (rather than our spouse's sins or shortcomings) that our marriages will fully express the character of Christ.

THE MARK OF CHRISTIAN MARRIAGE

Precisely this notion of sacrifice and service will help us reclaim spirituality for married couples. Dietrich Bonhoeffer wrote that "Christian marriage is marked by discipline and self-denial ... Christianity does not therefore depreciate marriage; it sanctifies it."[5]

This is an area where traditional Christian spirituality has been weak. We talked in chapter 1 about how, for centuries, Christian spirituality was virtually synonymous with celibate spirituality, that is, the idea that even married people thought we had to become like monks and nuns to grow in the Lord. We'd have to engage in the same spiritual exercises as celibates—long periods of prayer, seasons of fasting, times of quiet meditation—but many of these activities fly in the face of family responsibilities. One monk I read urged families to set apart a half day of silence, suggesting that giving the little ones a puzzle or two would keep them occupied until midafternoon. Only a monk who has never been around children could possibly believe that giving a toddler a puzzle is going to keep him quiet for longer than it takes him to figure out how to stick a piece of that puzzle in his sister's ear.

Rather than develop a spirituality in which marriage serves our sanctification, the church focused on how closely married people could emulate single spirituality without neglecting their family. The family thus became a barrier rather than a stepping-stone to spiritual growth.

The reason this perspective endured for so long may be that the vast majority of people do not enter marriage with a view to becoming a servant. The marriage relationship is often seen as a selfish one because our motivations for marrying often *are* selfish. But my desire is to reclaim marriage as one of the most selfless states a Christian can enter—and thus, it is an excellent tool of spiritual growth.

To fully sanctify the marital relationship, we must live it together as Jesus lived his life—embracing the discipline of sacrifice and service *as a daily practice*. In the same way Jesus gave his body for us, we are to lay down our energy, our bodies, and our lives for others.

Kathleen and Thomas Hart refer to the "paschal mystery" of marriage—the process of dying and rising as a pattern of life for married people.[6] Each day we must die to our own desires and rise as a servant. Each day we are called to identify with the suffering Christ on the cross and then be empowered by the resurrected Christ. We die to our expectations, our demands, and our fears. We rise to compromise, service, and courage.

IN THE SAME WAY JESUS GAVE HIS BODY FOR US, WE ARE TO LAY DOWN OUR ENERGY, OUR BODIES, AND OUR LIVES FOR OTHERS.

In this sense, a true Christian marriage proposal is an *offer*, not a request. Rather than saying in effect, "Will you do this for me?" when we invite another to enter the marriage relationship, the real question should be, "Will you accept what I want to give?"

If marriage is daily approached from this perspective, there can be no issue of disillusionment on the part of either partner, as both will become consumed with how well they are carrying out their duty of serving their spouse.

THE "WORTHY"

The important thing to remember is that service is a spiritual discipline we owe to God, and it can only be lived out as it is applied to others. I learned long ago that God has called me to serve him through people, regardless of whether those people are worthy of being served. For years I worked with a ministry that reached out to women facing crisis pregnancies. One of the challenges in raising support and recruiting volunteers was that some people thought these women were merely reaping what they had sown, so why should we help them?

To be sure, many people are in desperate straits because of sinful choices and actions. But the apostle John examines it from another angle: "If anyone has material possessions and sees a brother or sister in need but has no pity on them, how can the love of God be in that person?" (1 John 3:17). For John, there's no mention of a *sinless* brother or sister in need. His teaching is far more blunt—their *need* defines our obligation. It's a matter of God's love, not human evaluation or judgment.

IF THE HEART OF CHRISTIANITY IS SERVICE, ANY SITUATION THAT SHAPES THE SPIRIT OF A SERVANT IN YOU IS WORTHWHILE.

Jesus' example is particularly challenging. *None* of the disciples deserved to have their feet washed at the Last Supper—all of them would abandon him within a few hours—yet Jesus did it anyway (John 13:1–17). In fact, Jesus even washed the feet of Judas, *who was just hours away from betraying him.*

God doesn't tell us to love only those who deserve it or to serve only those who serve us back. If you are in a one-sided marriage where you feel like you're giving and giving and never receiving, my heart goes out to you. You can partially redeem such a situation by becoming more God-oriented. Remind yourself that you are also in a situation where you can grow spiritually by leaps and bounds. If the heart of Christianity is service, any situation that shapes the spirit of a servant in you is worthwhile—even a lopsided marriage.

Now, having said that, you could also make the case that one of the ways we can serve our spouse is to address spiritual failings such as selfishness. You don't serve an addict by buying them drugs. You don't serve an abuser by letting them hit you. You don't serve an angry spouse by letting their temper destroy their relationships. It's possible some could apply my earlier words in a way that would not be service but codependence. Let's keep that in mind.

THE SPIRIT OF SERVICE

One of the challenges of Christian virtue is living out the teaching of the Scriptures that stress the inner reality behind the external action. Jesus said we can do the right thing (give money, for instance) for the wrong reason (to show off), in which case we lose our reward (Matthew 6:1–4). Without a doubt, our service can be subject to wrong motivations.

It's certainly possible a spouse might render service in an attempt to exert their own superiority. Otto Piper writes, "Strong personalities are tempted to assume one-sidedly the whole responsibility for their marriage. Rather than ask the partner to perform certain services, they want to do everything themselves ... While it looks like sacrificial love, this is in fact a passion to dominate the other person."[7]

Service includes allowing your spouse to give—if, of course, they are willing to give. In other words, service isn't just washing someone else's feet; at times it's letting *your own* feet be washed.

Another aspect of true service is that it's performed willingly. A begrudging, complaining service is not a Christian one.

I've learned to guard not just my servant's actions but my servant's *spirit* as well. If I serve Lisa with little puffs of exasperation, grunting every time I lift a finger on her behalf, I'm exhibiting a proud, false-martyr's spirit, not the attitude of Jesus Christ.

I go back to imagining the scene that day as Jesus washed Judas's feet. Do you think Jesus was especially rough as he scrubbed Judas's toes? Do you think he maybe gave Judas's ankle a little twist, just enough to let him know he knew what was about to happen?

I don't think so.

This principle of marriage as a freely given arena of service leaves room for the understanding that each partner in the marriage will have different roles and different avenues of service. Lisa and I have settled into habits that have become as comfortable as an old pair of jeans. When we come back from a trip, we don't discuss who takes the suitcases in—that's my job. As we go through the mail, any checks or receipts go straight to Lisa. Every April, all I do for our taxes is sign my name on a government form. Lisa hates filling up the car's gas tank, so before I leave on a trip, I try to make sure it's full. If

Lisa knows I'm coming home, she'll nurse that tank until she's riding on nothing more than fumes.

I don't resent this, and Lisa doesn't resent the fact that she's usually folding laundry when she watches a movie while I just sit there like an all-star couch potato (in part because she knows that I'm likely the one who'll be doing the ironing after the next load of laundry is done).

We're not just after the imitation of Christ's *actions* in our home; we also want to model Christ's *spirit* and *attitude*. Our motivation and our thoughts about our actions become as important as the actions themselves. And as Jesus showed, there are both times to serve and times to receive service.

The beauty of this commitment is that it makes both Lisa and me God-dependent rather than spouse-dependent. If Lisa is faithfully serving me when I'm in a surly mood and not showing my appreciation, she still receives an inner affirmation and sense of fulfillment from God. She has the joy of an inner witness telling her that her Creator is pleased with her. And this is precisely where a Christian couple who is following God's plan for marriage has a leg up on non-Christian couples. We realize it's not about what we *get* out of our marriage but about what we *become* in our marriage. To become a servant is to become strong spiritually. It means we are free from the petty demands and grievances that ruin so many lives and turn so many hearts into bitter cauldrons of disappointment, self-absorption, and self-pity.

WE REALIZE IT'S NOT ABOUT WHAT WE GET OUT OF OUR MARRIAGE BUT ABOUT WHAT WE BECOME IN OUR MARRIAGE.

There is true joy when true service is offered up with a true heart.

MONEY, MONEY, MONEY

Service entails far more than occasionally helping out with the dishes or giving our spouse a night off from watching the kids. The spirit of service will color virtually every aspect of marriage, including how we spend our money and time. Dan Allender and Tremper Longman speak to this issue so well:

> Money is the medium of power. More often than not, the issue is not money, but power. The battle is not about who is most trustworthy or whose heart most deeply desires to sacrifice for the other but about who controls the most palpable means of setting the family agenda.
>
> Time becomes a commodity of contention as well. Should a wife work, requiring her husband to take care of the kids after he gets home from his job? Is the husband spending too much time with his colleagues and neglecting his wife?
>
> These conflicts over time and money cloud the real issue: Are we willing to sacrifice for the good and the glory of the other? Quarrels over money and time usually reflect a demand to "own" our life rather than to serve the other with our wealth and existence. The typical fight over who ought to pick up the kids usually is about whose time is more valuable, who works the hardest, and who is least appreciated. It is not wrong to alternate chores or divvy up responsibilities, but the hurtful interactions usually reflect drawing battle lines over more petty matters.[8]

The next time you battle it out with your spouse over time or money, pause and remind yourself that your prayers to become more like Jesus Christ are being put to the test. Be willing to honestly ask yourself this question: Am I playing a petty power game, or am I using the sometimes unpleasant realities of life to shape my stubborn nature toward having the heart of a servant?

How do a husband and wife use money and time to serve instead of to dominate or manipulate? By appreciating your spouse, by seeking first to understand them, by emptying yourself and not immediately assuming that your task, your time, your perceived need is the most important. By remembering that I will be most fulfilled as a Christian when I use *everything* I have—including my money and time—as a way to serve others, with my spouse getting first priority (after God). This commitment absolutely undercuts petty power games. If I humiliate my wife by pointing out how much more important I am to the family's financial well-being, or if she points out how utterly helpless I am to do certain chores, we don't just cheapen each other; we cheapen ourselves. We destroy the entire notion of Christian fellowship by denying that every part has its place in the body of Christ (1 Corinthians 12:14–31).

These little acts of sacrifice will not always be rewarded or even noticed by our spouse. That's what can make them all the more difficult over the passage of time. But if we guard our hearts from bitterness and resentment, we will receive affirmation where it counts and where it means the most — from our heavenly Father.

Just as the spirit of service colors the way we spend our money and our time, so it affects the way we relate to our spouse sexually. The marital bed is yet another area where our service skills are put to the test.

ABSOLUTE POWER CORRUPTS — OR SERVES?

Golf legend Gary Player was once asked by a reporter what he would do if he had to choose between his wife, Vivienne, to whom he had been married for forty-two years, and his favorite golf club.[9] Without hesitating, Player responded, "I sure would miss her." When he got back to his hotel, Player found his beloved driver on the bed, wrapped up in a negligee.*

The nature of sexual desire is such that it bestows tremendous relational power. The only sexual life a Christian spouse can legitimately enjoy is the romantic life a spouse chooses to provide. This makes manipulation and rejection ever-present spectators in the marital bed. Anything denied physically becomes an absolute denial, because there is no other legiti-

---

* *Sacred Marriage* has been translated into numerous languages, and in one instance, the misunderstanding that arose in relation to this anecdote is so funny that I just have to share it here. The person doing the translating didn't understand why Gary Player's "chauffeur" was draped in lingerie. She didn't understand that in English the word *driver* can refer to a golf club, not just to a person who steers a car.

mate outlet. (On the other hand, placing an unbearable sexual burden on a spouse in an attempt to meet other, unfulfilled needs can also be a manipulative abuse of power.)

The old adage "power corrupts, and absolute power corrupts absolutely" is particularly true in a microcosmic way in marriage. Few things in human experience match the absolute power of sexual desire in marriage. Sometimes if I'm in a foul mood, the mere knowledge that my wife is eager tempts me to be maliciously uninterested. This is a shameful and tyrannical display of power—"I have what you want, and you're not going to get it, so there!" It's a form of Hitlerism within a relationship, using power to destroy, condemn, and hate.

> THE ONLY SEXUAL LIFE A CHRISTIAN SPOUSE CAN LEGITIMATELY ENJOY IS THE ROMANTIC LIFE A SPOUSE CHOOSES TO PROVIDE.

A contrasting example of the appropriate use of power is seen most clearly during Jesus' last night on earth. The apostle John tells us that "Jesus knew that the Father had put all things under his power" (John 13:3), but instead of acting like a spiteful tyrant, Jesus got up from the meal and washed his disciples' feet. Instead of using his power to pout, chastise, or gloat, Jesus uses it to serve.

The spiritual beauty of sexuality is seen in service, lovingly meeting the physical desires and needs of our mate. The spiritual meaning of a Christian's sexuality is found in giving. When we have power over another and use that power responsibly, appropriately, and benevolently, we grow in Christ, become more like God, and reflect the fact that we were made to love God by serving others. But when we have power over another—particularly power in an area where someone feels so vulnerable and needy and where they can go nowhere else to be served—and then use that power irresponsibly, inappropriately, and maliciously, we become more like Satan, who loves to manipulate us in our weakness rather than like God, who serves us in our weakness.

Whether sexuality becomes a celebration of service or a

point of contention depends largely on one or both partners' selflessness. The sexual relationship thus provides an excellent opportunity for two Christians to experience the testing of their virtue in real-world ways. It is no exaggeration to say that the true nature of our spiritual character may be best demonstrated when we are engaging in sexual relations.

THE TRUE NATURE OF OUR SPIRITUAL CHARACTER MAY BE BEST DEMONSTRATED WHEN WE ARE ENGAGING IN SEXUAL RELATIONS.

Where sex becomes spiritually debilitating is when it ceases to become reciprocal. One of the problems with adolescent sexual awakening—as well as with a fascination with pornography and the like—is that it is usually divorced from the concept of giving. It too quickly becomes all about experiencing, receiving, trying to understand the mystery—in a word, about *getting*.

It is so easy, and yet so spiritually fatal, to take a shortcut here. Sex gives us a capacity to give to someone in a startlingly unique and human way. And yet sex is often used to take, to demand, to coerce, to shame, and to harm.

Honestly ask yourself these questions: Is sex something I'm giving to my spouse, or am I withholding it? Is sex something I am demanding, or offering? Is sex something I am using as a tool of manipulation, or as an expression of generous love? If God looked at nothing other than my sexuality, would I be known as a mature Christian, or as a near pagan?

There are many books that focus on the technical mastery of sex, and I suppose such books have their place. But the true challenge of sex is in its spiritual mastery. A growing, healthy, giving, and selfless sex life is not easy to maintain. And yet it provides the setting for tremendous spiritual growth.

Devoid of this emphasis on service, sex seems like the antithesis of an ascetic, self-controlled, and disciplined life. But looked at in the context of service, sex leads to the apex of spiritual maturity—being able to walk through something as powerful as the ultimate human pleasure and yet use it to serve rather than to demand, exploit, or abuse. Catholic philosopher Dick Westley observes, "The fact is that sexual activity, when it is truly lovemaking and the work of the spirit, is the antithesis of self-indulgence."[10]

Isn't it marvelous that God can use something as earthly and mundane as sexual angst to invite us to mature spiritually? Learning to give sexually instead of take, to lessen your own demands and to be more sensitive to your spouse's demands—these small choices will reap big dividends in your spiritual life because they are teaching you to become more selfless. You are imitating Jesus Christ and taking on the nature of a servant, which is your calling as a Christian.

It's wonderful when a husband and wife enjoy rich, fulfilling, and even exciting sexual relations. And there is nothing wrong with having this as one of your goals. But alongside this goal—in fact, *above* this goal—should be the desire to become a better Christian. Use the marriage bed to learn how to serve another and how to deny yourself, and the spiritual benefits will be many.

This same motivation can color all aspects of marital life. Household chores, conversation, time, money—enter these areas of need in your marriage with a desire to grow in the grace of giving. Pray that God might use them to root out your selfishness and to teach you to become gentle, forgiving, gracious, and kind.

Becoming more like Jesus is the essence of Christianity, and none of us can say with any degree of sincerity that we have cornered the market on being a servant. Our marriages provide opportunities every day for us to be pushed further in this direction.

Chapter 12

SEXUAL SAINTS

Marital Sexuality Can Provide Spiritual Insights and Character Development

> Like all truly mystical things, love is rooted deeply and rightly in this world and this flesh.
>
> *Katherine Anne Porter*

> We find God in the contact of our bodies, not just in the longing of our souls.
>
> *Evelyn and James Whitehead*

I was in junior high, walking toward a group of buddies, when my best friend at the time came out of the circle and stopped me.

"No," he said, "you don't want this."

"What are you talking about?" I asked, hurt that this guy, of all people, would spurn me.

"This isn't for you."

I learned later that my friend was keeping me from a book that was making the rounds at our school. It had something to do with sex—complete with pictures—and the dog-eared corners attested to its being quickly stashed in sock drawers and under mattresses in numerous adolescent-occupied homes.

Most of us are introduced to sex in shameful ways. The Internet has invited the younger generation into a carnal circus that few escape entering. First exposure usually comes long before the young boy or girl has the emotional, intellectual, or spiritual sophistication to process what they are seeing. What innocence they had left is ripped from their psyches with a malicious tear.

I truly feel sorry for what the younger generation has had to endure. I have mourned over the assault on their sexual development. Because our first encounter with sex is so often couched in perversion of various sorts, most of us have to overcome some deep-seated spiritual anxieties about sex. Many Christians see sex not as a gift for which to be thankful but as a guilt-ridden burden to be borne. And naturally, anything so intimately connected with guilt is difficult to view as a ladder to the holy.

Some of this guilt is justified. When we stray outside God's perfect will, we *should* feel guilty. But guilt is not infallible, nor does it always turn itself off when it is no longer applicable. And it's difficult for me not to believe that God is angrier at those who have enticed the young for their profit than he is with the young who have been enticed. It's not a fair fight to offer the possibility of seeing a naked woman at the click of button to a naturally curious twelve-year-old boy.

And yet — and what a colossal "yet"! — in spite of the discomfort with which we approach sexuality, most married Christians know that sexual intimacy can produce moments of sheer transcendence — brief, sunset-like glimpses of eternity. On the underside of ecstasy we catch the shadow of a profound spiritual truth.

Thus we are caught in the perplexity that sex often represents both the best and the worst moments of our lives. While sex may at times create moments that mark our deepest shame, it can also make us feel more alive than ever before.

In this chapter I want to move past the harm and shame brought about by sex that is experienced outside the protecting walls of virtue and examine how this very fleshly experience can sharpen our spiritual sensitivities. Please don't expect the typical marriage book discussion of sexuality; there will be nothing about sexual positions, keeping sex fresh and fun, or new ideas to maintain the spice. If you're looking for that, you're going to be disappointed and bored. Instead, we'll look at how we can reclaim some of the spiritual purpose and meaning behind marital sexuality.

WE ARE CAUGHT IN THE PERPLEXITY THAT SEX OFTEN REPRESENTS BOTH THE BEST AND THE WORST MOMENTS OF OUR LIVES.

If sex is going to turn us toward God and each other, it is vital that we examine it with Christian understanding. Christian spirituality serves us in at least three ways here:

1. It teaches us the goodness of sex while reminding us there are things that are more important than sex.
2. It allows us to experience pleasure without making pleasure the idol of our existence.
3. It not only teaches us that sex can certainly season our lives but also reminds us that sex will never fully nourish our souls.

To begin to view sex in this positive sense—as a mirror of our desire and passion for God—the institution of marriage becomes all-important. If we think about sex *only within the confines of marriage*, thereby sanctifying it as God intended it, the analogy of sex leading us toward God may not seem so far-fetched. To be sure, sex is abused within the marriage relationship as well, so let's take this a step further. Add in the notion (discussed earlier) that sex is to be used to serve our spouse, as well as the analogy that our restlessness for the sexual experience mirrors our restlessness for God—and the ability to use our sexuality as a spiritual aid may begin to make more sense.

To benefit from the insights of this chapter, try to move past the hurt, shame, guilt, and angst you associate with sex because of what you may have experienced, talked about, or seen depicted outside the marital relationship. Homosexuality, premarital sex, fantasy-laden masturbation, hard-core pornography—none of that constitutes sex as we're defining it here. Redefine sex as it was in Eden, as it was when Adam "knew" Eve and began to populate the world. Think of sex only in these terms, and *then* think of how God can reveal himself to you within your marriage through the gift of sexual pleasure.

It may sound shocking, but it's true: God doesn't turn his eyes when a married couple goes to bed. It only stands to reason that we shouldn't turn our eyes from God when we share intimate moments with our spouse.

AMBIVALENT ANCESTORS

For centuries, Christian spiritual writers have viewed sexuality as problematic at best. The Christian church has delicately tiptoed around the explosive reality of sex, attempting to rein in its power by regulating (in the Middle Ages) its acceptability to certain hours in the night, certain days of the year (including many weeks' prohibition before and after Easter, Christmas, and Pentecost), and requiring that the intent and purpose of procreation be behind every sexual encounter to deem it "sanctified." This view of sex continued in many Christian circles well into the twentieth century. Many young people have grown up with the idea that sex is dirty, sinful, and destructive. They have been given a hundred sermons about the awful consequences of premarital sex but have rarely been fed with solid teaching on the redeeming aspects of marital sex. This unbalanced view has left them confused, hurting, and ill-prepared to steward their own sexual desires.

All this reminds me of the time my children and I were at the beach. The tide was coming in—and the kids had built a sand castle. For forty-five minutes, we fought desperately to save the sand castle from the encroaching sea. We built large barriers around the castle and carried in large pieces of driftwood to serve as a block, but eventually, of course, the sea won, and the sand castle was ruined.

Trying to put so many burdensome restrictions (even within marriage) on such a powerful force as sexual expression is ultimately futile. It's like trying to hold back the sea. The desire to regulate marital sex comes, at least in part, from our fear of it. Common sense tells us that sex is necessary for the human race to continue—God's command to Adam that he "be fruitful and increase in number" (Genesis 1:28) was an *explicit commandment* to engage in sexual relations—but religious apprehension makes us think that the "most holy" among us will somehow shun its pleasure. This, tragically, would mean that only the *least* holy would actually raise children—which doesn't bode well for the faith of the next generation.

This fear of sex prepared its assault early on, particularly in the interpretation of the obviously erotic Song of Songs. The clear implication of Origen's work (around AD 185–254) was that fleshly, intoxicating pleasure had no place in this world. Only "spiritual delights" counted for anything. Dan Allender and Tremper Longman point out, "Origen interpreted the highly sensual Song of Songs in an allegorical, spiritual manner, doing to that book the same thing he did to his body when he took a knife and castrated himself."[1]

A century later, at the famous Council of Nicea (AD 325), certain radicals started suggesting that bishops must be celibate. A well-respected ascetic bishop, Paphnutius, opposed this suggestion vigorously, rightly arguing that it *was* chastity for a man to "cohabit" with his wife.[2] It was particularly significant that an ascetic bishop pledged to chastity had the wisdom to argue this position, as he clearly had nothing to gain from it. But Paphnutius was certainly the exception, and his opinion was soon buried by the weight of the famed church father Augustine (354–430).

Augustine, who stamped Christian thought like few others, taught that sexual intercourse transmitted original sin, thereby entangling sin and sex for centuries to follow. As a result, the church often had a difficult time reconciling sanctity with a sexually active life. The number of married saints who ended up being canonized were few and far between, and those canonized specially for marital sanctity are virtually nonexistent. More likely, married people got canonized for what they did *in spite of* being married, or after their spouses had died.

By the fourth century, Ambrose was calling marriage "honorable," but he tempered the compliment by calling chastity "more honorable." Institutionally, there was still a sense in which sexual intercourse was excused, *provided* it was carried out for the sake of procreation. All other sexual relations within marriage still constituted "venial sin" (excusable, but a black mark nevertheless).

There *were* moments of enlightenment, however. There is evidence that in medieval times, priests would sometimes bless a newlywed couple in their bridal bed. Interestingly enough, the Puritans seemed unusually at ease when it came to embracing sexual pleasure. Despite the Puritans' reputation as sexual killjoys, one of their most eminent and revered churchmen, Richard Baxter, wrote that husband and wife should "take delight" in the love and company and conversation of each other. He wrote, "Keep up your conjugal love in a constant heat and vigor." He added that spouses must not suffer their love "to grow luke-warm."[3] He's literally telling his congregation, "Don't become complacent in the bedroom."

An ancient Sarum rite (on which the 1549 Anglican Prayer Book was based) had, since at least AD 1125, nuptial rites that included the words "with my body I thee worship." This was rather bold and provocative for any period in the church, let alone the Middle Ages, so perhaps it is not surprising that these words were cut from the Anglican Prayer Book in 1786.

Perhaps we can be charitable toward the ancients' (and our own) uneasiness with sex, in part because few of us can deny the truth that, in one sense, "sex is a heavy burden that God has laid upon mankind."[4] While it is beyond doubt that the Bible has a favorable and positive view of sex—witness Song of Songs, for instance—biblical writers are also acutely aware of the snare of sexual sin and our propensity to spoil the good gift God has given us.

LAYING THE GROUNDWORK FOR SPIRITUALLY MEANINGFUL SEX

This human inclination is precisely why the institution of marriage is so crucial as we seek to navigate the sea of sexual desire. It is the only context in which sexuality becomes spiritually meaningful and helpful.

A Biblical View of Sexuality

In our pursuit of a fully biblical view of sexuality that will allow us to incorporate the experience of physical intimacy into a spiritually meaningful vision of faith, we Christians can learn a thing or two from the Jewish foundations of our faith.

There are theological reasons that the Christian church has had more difficulty dealing with sexual activity than our Jewish ancestors. To the ancient Jew, nothing was more important than the preservation and purity of the family line. As the chosen people, Jews viewed divorce in the case of barrenness as perfectly acceptable. Practically the worst thing you could do to a spouse was to deny him or her children, because progeny was how the unpolluted, God-chosen race would continue.

IN OUR PURSUIT OF A FULLY BIBLICAL VIEW OF SEXUALITY, WE CHRISTIANS CAN LEARN A THING OR TWO FROM THE JEWISH FOUNDATIONS OF OUR FAITH.

Jewish views about sex went beyond procreation. Ancient Jewish women were given three fundamental rights: food, clothing, and sexual intercourse apart from the duty of procreation. A religion based on bloodlines can ill afford to look down on procreative activity.

The ancient Jewish text *The Holy Letter* (written by Nahmanides in the thirteenth century) sees sex as a mystical experience of meeting with God: "Through the act [of intercourse] they become partners with God in the act of creation. This is the mystery of what the sages said, 'When a man unites with his wife in holiness, the Shekinah is between them in the mystery of man and woman.'"[5] The breadth of this statement is sobering when you consider that this *shekinah* glory is the same presence experienced by Moses when God met with him face-to-face (Exodus 24:15–18). In other words, God is present in a particularly intense way when husband and wife are joined together and a child is formed.

In contrast to medieval Christian prohibitions, Nahmanides recommends that married couples regularly experience sexual intercourse on the Sabbath in celebration of their faith. The reason he could advocate this was his firm belief that everything God made—including the sexual organs, and thus the sense of sexual touch—is good because God has declared it so (Genesis 1:31).

With Christians, however, salvation is not about family blood but spiritual faith. Procreation is no longer the highest end; faith is. Thus if someone avoids a sexual union so they can foster a deeper faith, they are frequently assumed to have chosen the higher way. But just because (in the Christian view) sex no longer services salvation or the propagation of God's kingdom on earth doesn't mean sex has nothing to teach us in the way of sanctification (or growth in holiness). We can continue to believe that for the purpose of salvation faith takes precedence over procreation while still appreciating the Jewish aspect of seeking the *shekinah* glory in the marital bed.

To use our sexuality as a spiritual discipline—to integrate our faith and flesh, so to speak—it is imperative that we become theologically grounded enough to incorporate into our thinking a Jewish view of sexuality. God made flesh, and when God made flesh, he created some amazing sensations. While the male sexual organ has multiple functions, the female clitoris has just one—sexual pleasure. By design, God created a bodily organ that has no other purpose than to provide women with sexual ecstasy. This wasn't Satan's idea; it was God's. And God called every bit of his creation "very good" (Genesis

1:31). For some of you, one of the most important things you can do for your marriage is to begin to see sexual pleasure as something morally and spiritually good and to be desired—something that God wants you to experience often and that gives you his blessing when you do it. God created it for your and your spouse's benefits. It is worth whatever effort it takes to free ourselves from the guilt-ridden view of sex that keeps us spiritually and sexually frustrated. A pastor told me about a seventy-year-old woman in his congregation who attended a Sacred Marriage conference and, after hearing me talk about this, for the first time in her marriage felt free to pursue this experience with enthusiasm. With gleeful exuberance, she told her pastor that she and her husband were making up for lost time. Amid the joy of this newfound discovery was a sense of loss over the decades that had been sexually squandered—all because of a misguided theological understanding of sex.

Betsy Ricucci comments on this issue from a feminine perspective: "Within the context of covenant love and mutual service, no amount of passion is excessive. Scripture says our sexual intimacy should be exhilarating (Proverbs 5:19 NASB) ... Believe it or not, we glorify God by cultivating a sexual desire for our husbands and by welcoming their sexual desire for us."[6]

If guilt rather than gratitude casts a shadow over your experience of sex, practice thanking God for what sex involves. For instance, a woman could pray, quite explicitly—but in all holiness—"God, thank you that it feels enticing when my husband caresses my breasts." Couples could even pray together, thanking God for the pleasure surrounding the act of marital consummation. This simple act of thanksgiving can sanctify an act that too many Christians divorce from their spiritual life with God. The reason it feels good is that God designed it so.

Gratitude Must Replace Guilt

Once we evaluate the theological foundations on which we build our view of marital sex, we also need to examine our emotional attitudes. In this case, gratitude must replace guilt.

In his book *Music Through the Eyes of Faith*, Harold Best tells the true story of a young man who became deeply involved in a satanic cult that developed a sophisticated and elaborate liturgy focusing on the compositions of Johann Sebastian Bach. The young man later became a Christian and started attending worship services at a local church. Everything went well until the church organist belted out a piece composed by Bach. The young believer was overcome by fear and dread and fled the sanctuary. Best writes that Bach's work "represents some of the noblest music for Christian worship. To this young man, however, it was not noble at all, but rather epitomized all that was evil, horrible, and anti-Christian."[7]

Sex is that way for some Christians. Past associations and guilt feelings have created severe spiritual roadblocks. While few would suggest that Bach's compositions are inherently evil, the young man *felt* they were because of how Bach's works had been abused in his past experience. In the same way, some Christians try hard not to believe that sex is inherently evil, but because of previous negative experiences, to them it certainly feels evil. The effects of these roadblocks can be lessened through a proper biblical understanding of sex, as well as through the practice of confession and repentance. If your history contains abuse, you may want to consider seeking counseling as a way to help you gain a new, and hopefully more favorable, perspective on sex.

Sex cannot pay spiritual dividends if its currency is shrouded in illegitimate guilt. Gratitude to God for this amazing experience is essential; otherwise, the powerful feelings associated with sex will lead us to focus on self.

Ironically, the idolatry of sex and obsessive guilt over sex accomplish the same thing—they keep the focus on self, whether it is out of enjoyment or despair. Gratitude, on the other hand, turns our hearts toward God.

It took me a while to realize how I was inadvertently insulting God by my hesitation to accept the holiness of sex and pleasure. I don't have any problem imagining someone seeking

God by enduring the pain of a fast. But what kind of God am I imagining if I can allow pain but not pleasure to reveal God's presence in my life? Instead of being suspicious of pleasure and the physical and spiritual intimacy that comes from being with my wife, I need to adopt an attitude of profound gratefulness and awe.[8]

VIEW YOUR SPOUSE AS MORE THAN A LOVER

Once we have reevaluated our theology and our emotional attitudes, we also need to reconsider our expectations—that is, what type of intimacy we are seeking.

The third step to becoming fully prepared to use sexuality as a spiritual discipline is to remember that in Christian marriage, husband and wife are more than lovers; they are brother and sister in Christ.

During my engagement to Lisa, I gave her a poem titled "My Sister, His Bride," in which I talked about how the step we were taking toward marriage was monumental in this world, but that there already existed an even more significant eternal bond between us that would actually outlive our status as husband and wife—the bond of being brother and sister in Christ. There is a depth to this spiritual brother-sister relationship that is all too frequently left unexplored.

Otto Piper explains it this way: "The believer who conducts his marriage as in the Lord will seek to make his marriage transcend mere sexuality by emphasizing his fellowship with God. Then the spouse is not only a sexual partner but also and above all a brother or sister in Christ. In this way the instinctive longing inherent in all love becomes real: our earthly lives are transmuted into lives with God."[9]

Therefore, while physical pleasure is good and acceptable, we mustn't reduce sex to a merely *physical* experience. It is about more—much more—than that. Sex speaks of spiritual realities far more profound than mere pleasure.

When Paul tells us that our bodies are temples of the Holy Spirit (1 Corinthians 6:19), our contemplations on the significance of sex take on an entirely new meaning. What a woman is allowing inside her, what a man is willingly entering—in a Christian marriage, these are *sanctified* bodies. These are bodies in which God is present through his Holy Spirit, bodies coming together, celebrating, but in a spirit of reverence and holiness.

If Paul tells us that a man is not to join himself to a prostitute because his body is a holy temple—that is, if we are to use such imagery to *avoid* sinning—can a Christian not use the same imagery to be drawn into God's presence in a unique way as he joins his body with his wife? Isn't he somehow entering God's temple—knocking on the door of *shekinah* glory—when he joins himself to a fellow believer? And isn't this a tacit encouragement to perhaps even think about God as your body is joined with your spouse?

Otto Piper urges us to view the sex act as a physical picture of a deeper spiritual reality: "We have come together in [God], called by him, creating a family, serving him, he living in both of us, we now expressing, physically, the spiritual truth that he has created—we are no longer two, but one."[10]

Addressing this spiritual element of sex is crucial in helping men experience deliverance from sexual addictions. When sex is reduced to pleasure alone, no wife can possibly meet a husband's expectations. Pleasure, by nature, is fleeting and fickle and easily bored. I read an article written by a Christian (back in the days before the Internet) who had overcome a serious addiction to pornography, and he made it quite clear he always needed a new magazine. Although he possessed enough naked pictures to wallpaper his house (more than he could possibly look at in the course of a day), he needed the thrill of getting *new* pictures of *new* women.

A wife can't reinvent herself on a daily basis, so a man can't kick a passion for pornography by trying to turn his wife into a centerfold. He must search for and find something much different in the marital bed. He can seek the deeper (but oftentimes quieter) fulfillment of spiritually meaningful sex, looking for God and for Christian fellowship behind the pleasure—not running from the pleasure, to be sure, but not making an idol of that pleasure either.

EVERY HUNGER THAT ENTICES US IN THE FLESH IS AN EXPLOITATION OF A NEED THAT CAN BE BETTER MET BY GOD.

Remember, every hunger that entices us in the flesh is an exploitation of a need that can be better met by God. The only context for godly sex is marital sex. Illicit sex is spiritual junk food—immediately sweet, but something that will poison our spiritual appetite until we crave that which will ultimately destroy us. Illicit sex will do nothing but diminish our sensitivity to holiness, righteousness, and God's presence in our lives.

The deeply physical and fleshly experience of sex can be enjoyed without guilt, but there is an even deeper spiritual fulfillment inherent when a man and woman engage in sexual relations. Don't reduce sex to either a physical or spiritual experience. It is both—profoundly so.

RECONCILING THE POWER OF SEX

Now that we've examined our theology, our emotional attitudes, and our expectations regarding sex, we must become comfortable with the oftentimes fearful yearning inherent in sexual desire.

Sex is not a physical need in the same way that food is; you can survive a lifetime without a single orgasm. But it is certainly a physiological *drive*. It is predictable, and it is physical as well as emotional. Most important, this physical desire—which feels like a need—that a man and woman have for each other is there *by God's design*. God put this need in us.

How do we approach this sense of need from a Christian perspective? It may help if we see hidden in this analogy the sense of need that represents our longing for God—that we are incomplete without him and need to join ourselves to him anew. Thomas Hart observes that "our fascination with sex is closely related to our fascination with God."[11]

Sex cannot replace God. Sex will not suffice as a substitute for God. But a healthy look at sex can provide fruitful meditation on our need and desire for God — the sense of incompleteness followed by the joy and fulfillment made all the sweeter after finally giving ourselves to another.

If there were no great need, the fulfillment would be less sweet. It is only when I am truly hungry that I fully appreciate a good meal. Passion is a fearful thing to some of us. The sense of longing reminds us that we are incomplete by ourselves, but the fact is that God made us incomplete. We need him; we need others.

I remember reading Song of Songs as a young man with great discomfort, in large part because I was terrified of ever wanting someone as desperately as those two lovers wanted each other. Such wanting, I knew even at a young age, can lead to tremendous pain, disillusionment, and grief.

It is frightening to want God. What if he doesn't show up? It is even scarier to want another human. What if they spurn our advances or use our desire as a weapon against us?

Here is the difficulty: There is no guarantee that our spouse will not use our desire against us. But while this provides a point of possible manipulation, it also provides an avenue of spiritual growth. We can use this sense of need as a way to grow as servants of each other. In a healthy Christian marriage in which both husband and wife lovingly seek to fulfill the sexual desires of each other, both can learn that God will minister to them as well. Just as Jesus uses the example of an earthly father who will not give his son a stone when he asks for bread (Matthew 7:9) — and then encourages his followers to likewise trust God to give good gifts — so a man or woman may be able to open up their heart to God when they experience how their spouse is generous in meeting their need for sexual expression.

The truth is, without this physiological drive many couples would slowly drift apart. We are by nature selfish beings who hide from each other. Maintaining a steady pursuit toward and empathy for another human being goes against our sinful, egocentric bent. By creating a physical desire, God is inviting us to participate in the spiritual reality of learning to share, have fellowship with, and enter the life and soul of another human being in a profound way.

MAINTAINING A STEADY PURSUIT TOWARD AND EMPATHY FOR ANOTHER HUMAN BEING GOES AGAINST OUR SINFUL, EGOCENTRIC BENT.

The above thoughts are intended to legitimize the use of sexual expression as a tool of spiritual development. It would take an entire book to fully explore this subject, but in the next section we're going to consider a few representative examples of how a married couple might use aspects of their physical intimacy to grow spiritually.

SPIRITUAL DEVELOPMENT THROUGH SEXUAL EXPRESSION

Bernard of Clairvaux (1090–1153) taught that carnal or earthly love is actually the first step in human experience that leads us to love God—sort of like in kindergarten, where we learn to get along with others and sit behind a desk before the "real schooling" begins in first grade. He took this one step further when he suggested that, carnal as we are, our love for God in this life will fittingly have a carnal element. Certainly, as you read some of the testimonies of mystics, their unabashed love for God has this near-erotic element.

Many books provide guidance on a variety of sexual positions and on ways to keep sex fresh. I want to now look at the spiritual side of sexuality, examining how we can be transformed spiritually through this very physical act. We'll do this by seeking to have our notion of beauty transformed, learning to give what we have, being called out of ourselves, learning to become passionate, and cultivating the art of celebration.

GAINING GOD'S VIEW OF MARITAL BEAUTY

Marriage takes the raw force of sexuality and connects it with emotional intimacy, companionship, family responsibilities, and permanency of relationship. In so doing, it provides a context that encourages spiritual growth by moving us to value character, virtue, and godliness over against an idealized physical form.

To prepare for a part in a major motion-picture release in which nudity would be prevalent, an internationally famous actress spent up to five hours a day in a gym, working out with a personal trainer. All this would refine the body-enhancing surgery that had taken place earlier in her life. With enough time and money, and a professional hairdresser and makeup team, virtually any woman can look good.

I won't deny that one of the reasons I was first attracted to Lisa was because I thought she looked good. But what if looking good became Lisa's obsession? Does God think three hours a day in a gym, working feverishly against the realities of nature to preserve an adolescent stomach (with the hips of a mature woman and the breasts of a nursing mother), is a good and profitable use of time?

Peter doesn't leave us to guess the answer. He says, quite explicitly, that women shouldn't focus on an external beauty that requires "outward adornment," but instead aspire after a beauty "of your inner self, the unfading beauty of a gentle and quiet spirit, which is of great worth in God's sight" (1 Peter 3:3–4).

Notice that in their pursuit of beauty, wives are directed toward creating a beauty that is of great worth *in God's sight*. Husbands might focus on the wrong things, but Peter still urges wives to direct their lives toward God's view of beauty. This instruction is crucial for a number of reasons.

In C. S. Lewis's *The Screwtape Letters*, the demon Screwtape laments that Wormwood has allowed his man to get victory over sexual temptation. Screwtape's next step is this: "If we can't use his sexuality to make him unchaste we must try to use it for the promotion of a desirable marriage."[12] Keep in mind that "desirable" is from a *demonic* perspective, meaning "disastrous" from a Christian perspective. Referring to demonic hosts, Screwtape continues:

> It is the business of these great masters to produce in every age a general misdirection of what may be called sexual "taste." This they do by working through the small circle of popular artists, dressmakers, actresses, and advertisers who determine the fashionable type. The aim is to guide each sex away from those members of the other with whom spiritually helpful, happy, and fertile marriages are most likely ...
>
> As regards the male taste we have varied a good deal. At one time we have directed it to the statuesque and aristocratic type of beauty, mixing men's vanity with their desires and encouraging the race to breed chiefly from the most arrogant and prodigal women. At another, we have selected an exaggeratedly feminine type, faint and languishing, so that folly and cowardice, and all the general falseness and littleness of mind which go with them, shall be at a premium ...
>
> And that is not all. We have engineered a great increase in the license that society allows to the representation of the apparent nude (not the real nude) in art, and its exhibition on the stage or the bathing beach. It is all a fake, of course; the figures in the popular art are falsely drawn; the real women in bathing suits ... are actually pinched in and propped up to make them appear firmer and more slender ... than nature allows a full-grown woman to be ... As a result we are more and more directing the desires of men to something which does not exist—making the role of the eye in sexuality more and more important and at the same time making its demands more and more impossible. What follows you can easily forecast![13]

The Christian duty of married men is to reverse this propensity and make the "role of the eye in sexuality" less important as we embrace the spiritual reality of what is taking place. Sight will always matter to men—that's how God wired us—but we can become mature in what we long to see. *Appetites can be cultivated.* Different cultures enjoy different foods because the inhabitants have eaten such foods all their lives. My kids would wrinkle their noses if my wife dropped rice in front of them for breakfast; in China, children would look askew at a bowl of Cheerios.

The same principle holds true for taste in sexual desirability. Different eras appreciate different shapes in women because of whatever happens to be in fashion. While today's supermodels lean toward waifishness (with adult-sized breasts but adolescent stomachs and thighs), an old Sanskrit word (*gajagamini*) describing the then-ideal of female beauty in ancient India is literally translated "woman who has the gait of an elephant." History has not come up with *the* definitive beauty. The debate has never been resolved. What men and women obsess about, fantasize over, and concentrate on will shape what they desire.

A GODLY MARRIAGE SHAPES OUR VIEW OF BEAUTY TO FOCUS ON INTERNAL QUALITIES.

A godly marriage shapes our view of beauty to focus on internal qualities. Beauty is wonderful, but it is not the only or even the highest value when we seek Christian marriage.

A single woman is likely to face strong temptations to become the type of woman a man would want to marry—and that might very well compete with the type of woman who lives a responsible life before God. But single women know that men are attracted to a certain physical shape and so might be inclined to put more effort into changing physically than changing internally by growing in godliness. Marriage can set women free from this vain pursuit; once they are married, they can focus more intensely on the internal beauty that God finds so attractive.

This is not to suggest that either men or women should shun the care of their physical bodies and become unfit. Keeping in good shape is a gift we can give to our spouse. But so is the grace of *acceptance*—particularly on the part of husbands—in recognition that age and (in the case of women) childbearing eventually reshape every individual body. Marriage helps to move men from an obsession over a body "which does not exist" into a reconsideration of priorities and values.

For instance, marriage calls us to redirect our desires to be focused on *one woman* or *one man* in particular rather than on society's view of attractive women or men in general. We men are married to women whose bodies we know intimately. And out of these bodies, our own children have been born. God gives us each other's bodies as gifts in which to delight. But in receiving our gift, we must not covet another's.

On the day I was married, I began praying, *Lord, help me to define beauty by Lisa's body. Shape my desires so that I am attracted only to her*. I knew from the book of Proverbs that I was to take delight in *my wife*, not in women in general. The writer says, "May you rejoice in the wife of your youth. A loving doe, a graceful deer—may her breasts satisfy you always, may you ever be intoxicated with her love. Why, my son, be intoxicated with another man's wife? Why embrace the bosom of a wayward woman?" (Proverbs 5:18–20).

I cannot fully explain this without embarrassing my wife, so I'm going to speak generally. God has answered my prayer. The physical characteristics that distinguish my wife are the characteristics I generally find most attractive in other women.

But just as important is a wife who works on internal beauty, who makes the pursuit of sanctification an even greater pursuit than wanting to fit into a size 0 dress. This is a beauty that never goes out of style.

Married sexuality helps form us spiritually by shaping the priorities of what we value and hold in high esteem. Many of us don't realize how truly shallow this world and its values really are. A young man or woman can become ridiculously wealthy and incredibly famous—regardless of whether they are a person of character, high morals, or exemplary wisdom—if they're willing to disrobe in the latest Hollywood blockbuster. The net effect is that many people who aren't able to display one particular body type feel devalued.

I'm convinced that, with God's Spirit within us, we can become enamored with the things that enamor God. By denying myself errant appetites and by meditating and feeding on the right things—including being "intoxicated" with my wife's love—I will train myself to desire only what is proper to be desired. This doesn't mean I can't appreciate another person's beauty. It does mean I can appreciate without obsessing. I can see without wanting to enter into a sexually or emotionally inappropriate relationship.

Maturity demands we adopt this view. Evelyn and James Whitehead put it simply and powerfully: "When the body is love's only abode, change becomes an enemy."[14] From a Christian perspective, change is not an enemy, but it is, in fact, *the purpose of marriage*—assuming the change we desire is to become more holy. If my acceptance of my wife is based only on my feelings about her outward appearance rather than on her inner qualities, time will slowly but surely erode my affection.

Those who live only for sexual pleasure and stimulation know only a very limited life—and probably experience a high degree of frustration as time inevitably takes its toll on their aging bodies. Those who find meaning and fulfillment not just in sexuality but in parenting their children, serving God, engaging in a consistent prayer life, and living virtuously have a much broader base from which to enjoy life. A thoughtful and godly marriage will move us in this direction.

GIVE WHAT YOU HAVE

Do you remember the first time you saw your spouse naked? Some good friends of mine tried to ease into it on their wedding night. They decided to take a shower together, with the lights out. Unfortunately, the tub began to overflow. It was dark, remember, so they couldn't figure out what was going on with this unfamiliar hotel bathtub drain. Much to their chagrin, they were forced to turn on the lights and start mopping up *in the nude*. Their "twilight transition" turned into a spotlight extravaganza!

It is one thing to stand naked and relatively trim in front of your partner in your early twenties. But what about in your late thirties, forties, or sixties? What about after the wife has given birth to a child (or two or three) and the husband's metabolism has slowed down, depositing "love handles" around his waist?

Continuing to give your body to your spouse even when you believe it constitutes damaged goods can be tremendously rewarding spiritually. It engenders humility, service, and an others-centered focus, as well as hammering home a very powerful spiritual principle: Give what you have.

There are many times when we are called to keep serving God, even though we know the situation is less than ideal. Maybe we want to share the gospel with a neighbor, but we just don't think we're smart enough or that we know the Bible well enough. Or perhaps we hear about a worthwhile charity and wish we could give thousands of dollars, all the while knowing it will be difficult to come up with even a twenty-dollar bill.

MARRIAGE TEACHES US TO GIVE WHAT WE HAVE.

Marriage teaches us to give what we have. God has given us one body. He has commanded our spouse to delight in that one body—and that body alone. If we withhold from our spouse our body, it becomes an absolute denial. We may not think it is a perfect body, but it is the only body we have to give.

By no means am I suggesting it is *easy* to give, but I am saying it is *worthwhile* to give. It is rewarding to say, "I'm willing to give you my best, even if I don't think my best is all that great." That kind of commitment reminds me of Peter, who told the Jerusalem beggar, "Silver or gold I do not have, but what I do have I give you. In the name of Jesus Christ of Nazareth, walk" (Acts 3:6).

So many people fail to give God or others anything simply because they can't give everything. Learn to take small steps of obedience toward God by offering to your spouse what you have, with all its blemishes and limitations.

CALLING US OUT OF OURSELVES

One of the most perplexing problems for me when considering Christian spirituality has been admitting how much we are affected by chemistry. It is sobering to see someone virtually cured from serious disorders through a readjustment of their chemical imbalance.

Scientists have shown that men become more nurturing as they age and as their testosterone level decreases, and older women often become more ambitious as estrogen levels go through adjustments. As hormones play less of a role, the sex differences begin to blur somewhat (but are never entirely eclipsed).

Our sexuality is indelibly connected with bodily urges that are chemical in nature. I can abstain for quite some time, but abstinence changes in nature as time builds. I don't always like the fact that a spiritual struggle has such a physical relief, but it's the way God made me—and you.

There's another way to look at this, however. Sex may be God's way of calling us to connect with each other. This need for physical expression will sometimes literally force us to work through and resolve emotional and spiritual conflict. This is where a biblical view of divorce and remarriage is essential. Too many Christians enter the process of divorce assuming they can automatically remarry as soon as the divorce papers are finalized. But let's say we were to accept the biblical view (and our civil laws and church leaders were to support this), which would in most cases declare something like this: "You may opt for a divorce, but you cannot ever engage in sex again with anyone else for the rest of your life." Most, if not all, of the men would find or create a way to be reconciled. They would not choose celibacy.

I remember talking frankly to two Christian men once about the ideals of Christian marriage. I cracked them up when I freely confessed, "You bet I've swallowed arguments because I wanted something from my wife later that night." They both admitted, somewhat sheepishly, that they had done the same thing. I'm not proud of the fact that I'm less willing to stand up for my beliefs when I feel "the urge"—and I particularly don't like the fact that what feels like a physical need directs my spiritual attitudes—but I can learn to use that physical need for spiritual benefit.

Let me put this succinctly: We can learn to use the sex drive to groom our character. Out of a need to be intimate with their wives, husbands may learn to show tenderness and empathy. Wives may use physical intimacy to help capture their husbands' interest emotionally. Idealistically, we would seek opportunities to grow because that's what we're called to do as Christians. Realistically, it doesn't hurt to have such a physical need pushing us in that same direction of growing in character.

Remember, we are *fallen* saints. God has redeemed us, to be sure, but all of us are still mired in sin. Our sanctification will never be perfect this side of heaven. Something as important as preserving marriage—especially in the earlier years when the kids are small and stability is supremely important—can't be left merely to altruistic motives.

The sex drive literally calls us out of ourselves and into another. Provided the "other" is our spouse, this is a fruitful exercise. It reinforces the "falling forward" concept we talked about in chapter 10. As we are called out of ourselves, we nurture interdependence and fellowship, two very valuable Christian practices.

THE PRICE OF PASSION

From the record of King David's life and his psalms, it is clear he was an unusually passionate man. There is also no doubt David's passion occasionally got him into trouble—the story of Bathsheba is well-known—but nowhere in Scripture are we told to go to the other extreme and choose a passionless existence. In fact, we are told in the book of Revelation that God would rather have us hot or cold, anything but the putrid "lukewarm" (Revelation 3:16).

The German philosopher Martin Heidegger argued that our passions tune us into the world. *Tune us into the world*—think about that for a moment. A sexually fulfilled and active wife radiates a certain energy. A man who is sexually satisfied with his wife exudes a sense of well-being. Passion is a very healthy thing.

Just as love expands us, passion can as well. The more passionate we become about one thing, the more passionate we tend to become about many other things. A man who is passionate about his wife can be passionate about justice, about God's kingdom, about his own children, about the environment. On the flip side, if he is facing serious sexual problems within his marriage, a feeling of apathy and a certain despondency may well settle like a cloud over his work, his faith, and his fellowship. He is likely to become selfishly preoccupied and self-absorbed.

THE SOLUTION IS NOT LIVING A LESS PASSIONATE LIFE BUT FINDING THE RIGHT THINGS TO BE PASSIONATE ABOUT.

Stoicism has never been a Christian philosophy. We serve a passionate God who feels deeply.

Our passions are what make us come alive. The apathetic person is a pathetic person. While we often fear our passions because they can carry us into an affair, a fight, or some other destructive behavior, the solution is not living a less passionate life but finding the right things to be passionate about.

The history expressed in the Bible and in the two thousand years of Christian experience attest to the fact that Christian spirituality is largely about maintaining our thirst and passion for God and his purposes in this world. Admittedly, at times our passions can lead us astray, but Christian marriage teaches us to manage these passions, like the dam keepers in Washington State. You can hardly drive a hundred miles on the western side of Washington without coming across a dam of some type. Sometimes dam managers opt to let the water flow rather freely; other times they hold it down to a trickle.

That's what marriage teaches us to do. Sometimes it is healthy and good to let marital passions run free, even if we fear we are almost crossing over the line into lust. Some people make the mistake of believing that because they have been burned by their passion and their sexual hunger, the antidote is to completely cut it off. They do to sex what an anorexic does to food: I don't want to overeat and become fat, so I won't eat at all.[15] This isn't a healthy attitude; it's an irrational one.

The healthy life is a life of saying yes and no. I travel quite a bit, so my wife and I must fast from sexual expression many times. Couples with young kids, particularly babies, soon learn they can no longer express themselves sexually whenever they get the inclination. At other seasons, our spouse may be ill or worn-out, and it would be unkind to place sexual expectations on them. In such situations, sexual fasting is appropriate and necessary.

But times of feasting are also necessary. In fact, every no we say to sex should be placed in the context of a corresponding yes. Marital abstinence is not a cul-de-sac or dead end; it is a long on-ramp. My denial of sexual expression when I'm apart from my wife is empowered by what the future holds when I get home. I am not truly saying no, but rather, *wait.* Rather than being a complete denial, it is a channeling of desire into the proper place. Faithfulness seasons the marital bed in many delightful and profound ways.

I don't want to overspiritualize this. We don't always have to think spiritual thoughts when we are enjoying conjugal relations. Passions call us to enter fully into life. Passion is at the heart of the Sabbath commandment, which has two sides: Six days you shall do all your work—engage yourself vigorously—and on the seventh day you shall rest. Work hard; then rest well. Both are necessary for a meaningful life. At times, sex will have distinctly spiritual overtones; at other times, it will be a celebration of physical pleasure. Both are holy within marriage.

The bottom line is this: Passion and engagement are extremely important. They should be cultivated in marriage and brought to bear on all of life.

CELEBRATION

I tend to be overly serious in my faith, which is a problem if you become more serious than the Bible. There were at least three major celebratory feasts prescribed in the Old Testament—Passover, Weeks, and Tabernacles—as well as many other religious celebrations (Leviticus 23; Numbers 28–29). These often were elaborate affairs. The Feast of Tabernacles, for example, involved a seven-day feast in which the Israelites were commanded to rejoice and forbidden to mourn.

I have to constantly break out of my "serious" rut. That's just my nature. I tend to view celebration as flighty or less reverent—but that's a personal prejudice I'm trying to overcome.

You're celebrating a deeply human dance, a transcendent experience created by no less a preeminent mind than that of Almighty God himself.

Marital sexuality provides a unique context for celebration. Naked in each other's arms, it doesn't matter if you have a portfolio worth a million dollars or if you're struggling with the realities of a negative net worth. You could be lying in a luxurious bed on the top floor of the Waldorf Astoria Hotel or enjoying a night away from the kids at a Motel 6 (well, my wife could never relax under the bedspread in a Motel 6, but you get the point …). You could be delighting in a honeymoon as you celebrate life in your twenties or thirties, or renewing your passion as you celebrate life in your sixties or seventies. Regardless of your station or status in life, you're celebrating a deeply human dance, a transcendent experience created by no less a preeminent mind than that of Almighty God himself.

There is a time to fast. There is a time to "take up [your] cross," to be "salted with fire" (Mark 8:34; 9:49). But there is also a time to be virtually transported to another world through the intimate sharing and exploration of our spouse's body.

Some of us need to be reminded to celebrate with zeal; others need to be reminded there is a place for thoughtful sobriety, quiet reverence, and deliberate duty. The marriage relationship makes available to us a full, responsive, and responsible human experience—assuming responsibility, to be sure, but along with that responsibility relishing the very real and earthy pleasure of sexual activity, an intense celebration that gently reminds us of the heavenly existence that awaits all God's children.

BEYOND TOUCH

Sex is about physical touch, to be sure, but it is about far more than physical touch. It is about what is going on *inside* us. Developing a fulfilling sex life means I concern myself more with bringing generosity and service to bed than with bringing washboard abdomens. It means I see my wife as a holy temple of God, not just as a tantalizing human body. It even means sex becomes a form of physical prayer—a picture of a heavenly intimacy that rivals the *shekinah* glory of old.

Our God, who is spirit (John 4:24), can be found behind the very physical panting, sweating, and pleasurable entangling of limbs and body parts. He doesn't turn away. He wants us to run into sex, but to do so with his presence, priorities, and virtues marking our pursuit. If we experience sex in this way, we will be transformed in the marriage bed every bit as much as we are transformed on our knees in prayer.

Chapter 13

SACRED PRESENCE

How Marriage Can Make Us More Aware of God's Presence

> The Christian family is a product of faith. It offers the matchless opportunity of suffusing every relationship of daily life with the Spirit of God. Since the spouses have to live together and are unable to escape each other, every moment of the day and every activity in the home form a challenge to live in common according to the divine purpose. *Otto Piper*

Sincerity isn't enough.

I found this out the hard way early on in my marriage. Just weeks after our wedding, Lisa had her twentieth birthday. I was a new husband, completely uninitiated in the finer arts of marital conversation, so when Lisa said, "Don't worry, my birthday's no big deal," I made a terrible mistake.

I believed her.

What else could I do? My campus pastor had told me, "Go for the godly ones," so I had. Lisa was, indeed, one of the godliest women I had met in college. The only problem was that my college pastor never warned me godly women can occasionally lie.

Consequently, I didn't put much thought into what I should do for Lisa's birthday. Besides, I was in a new job and feeling slightly ill as well, so I wasn't at all prepared to meet the high expectations of something that was "no big deal."

The day before Lisa turned twenty, I stepped into a bookstore and bought her three books. Early the next morning, I handed them to her with a smile.

It's a good thing *I* was smiling that day, so at least one of us was. I had to learn that getting Lisa books because *I* like books isn't love—no, that's hope! (I get the two confused sometimes.) Love is choosing something that will affirm Lisa and show her that I know her and appreciate her.

Husbands need to learn that when it comes to loving our wives, sincerity isn't enough; we need substance.

James, the writer of the biblical book that bears his name, tells us the same thing is true when it comes to our relationship with God. The highest value many people place on spirituality these days is sincerity. According to the popular view, it doesn't matter what we believe or even who we believe in, as long as we are sincere about it.

This is, however, not biblical truth. James 1:27 puts this idea to rest with a dozen words that introduce the truth about spirituality: "Religion that God our Father accepts as pure and faultless is this ..." If there is a religion God finds acceptable, then there must be a religion he finds unacceptable. If there is a way God wants to be loved, then there must be a way he doesn't want to be loved.

In other words, for God and our wives, sincerity alone isn't enough.

One of the most important components of Christian spirituality is relationship. Christian spirituality is not a search for spiritual enlightenment, new experiences, or esoteric wisdom. It is rather rooted in a passionate pursuit of and response to a spiritual being—God himself. I like the Whiteheads' definition: "Christian spirituality can be described as our consistent efforts to respond to the delights and demands of God's presence in our life."[1]

The operative word here is *presence*. The great Christian writers of the past stressed the importance of living in constant awareness of God's presence. Those who have advanced in the Christian life have learned to develop almost a mystical memory that keeps them attuned to the fact that God is always with them, always ready to whisper his words of challenge, encouragement, affirmation, and loving rebuke. He is always watching, always caring, always hearing.

One of the ways to describe practicing God's presence as a discipline is *turning*. François Fénelon wrote the following:

> A general rule for the good use of time is to accustom oneself to live in a continual dependence on the Spirit of God, receiving from moment to moment whatever it pleases him to give us, referring to him at once in the doubts which we necessarily run into, *turning* to him in the weakness into which goodness slips from exhaustion, calling on him and lifting oneself to him, when the heart, swept away by material things, sees itself led imperceptibly off the path and finds itself forgetting and drifting away from God.[2]

Perhaps the classic literary work on this aspect of the Christian life is Brother Lawrence's *The Practice of the Presence of God*. Writing in the seventeenth century, Lawrence, a humble monk, learned to take special delight in God's continual presence, with the result that he felt equally close to God peeling potatoes in the kitchen as kneeling at the altar in prayer.

Brother Lawrence said we should establish ourselves in God's presence by continually talking with him, suggesting it was a shameful thing to allow trivial thoughts to break into this spiritual conversation. He urged us to feed our souls on lofty thoughts of God, and so find great joy in being with him.[3]

Early on, practicing the presence is largely a discipline; over time, the discipline of practicing God's presence begins to feel more natural. Brother Lawrence observes that in the beginning a persistent effort is needed to form the habit of continually talking with God, but after a little care, his love brings us to it without any difficulty.[4]

It was this pursuit of God's presence that sent so many men and women into monasteries and convents. These earnest souls believed they could best experience the delight of God's presence by engaging in a life free from the encumbrances of earning a living and caring for a family. Although ancient religious orders differed substantially, most often a monk's or nun's life was structured around this remembrance—this constant awareness—of God. The day began and ended with prayer; there were often long periods of enforced silence; and the community itself created an environment that encouraged its citizens to look heavenward.

RATHER THAN ALLOWING MARRIAGE TO BLUNT OUR SPIRITUAL SENSITIVITIES, CAN WE USE IT TO AWAKEN OUR SOULS IN NEW AND PROFOUND WAYS?

How can we, as married saints, use the daily rush of activities and the seeming chaos of family life as a reminder of God's presence? To be sure, we have many challenges to overcome, but isn't there a way we can use marriage to draw us to God rather than let it dull our senses and lead us into a practical atheism where we give lip service to God but live as if he simply does not exist? Rather than allowing marriage to blunt our spiritual sensitivities, can we use it to awaken our souls in new and profound ways?

There is a marvelous picture in the Old Testament that suggests we can indeed!

BETWEEN THE CHERUBIM

The ark of the covenant law was constructed with two cherubim of hammered gold that faced each other and touched wings. In this joining of the two, we are told, "There, above the cover between the two cherubim that are over the ark of the covenant law, I [God] will meet with you" (Exodus 25:22).

God's presence between the cherubim came to be a popular Old Testament image. In Samuel's time, the Israelites wanted to bring back the ark, referring to "the LORD Almighty, who is enthroned between the cherubim" (1 Samuel 4:4). The psalmist writes, "Hear us, Shepherd of Israel ... you who sit enthroned between the cherubim" (Psalm 80:1). Isaiah uses the same imagery: "LORD Almighty, the God of Israel, enthroned between the cherubim" (Isaiah 37:16). This imagery even makes its way into the New Testament: "Above the ark were the cherubim of the Glory" (Hebrews 9:5).

The presence of God comes to us as two beings are joined. God dwells in the midst of this coming together. It's a beautiful picture.

There is a long tradition of seeking God in solitude, but clearly there is also biblical warrant to seeking God in relationship and community. Consider Jesus' words, "I tell you that if two of you on earth agree about anything they ask for, it will be done for them by my Father in heaven. For where two or three gather in my name, there am I with them" (Matthew 18:19–20).

Notice that Jesus says "where two or three gather ..." There seems to be something that is quantitatively different from just a solitary pursuit. Jesus qualifies this even further when he mentions the two coming together "in my name." The family that will enjoy Jesus' presence as a customary part of their union is a family that is joined precisely because husband and wife want to invite Jesus into the deeper parts of their marriage. They are not coming together in order to escape loneliness, more favorably pool their financial resources, or merely gain an outlet for sexual desire. Above all these other reasons, they have joined themselves to each other as a way to live out and deepen their faith in God.

Even if you didn't enter marriage for this reason, you can make a decision to *maintain* your marriage on this basis. The day you do this, you will find that marriage can be a favorable funnel to direct God's presence into your daily life. Marriage invokes the presence of God through prodding us to communicate, reminding us of our transcendent ache, helping us to behold the image of God, and allowing us to participate in creation.

CONVERSATION

As a young man, I always thought silence was the preferred pathway to the heart of God. The church I attended put a comment in the weekly bulletin that went something like this: "Please maintain an attitude of reverence and quiet as we prepare our hearts for worship." And, indeed, there are deep roots in Christian tradition testifying to the spiritual value of silence. For instance, because a Trappist monk's duty is to maintain silence, members of this order often communicate with sign language. There are records of ancient monks who didn't talk for three decades or more.

Just as the silence of the Trappist monks is a discipline designed to draw them into the realm of the holy, so the conversation of marriage can bend us toward God. Earlier in the twentieth century, there developed in France an idea that talk should be seen as a spiritual exercise. Out of this arose *le devoir de s'asseoir*, which literally translated means, "the duty to sit down."[5]

In marriage, it is our duty to communicate. In our relationship with our spouse, communication is a discipline of love. Our reaching out to each other mirrors God reaching out to us, and as he does so, his presence and character become better known to us. The fact that God uses dreams to communicate in the Old and New Testaments reveals that he is reaching out to us at all hours of the day and night. God loves us with words rather than with physical arms that embrace us. We can love our spouses with those same words and grow more like Christ in the process.

Dan Allender and Tremper Longman observe that "we are called to cultivate Christ in our spouses by the power of the spoken word."[6] How can words do this? This way—at least in part: "Good speech quells chaos and produces joy and life; bad speech produces chaos and leads to despair and death."[7] In this view, our tongue invites God's presence or pushes him away. Every word spoken to a family member is either an invitation to the experience of the holy or to the experience of chaos.

The letter of James (3:2–6) views controlled speech as one of the fundamental Christian disciplines:

> We all stumble in many ways. Anyone who is never at fault in what they say is perfect, able to keep their whole body in check.
>
> When we put bits into the mouths of horses to make them obey us, we can turn the whole animal. Or take ships as an example. Although they are so large and are driven by strong winds, they are steered by a very small rudder wherever the pilot wants to go. Likewise, the tongue is a small part of the body, but it makes great boasts. Consider what a great forest is set on fire by a small spark. The tongue also is a fire, a world of evil among the parts of the body. It corrupts the whole body, sets the whole course of one's life on fire, and is itself set on fire by hell.

In James's view, our tongue serves as a spiritual thermometer inasmuch as its words register our spiritual temperature toward God.

The tongue can be cruel in two ways: by speaking evil and by refraining from speaking good. We need to recognize the offensiveness of pervasive silence within marriage. There comes a time when silence is healing, but there is also a malicious silence. You know your heart. You know whether you are being silent in order to promote healing or whether you are being self-centered, cowardly, or malicious. When I refuse to speak out of cowardice, malice, or weariness, I am taking a step back as a Christian.

God calls me to speak, *but to speak carefully*. I had to learn how to communicate with my wife, to find out why I sometimes exasperate her either by not speaking at all or by speaking in the wrong way. In other words, to be lovingly married, I had to learn how to better tame my tongue.

Communication forces us to enter into another's world. To communicate with my wife, I have to get beyond my own frame of reference and understand how the same word can mean two different things to each of us. This is an ego-emptying exercise that harbors enormous spiritual benefit. Learning to communicate effectively is part of the process of the two becoming one.

COMMUNICATION FORCES US TO ENTER INTO ANOTHER'S WORLD.

Words spoken with malice can cut deeply. Words can destroy, pummel, and build walls. Dan Allender and Tremper Longman encourage us to choose our words carefully:

> I am to sow words like seeds to bring a harvest of fruit that blesses God.... We must choose our words as if we were choosing an instrument of life or death. If we know the power of words, then we will neither refuse to speak because of fear nor speak often and sow seeds of destruction. We are to speak words of encouragement to draw forth the heart of God in those we love; we are to speak words of rebuke to disrupt the natural bent of our hearts to pride and self-righteousness.[8]

The other side of communication is learning to listen, and it is in this area that I often struggle mightily. I'm often lost in my own thoughts and consequently resent the fact that someone wants me to stop my thinking and share hers. But when I married Lisa, I committed to communicate with her.

Early on in our marriage, my wife was an inveterate reader of *Guideposts* magazine. She loved the stories of tragedy and near tragedy and the often teardrop-producing effects of the regular column titled "His Mysterious Ways." As coincidence would have it—I'm not making this up!—as I typed these words for the first edition of this book, Lisa asked me to take a break so she could read a *Guideposts* story to me.

Lisa knows this isn't really the type of thing I would read on my own. I read about forty to fifty books a year and numerous magazines, but usually not the personal-experience type of literature. Even so, listening to these stories has become part of my commitment to enter into my wife's world. Love is an intentional movement toward another.

How does listening invite God's presence? A significant part of prayer involves listening to God. I think back to chapter 4 where I quoted Dr. John Barger. An abbreviated reminder might be in order here:

> [When women] love, they love quietly; they speak, as it were, in whispers, and we have to listen carefully, attentively, to hear their words of love and to know them.
>
> Isn't God also this way?
>
> Doesn't he intervene in most of our lives in whispers, which we miss if we fail to recollect ourselves and pay careful attention—if we do not constantly strive to hear those whispers of divine love? The virtues necessary in truly loving a woman and having that love returned—the virtues of listening, patience, humility, service, and faithful love—are the very virtues necessary for us to love God and to feel his love returned.

Communication calls us out of ourselves, out of our own personal world and into another's. Learning how to do this is as much a prerequisite for building a meaningful prayer life as it is for building a meaningful marriage. The act of communication invites God's presence into our daily existence. The truth of the matter is this: By our words, we either draw forth God's presence or we push him away.

BY OUR WORDS, WE EITHER DRAW FORTH GOD'S PRESENCE OR WE PUSH HIM AWAY.

TRANSCENDENT ACHE

At some point in your relationship with the one who was to become your spouse, you were willing to leave all other possible suitors and cleave to this one person for the rest of your life. As a single man or woman, the options for a lifetime partner were virtually unlimited—as long as someone would have you, you could marry them. And yet, out of all the billions of people in the world, you chose this one person—your spouse.

As a spiritual exercise, remind yourself again that, regardless of the result of your choice, you *willingly chose* this man or woman. After considerable consideration, you asked this person to marry you—or you said yes when he asked you. At the time, your decision made perfect sense—you were literally willing to bet your life on it—and you had every reason to believe that being married to this person was a relationship you would cherish for years to come, till death intervened to separate you.

And yet, as we travel into marriage, there usually comes a moment when we wonder, "Is this *really* as good as it gets? Is this really all there is?" Instead of being turned away from our spouse when this disillusionment sets in, we can be turned toward God. It can remind us that even our best choice of a human partner isn't enough of a choice to fully satisfy us. It won't help us to change marital partners; instead, we have to change emotional focus, recognizing we can never receive all the love we need and desire from fellow humans. Instead of realizing that our true needs can be ultimately met only in and by God, some people keep trying to find their fulfillment in new relationships, thinking that what they really need is just to find "the right person," which, when translated, usually means a new person. Christianity does not direct us to focus on finding the right person; it calls us to become the right person. Our happiness is not determined by what is around us, but rather by how we deal with what is around us.

Use your dissatisfaction—or even your boredom with life and with your relationships—as a compass that directs you to the True North of your heart's passion: God himself. Remind yourself that in serial marriage the same process will inevitably repeat itself: great excitement, the thrill of discovery, and then, on some level, increasing disillusionment.

Let your relationship with your spouse point you to what you really need most of all: God's love and active presence in your life. Above all, don't blame your spouse for lack of fulfillment; blame yourself for not pursuing a fulfilling relationship with God. Monks and nuns who have found delight in their solitary pursuit of God bear witness to the fact that lack of marital intimacy is not a guarantee of misery or a prohibitor of spiritual enjoyment. When you discover this truth, it's amazing how satisfied you can be, regardless of who you're living with.

Marital dissatisfaction, on whatever level, is best met with the prayer, *That's why I need you, God.* We are reminded of the transcendent ache in our soul that even this one very special person can't relieve entirely on his or her own. As odd as it may sound, I have discovered in my own life that my satisfaction or dissatisfaction with my marriage has far more to do with my relationship to God than it does with my relationship to Lisa. When my heart grows cold toward God, my other relationships suffer, so if I sense a burgeoning alienation from or lack of affection toward my wife, the first place I look is how I'm doing with the Lord. Lisa is, quite literally, my God-thermometer.

BEHOLDING THE IMAGE OF GOD

Every night, I sleep with a God-mirror lying beside me.

The Bible teaches us that both men and women are made in the image of God (Genesis 1:26–27). Understanding this truth should remind us regularly of God's presence, for it allows us to realize that our mate is helping us to complete a fuller picture of God's nature and person.

Dan Allender and Tremper Longman point out how important it is for men and women to model elements of God's existence to each other: "Since a husband's strength helps him resonate God's strong qualities, he can help his wife understand that aspect of God's being more clearly by incarnating it, even though he does that imperfectly. On the other hand, a woman's tenderness and compassion can increase her husband's awareness of God's mercy (1 Peter 3:1–2)."[9]

I practically begged a close college friend not to get married. He and his girlfriend fought all the time when they were dating, in part because they were on opposite ends of the personality spectrum. Steve could be harsh, blunt, and amazingly tactless.

His girlfriend, Laura, was one of the most sensitive women I've ever known. On one occasion, Steve "confronted" Laura with seven ways she was failing as a girlfriend. When I expressed my incredulity that he could dump so much on her at one time, Steve responded, "But, Gary, I could have said so much more!"

And yet, as both Steve and Laura grew in their relationship with Jesus Christ, they both changed in many positive ways. Steve might have grown up without tact, but to his credit he began practicing the Christian virtue of humility, willingly learning from Laura's sensitivity. Laura respected Steve's courage to tell the truth, regardless of the consequences, and realized that always being "soft" wasn't appropriate in every circumstance. After thirteen years of wedlock, they have a marvelous relationship—in fact, one of the strongest marriage relationships I've seen. Each has helped the other draw closer to God in character, as each represented respectively (almost to an extreme) God's strength and God's tenderness.

Too often, however, when a mismatched couple gets together they start judging each other instead of learning from each other. They in essence ask, "Why can't you be more like me?" instead of asking, "How can I become more like Christ?" That's really the prayer we need to adopt, because to do so would solve many marital conflicts. Steve, though often frustrated with Laura's sensitive nature, realized her tenderness modeled something he lacked; Laura, though occasionally hurt by Steve's bluntness, realized his courage and passion for justice could also represent a side of God that her personality didn't reflect so accurately. If we would turn every, "How come you're not more like me?" into "How can your difference model to me how to become more like Christ?" we'd all benefit much more from our spiritual differences.

Not only can being married remind us of God's nature and character, but it also reminds us of his moral claims on our lives. One of the great problems of Christian spirituality is the seemingly simple problem of forgetfulness. God appeals to us to adopt and act on certain priorities, but we forget about these priorities and go our own way. God is always with us, yet we forget his immediate presence and treat our spouses or kids in a way we would never treat them if our pastor or other church members were seated around our kitchen table.

Godly husbands and godly wives make God seem more real and active in the home. I've always loved movies, but movies are not always a safe recreation. So in this activity Lisa acts as sort of a conscience for me. For some reason I'm not proud of, I suspect my standards would be a bit lower if I knew Lisa wouldn't be in the room watching the movie with me. Watching a movie with Lisa feels a little more like watching it in the sight of God. I can imagine her thinking, *You picked* this?

Dietrich Bonhoeffer shocked the theological world when, as a Lutheran theologian in the early part of the twentieth century, he began advocating that Protestants reinstitute the practice of confession. He did so, not because he felt confession to a human was necessary in order to gain forgiveness from God, but because human confession has a practical purpose: It makes our sin seem more real to us.

If you question the truth of this, ask yourself why it's so much easier to confess sins to God than to your pastor. Why is there more shame when another sinful human being observes my weakness than when I pronounce it before an all-holy God?

Could it be that God's presence is so weak in our lives? If we truly understood and cherished the beauty and holiness of God, we would shake a little bit more when approaching him. But his invisibility often creates a buffer, thereby softening the impact of his presence.

In and through our spouse, God becomes real to us in human form. There is a flesh-and-blood person sitting next to me who flinches when she sees what should make *me* flinch but doesn't—and I see my hard heart exposed by her soft one.

It goes both ways, of course. Sometimes I'll try to help Lisa understand how she sounds when she's tired and letting the kids have it verbally. When she sees the reaction on my face, she knows she's allowed the sins of others to incite her own sin.

We can help each other become aware of God's presence by gently encouraging each other toward growth in holiness. Yet we need to be sure to undertake this with extreme caution. We want to bring God's presence into the other's life, not our own judgment. But pointing each other to God's presence is certainly a fundamental spiritual discipline for spouses.

A SPIRITUALLY DISCERNING MARRIAGE WILL BE A TOOL OF SANCTIFICATION.

A spiritually discerning marriage will be a tool of sanctification. As we look at our spouse, we are reminded of God's presence and image. And in the presence of God, we long to become more holy. "Make every effort to live in peace with everyone and to be holy," the author of the book of Hebrews writes. "Without holiness no one will see the Lord" (Hebrews 12:14).

It is no easy discipline, this cooperating in sanctification. My tendency is to *hide* my faults rather than work on trying to transform them. Every day, either I am choosing to spend my energy covering up my mistakes and trying to create a false, glittering image, or I am repenting and cooperating with God to become a person who looks a little more like Jesus. Living with a woman made in the image of God calls me to honesty and to growth in sanctification—provided I allow my marriage to remind me of God's presence and his claims on my life.

CREATING

I stood on the top of Marye's Heights in Fredericksburg, Virginia, site of a horrible Civil War battle in 1862, and kept whispering, "What a waste." On this spot, Union troops had foolishly tried to take an impenetrable wall, charging uphill in an effort to capture the city. It was nothing more than target practice for the Confederates. The first wave of the Union assault group was massacred. Ambrose Everett Burnside, the Union general, ordered another wave. The Confederates cheered their bravery, waited until the soldiers were in range, and then shot every last one of them.

Burnside sent yet another wave, with the same result. Every man lost was a son, husband, uncle, father, or brother. Every lost life was no doubt felt keenly by at least one other person. And these lives were virtually thrown away on a fool's errand.

Few things anger me more than wasted life. When I hear about high school kids who drive foolishly and end up dead before their nineteenth birthday; when I read about college students who go on a fatal drinking binge and die of alcohol poisoning before they reach their twenty-first birthday; when I read anything about a preventable loss of life, I feel a profound sadness.

Part of this springs from my theological belief that as people created in the image of God, we have a responsibility to create. Whether we build a business, a house, a family, a book, a life (through education or the practice of medicine), or whatever else we choose to build, we shouldn't waste our lives but spend them productively.

Marriage leads us into the domain of creation. It goes without saying that there is no holy way to conceive children and help create a new life if you are not married. The sheer mystery, awe, and absolute wonder of birth simply transcend this world. When that first bloody and naked baby was placed in my wife's arms, I felt emotions I had never known before. Overnight I quit being a pacifist. I didn't rethink my intellectual positions on Christians being involved in military combat. I just knew, at the core of my being, that I would do whatever it took to protect this child and the wife who bore her.

Creating a family is the closest we get to sharing the image of God. Seeing this child, made partially in your image, is almost too frighteningly comparable to us being made in God's image. I was an inveterate teaser with little kids. I loved to play around and trick them. I watched as my then nine-year-old son did the same thing when he was with younger kids. And it never failed to amaze me how, when I sensed a renewal of my faith, I could wake up and see that my son had also discovered a new thirst for God. It was sobering to realize that by my actions, I was shaping three little lives.

But this kind of creation takes effort. I once visited a pastor's house, and his kids were almost unbelievably well behaved. After his teenage daughter displayed her usual good grace, I turned to another friend and asked, "They *do* bleed if you prick them, right?" and the friend laughed.

But the next morning, as I was having breakfast with this pastor, he confessed he had spent more than an hour and a half talking through a tough issue with his daughter after I had left their house the night before. And he was participating in similar lengthy talks with his son on a daily basis. Something was always coming up that called for his attention.

I was shocked at the effort, time, and purposeful attention this godly man was pouring into his family. He was engaged in a way I wasn't. He was sacrificing enormous amounts of his own life to pour his efforts into helping create other lives. And I realized that building a family of deep faith takes enormous energy, concentration, and self-denial.

When this sense of creation is lost, marriage loses some of its spiritual transcendence. When we grow lazy in our family life and stop actively trying to create and re-create it, we lose a sense of God's presence in that his empowering work isn't called on. Dan Allender and Tremper Longman tell the story of a man named Jack, whose withdrawal from the act of creational family living had severe consequences:

> [Jack] refused to imagine what he could be if God were to rule his heart more deeply. Jack's refusal to see his own soul as the prime ground for creation left him dreamless as he thought about his wife and children. He had no more vision of who they were and who they were meant to be than he had for himself. In harsh terms, Jack loved them, but he never dreamed about their existence. He was a creator in his job but not in his family. Therefore the family was left in middle-class chaos—moving aimlessly, circling in the tiresome, dark loneliness of the status quo.[10]

In other words, Jack had no purpose or vision for his family, no dream for what each of his children could become. As a result, they found no vision for themselves beyond chasing a status quo. By refusing to shape his children and family, he let the world around him shape them. If we don't nurture a godly sense of creativity, we will experience an emptiness we may perversely and wrongly blame on our marriage. The emptiness comes not from our marriage, however, but from the fact that we're not *engaged* in our marriage. We're not using this powerful relationship in order to create something. Families don't grow themselves; we have to grow them. Kids don't naturally mature toward God; they have to be trained. Husbands and wives don't "fall" into intimacy and oneness; those things have to be chosen and pursued. Family living is creational living. Families fall apart when we stop creating and become content with just existing.

We were made to worship. If we don't grow in our worship of God, we will descend to worship something or someone else—power, money, our reputation, a sports team; it could be anything. In the same way, if we are not creating in our marriage—if we are not filling our souls with the meaning that comes from doing what we were made to do—we will become dissatisfied very quickly. Getting a promotion won't fill our souls—at least not for long. Keeping up with the latest sitcom or soap opera certainly won't create soul satisfaction either.

Have you ever noticed how our culture lives off other people's acts of creation? Consider how many awards shows fill the television schedule—the Grammys, the People's Choice Awards, the Academy Awards, the MTV Awards, the Golden Globes, the Dove Awards, the Emmys—and the list goes on and on—as our culture lives vicariously through the achievements and recognition of others.

You were made by God to create. If you don't create in a thoughtful and worshipful manner—whether preparing meals, decorating a home, achieving a vocational dream, responsibly raising children, building a relationship—you will feel less than human because you are, in fact, acting in a subhuman mode. A life spent in a dead-end, joyless job with evenings spent in front of a television set and weekends spent passing the time will feel like hell on earth *because it is*. It's a wasted life, devoid of God's creative energy. There hasn't been a single marriage in all of human history that could fill a soul that has been emptied of purpose through noncreative living.

Marriage calls us to create—every day. It leads us into many and varied acts of creation. The creation, of course, must have a proper focus—namely, the glory of God. Creating children who are just as shallow as we are is not the same thing as creating children who are mature in the Lord and who live to serve him. Building a business to honor God is not the same thing as creating a monument to our success. Selfish hospitality—when it is done primarily to impress and elicit appreciation—is easily detectable and is far removed from genuine service.

MARRIAGE CALLS US TO CREATE—EVERY DAY.

But a man and woman dedicated to seeing each other grow in their maturity in Christ, to raising children who know and honor the Lord, to engaging in business that supports God's work and is carried out in the context of relationships and good stewardship of both time and money—these Christians are participating in the creativity that gives a spiritually healthy soul immeasurable joy, purpose, and fulfillment.

PURPOSEFUL MARRIAGE

Clearly, then, marriage, on its own, should not and does not make it difficult to pursue God and enjoy his presence. What makes spirituality in marriage difficult is a laissez-faire attitude within marriage. When we don't seek to communicate; when we ignore the divine ache in our soul and try to soothe that ache with human companionship alone; when we fail to behold the image of God in our spouse and instead embark on a deceitful life; when we become disengaged as married people and do not revel in marriage's call for us to create—*this* is what can lead us ultimately to separation from God.

In many ways, marriage is a slippery slope. If we are not vigilant, we will fall backward. If we are lazy, our spiritual sensitivity will become frozen. But if we engage in marriage thoughtfully, purposefully, and with godly intentions, our wedlock will shape us in a way that few other life experiences can. It will usher us into God's own presence.

CHAPTER 14

SACRED MISSION

Marriage Can Develop Our Spiritual Calling, Mission, and Purpose

> Christianity has long called us to this truth: Marriage must be about more than itself because love that does not serve life will die.
>
> *Evelyn and James Whitehead*

Está Lisa?" I asked.

There followed a torrent of Spanish, none of which I could pick up.

"Está Lisa?" I repeated, hoping the Mexican woman would catch the hint and put my girlfriend on the phone.

Finally Lisa was on the other end, but our connection was anything but a happy one. In all honesty, there was a long, half-frustrated sigh—from both of us. It was the summer before we became engaged, and Lisa was on a missions trip in Mexico City. Her letters had grown a little more distant over the summer—less and less about how she was doing personally and how she was feeling, with more and more information about *what* she was doing and that strong male assistant she was spending so much time with.

The virtual absence in her letters of any talk about us—or about missing me—had raised a red flag. Then, so casually that it hurt twice as much, Lisa dropped a line in one of her letters that she was thinking about extending her stay for an entire year. As I recall, the male assistant was pondering the same possibility.

I hadn't called Lisa before. This was back in the days when long-distance phone companies enjoyed a monopoly and international calling was frightfully expensive, especially for a near-penniless college student. E-mail was still the stuff of science-fiction novels as far as the general public was concerned.

I don't remember how the phone call started, but in the middle there was a long silence—more than a minute at least. I finally broke it with the not-too-gentle (and not-too-bright) comment, "Do you have any idea how much that silence just cost me?!"

Our struggle to be together *and* serve the Lord had begun before we were even engaged. I wanted Lisa to serve the Lord, all right—as long as she did it with me. At the time, I wasn't open to any other possibility.

This "crisis" ended happily and rather quickly. When one of the Mexican nationals actually proposed to her, trying to keep her in country, Lisa kept thinking, *I've* got *to get back to Gary*. She returned from Mexico a month later, and we were engaged by the end of the year.

I could have learned a few things from one of my heroes at the time, the German pastor Dietrich Bonhoeffer, who was himself engaged to be married when he entered his Tegel prison cell after having been arrested for his part in a plot to overthrow Adolf Hitler. Flush with the passion of a new love and the confirmation of returned love, Bonhoeffer was no doubt tempted to reconsider the harsh effects of his personal mission to stop Hitler at virtually any cost. If he were to hold back, he could expect a rather easy and enjoyable life—being married to Maria and living out his days as a seminary professor. Yet Dietrich willingly risked a life of relative ease for the uncertainty of revolutionary involvement.

Tucked away in his prison cell, Bonhoeffer asked some hard and fundamental questions. In one poem written during confinement, Bonhoeffer posed the question, "Who am I?" He observed how he was often complimented for being friendly, cheerful, and agreeable. Yet inside himself, he was experiencing a different sense of who he might be. In the midst of anguish of spirit, he proceeded to ask himself some heartrending questions:

Who am I? This one or the other?
Am I this one today and tomorrow another?
Am I both at once? Before others a hypocrite,
and in my own eyes a pitiful, whimpering weakling?...
Who am I? They mock me, these lonely questions of mine.
Whoever I am, thou knowest me; O God, I am thine.[1]

It's this last line I want to focus on: "Whoever I am, thou knowest me; O God, I am thine."

The intimacy of the marriage relationship is something most of us desire, but how do we enter this union without sacrificing our sense of personal mission before God? How do we promise to be unreservedly faithful and continue to fall forward toward our spouse when we have already pledged to be unreservedly available for God's service?

HOW DO WE PROMISE TO BE UNRESERVEDLY FAITHFUL TOWARD OUR SPOUSE WHEN WE HAVE ALREADY PLEDGED TO BE UNRESERVEDLY AVAILABLE FOR GOD'S SERVICE?

It's not easy to balance the competing demands of an intense human relationship and an overarching, all-embracing spiritual devotion. One of the great (and often unexplored) challenges of marriage is maintaining a sense of individual mission while living in a cooperative relationship.

Not much has been written about this for the simple reason that most ancient Christian writings assume that "really" serious Christians will remain single. I've found one classical Christian writer, however, who addresses this challenge head-on—a man named Francis de Sales (1567–1622). De Sales was learned in both law and theology and carried on an active spiritual-direction-by-letter ministry, making him somewhat of a seventeenth-century advice columnist. His advice is so insightful, practical, and helpful that I want to devote an entire section in this chapter to his responses to letters sent from earnest Christians living "in the world."

LETTERS TO PERSONS IN THE WORLD

A married woman wrote Francis to express her concern that her marital and spiritual devotion were at conflict. De Sales dismissed this concern out of hand, encouraging her, "Let us be what we are, and let us be it well." In other words, if we are married, we are married, and we must not try to live as if we were otherwise. Francis noted that by living with this attitude, we "do honor to the Master whose work we are."[2]

To accept this counsel entails we do not make the mistake John Wesley made, which was to get married but refuse to adjust his life accordingly. Wesley said he wouldn't let being married slow him down by even one sermon. This kind of vision is unrealistic and unfair to our spouse, to be sure. Being married brings obligations—some particularly intense ones for those who are by nature ambitious. There are times when I must sacrifice my ambition to succeed in God's service so I can be fully present and involved in the lives of my wife and children. Most assuredly, the tension should lead us to ask the question, "If I ignore God's daughter [God's son] to do God's work, am I honoring God?"

De Sales warned that even spiritual devotion can be taken out of bounds. When we get married, we make a certain promise to our spouse that we will devote a considerable amount of energy, initiative, and time into building and nurturing the relationship. It is spiritual fraud to enter marriage and then to live like a single man or woman.

To another woman with a similar concern—she longed to become a nun but felt yoked within her marriage—Francis counseled that God does not compensate his servants according to the dignity of the office they exercise but according to the *faithfulness* with which they exercise it. Whether a woman is overseeing a hospital or homeschooling her children makes little difference in God's eyes, as long as that woman is being faithful to her particular calling in life.

To yet another woman, who wrote that she had great difficulty harmonizing marriage and devotion, Francis wrote, "The means of gaining perfection are various according to the variety of vocations: religious, widows, and married persons must all seek after this perfection, but not all by the same means."[3] He encouraged the woman by suggesting several spiritual exercises, but then he warned, "In all this take particular care that your husband, your servants, and your parents do not suffer by your too long stayings in church, your too great retirement [for prayer], or by your failing to care for your household ... You must not only be devout, and love devotion, but you must make it lovable to everyone."[4]

I love that phrase: we must love devotion in such a way that we *make it lovable* to our family members. True devotion serves and blesses our family; it doesn't compete with them. God is not served well if we turn off everyone around us in our selfish pursuit of devotion. "We must sometimes leave our Lord," Francis affirmed, "in order to please others for the love of him."[5]

I've met women who, because they are married to unbelieving husbands, feel frustrated that they are not able to participate as fully in the life of the church as they might wish. This is a frustration Francis would urge wives to live with; he would argue it is not the better part of godliness to let one's spiritual duties eclipse one's marital responsibilities.

One of the great challenges of marriage for me is the seemingly endless tasks that accompany married life. How can I experience peace and serenity, focus on the presence of God, and devote myself to worship when the lawn needs to be mowed, the garbage needs to be taken out, the kids want time alone with me, laundry needs to be done, meals need to be cooked, cars need to be fixed . . .

To a woman who had this same concern, Francis was gentle rather than condemning. "I remember you telling me how much the multiplicity of your affairs weighs on you," he wrote — and then, rather than chide her, he encouraged her, "[This] is a good opportunity for acquiring the true and solid virtues."[6]

De Sales wrote with the wonderful assumption, so foreign to our contemporary culture, that the more difficult something is, the more spiritually beneficial we will find it to be as it builds our character. It is only natural when facing all these responsibilities that our souls cry out for relief. But Francis urges us to draw maximum benefit from them by crying out for patience and virtue and growth in Christlikeness. We can learn to grow in God by focusing on serving him through even our daily chores. Accepting this with the right spirit shapes us into a different kind of person.

PATIENCE CAN BE FORMED ONLY IN THE CRUCIBLE OF FRUSTRATION — MAKING MARRIAGE, WITH ITS MULTITUDE OF TASKS, ONE OF THE BEST SCHOOLS OF PATIENCE THERE IS.

Here's the kicker: Patience can be formed only in the crucible of frustration — making marriage, with its multitude of tasks, one of the best schools of patience there is. De Sales entreats us to "resolve to restore yourself to patience throughout the day as many times as you sense yourself becoming distracted."[7]

He encouraged this same woman to further practice mortification by not losing "any occasion, however small it may be, for exercising gentleness of heart toward everyone."[8] The practice of this virtue of gentleness is particularly challenging (Francis admitted his correspondent will be able to succeed only by God's assistance), because it is one thing to do the right thing and it is another thing entirely to do the right thing *with the right spirit*—and our motives and character are surely being tested in marriage. Francis explained further: "I say 'gentle diligence,' because violent diligence spoils the heart and affairs, and is not diligence, but haste and trouble."[9]

Francis accepted the presupposition that becoming a more mature person is just as honoring to God as doing the right things. There is no question that marriage limits how much we can do, but it multiplies what we can become. If a man or woman focuses on spiritual growth rather than achievement and accomplishment, they'll see the marriage relationship as providing a wonderful environment for Christian mission.

Knowing that the juggling of many concerns can become burdensome, Francis encouraged the mother to persevere by remembering eternity:

> We will soon be in eternity, and then we will see how all the affairs of this world are such little things and how little it matters whether they turn out or not . . . When we were little children, with what eagerness did we put together little bits of tile, wood, and mud, to make houses and small buildings! And if someone destroyed them, we were very grieved and tearful at it; but now we know well that it all mattered very little. One day it will be the same with us in heaven, when we will see that our concerns in this world were truly only child's play.[10]

This is not to suggest, Francis hastened to add, that these affairs of this world have no value at all: "I do not want to take away the care that we must have regarding these little trifles, because God has entrusted them to us in this world for exercise; but I would indeed like to take away the passion and anxiety of this care."[11]

Marital concerns necessarily give rise to more emotional swings than celibate living. I remember one Sunday morning in particular. I had spoken at a banquet the previous night, and I was scheduled to preach at all four services at a local church. Two of my children decided to initiate World War III in my kitchen. Lisa was getting ready for church, and I had to take care of disciplining the kids. I was so frazzled that I lost my temper.

"This is just *great!*" I wanted to scream. "How am I supposed to preach when I live in chaos?"

I limped emotionally to church that morning and asked several people to pray for me, explaining what had happened. It wasn't until after the first service that I really got warmed up. While I wished things had turned out differently that morning, looking back on it now, the entire experience was in all likelihood beneficial in the long run (as far as my character growth), though it certainly wasn't the best preparation for a "performance."

De Sales did not view marriage as a compromise to our mission before God, precisely because if we are led into marriage, then marriage becomes an essential element of our mission—not our only mission, to be sure, but at least the front lines from which our mission is launched.

We can draw this conclusion because mission includes not just what we *do* but also what we *become*. Christianity is one of those rare religions that marries internal reality with outward obedience. We cannot simply focus on external adherence; doing that was the spiritually fatal mistake of the Pharisees. On the other hand, internal piety that shows no concern for service in and for the world is just as grievous an error. Our marriages will, as a matter of fact, be strengthened by an outward focus.

IF WE ARE LED INTO MARRIAGE, THEN MARRIAGE BECOMES AN ESSENTIAL ELEMENT OF OUR MISSION.

OUTWARD BOUND

A friend of mine named Mike is an unusually gifted man. He is one of the best oral communicators I have ever heard—one of those rare individuals who can leave you laughing until your sides ache and then slip in a spiritually penetrating challenge—and his written material is equally well done.

He built a college ministry from sixty participants to over six hundred in just a few years. He then surprised many people by leaving the ministry and launching a very successful management and consulting business. "On the side" he published a newsletter for college pastors, organized a national campus pastors conference, and wrote articles (he's since returned to the pastoral ministry).

You get the picture—this is a very capable man!

Yet I remember one day, years ago, when he came into the church office (I was his associate at the time) raving about his wife. "You should have seen her last night," he gushed. "I was so proud of her!"

Sherri had approached her church board with an idea for a ministry to new mothers. Sherri recognized that if someone isn't won to the Lord in college, they may be most open to considering God's claims on their lives when they give birth to their first child. With that in mind, she drew up plans in which the church would send a small gift and letter to every woman in our community who gave birth, inviting her to worship and find fellowship at their church if the recipient didn't already have a church home. In that small town, every birth was published in the local newspaper, which made Sherri's plan surprisingly easy to carry out.

By focusing on extending God's kingdom, Sherri won her husband's heart. It's ironic but true: by serving something outside her marriage, Sherri strengthened her own.

A spiritually alive marriage will remain a marriage of two individuals in pursuit of a common vision outside themselves. This has been true throughout history. I was particularly moved when reading the letters of another German hero, Count Helmuth James von Moltke, who, like Dietrich Bonhoeffer, was a conspirator against the Nazis.

Von Moltke's passion for his wife was obvious in his letters. Consider this: "You are not one of God's agents to make me what I am, rather you are myself. You are my thirteenth chapter of the First Epistle to the Corinthians ... It is only in our union—you and I—that we form a complete human being. We are ... one creative thought."

While von Moltke loved his wife deeply, his life was equally charged by his participation in God's work on earth. Just hours before he was executed, von Moltke wrote another passionate letter to his wife. Before you read this, ask yourself, "What would I write to my spouse if I knew it would be my last letter?"

> My dear, my life draws to its close, and I can truthfully say of myself, "He died in fullness of years and of life's experience." That does not imply that I would not gladly go on living, that I would not gladly walk further at your side on this earth. *But for that I should need a new commission from God*, since the one for which he created me stands completed.[12]

Even with such a passionate, rich, and rewarding marriage relationship, von Moltke says that to go on living, he would need a new commission from God. What a remarkable statement from a man only hours away from being hanged! What helped to make his marriage so rich was that von Moltke looked outside his marriage to find meaning—which, ironically enough, infused his marriage with even more meaning. Their marriage was so exciting because it was fed by a commission from God.

Earlier in this book, I spoke about how essential it is that in marriage we view ourselves as "we" instead of "I." This "we," however, is not achieved through the absorption of one mate into the other—either wife into husband or husband into wife. The apostle Paul is clear that each of us is given our own gifts and our own role to play in the kingdom of God (Romans 12:4–8; 1 Corinthians 12:1–11). Each of us must be passionately devoted to our own faithful service.

A mature marriage looks beyond itself, forfeiting not just the tyranny of individual desires, but also the tyranny of the couple's comfort. It has been described by one couple as the transition from "we are" to "we care." Such a transition settles gradually. A couple's sex and recreational life is radically transformed when children are born; even such a simple act as getting ready for church can become an exhausting experience as the baby must have its diaper changed and the diaper bag packed. The selfishness of early infatuation and the virtual intoxication of young love are stretched to welcome this tiny and demanding person.

In this early stage of rearing children, couples gradually begin to learn the value of serving. What they are able to do outside the home is limited. Ideally, as the children become independent and move out, the couple will continue to nurture the vitality of service. Freed from the demands of parenting young children, a man and woman are released to focus on a broader world.

I've seen my own parents go through this process. Now past eighty, my dad has been in "retirement" for two full decades, but his vocational freedom has in reality become merely a redirection of service. My parents end up as servants even on vacation.

We once visited them at a remote campground, and they recounted how, the night before, they had spent two and a half hours comforting a man who had recently lost his wife. They had never met this man before, but he sensed in them a listening ear, and they obliged, giving up participating in a campground musical fest to ease a grieving man's loneliness.

A SELFISH MARRIAGE IS A HOLLOW MARRIAGE.

Soon thereafter, a young man who had just been released from a psychiatric ward moved into the campground with his family. He homed in on my parents almost immediately, even to the point of calling them "Grandpa" and "Grandma" before his stay ended.

Retirement can be a lonely time, but my parents have plunged headlong into making that phase of life represent some of the most rewarding and even busy years of their lives. While it is appropriate to slow down and enjoy an occasional vacation or cruise, in the main their meaning and fulfillment have come from ongoing service. My dad has often remarked, "I don't know when I found the time to work!"

Without this involvement in and commitment to service, marriage gets very lonely very fast. A selfish marriage is a hollow marriage. We were made to serve God, and no human affection can appease that hunger for very long.

TWO VISIONS, ONE LIFE

Ambition can be fatal.

Lou Kasischke joined a commercial expedition to climb Mount Everest in the spring of 1996. He was witness to one of the worst climbing disasters in history, a calamity that made worldwide news when several people perished on the world's highest peak. As that fateful day wore on, many climbers refused to turn back, even though it was getting ridiculously late to be up so high. Lou decided to turn back, and that decision in all likelihood saved his life.

Although Kasischke was serious about reaching the top, he wasn't willing to put his life at grave risk in order to get there. He explains why:

> I didn't think I could get there and back alive or, best case, I'd lose some fingers and toes. And the other thing, too, is ... I wasn't really subject to a lot of the same pressures ... In my perspective of things, it wasn't life-and-death to me, it wasn't the most important thing in the world, and I wasn't going to have newspapers writing stories about me. And media, fame and fortune, world records, and all that kind of stuff, which were kind of the stakes for ... some of the others in our expedition ... It meant a lot to me, I don't want to suggest that it didn't. But ... my ambition to get there just wasn't suffocating every other thought that I had in my mind.[13]

That last line ("my ambition to get there just wasn't suffocating every other thought that I had in my mind") is particularly telling. I've seen men and women blinded by their own ambition, even religious ambition, and that kind of blind ambition does have the tendency to suffocate everything and everyone around them. They don't see the price they're making their loved ones pay for their blind, obsessive pursuit. If their spouse doesn't fall in line, a sort of spiritual murder often can result. Something will die—affection, the relationship, virtue. Some kind of casualty is certain.

Mixing ambition and relationships is like mixing fire and dynamite: an explosion is inevitable. If we are going to learn how to live out our mission in the marriage relationship, we must learn to be more selfless, and we have to become more connected with each other. We have to remember that our spouse is called, just as we are, and we have to be interested enough in *their* call to know what it is that moves them and gives them energy.

MIXING AMBITION AND RELATIONSHIPS IS LIKE MIXING FIRE AND DYNAMITE: AN EXPLOSION IS INEVITABLE.

When Lisa and I got married, we were pursuing two seemingly disharmonious missions. More than anything, I wanted to be a writer, and most professional writers will tell aspiring writers what I typically say to such folks: "You really want to be a writer? Marry a spouse who can support you for ten years!"

Lisa never wanted to work outside the home. She was dedicated to the thought of homeschooling and creating a home environment that was conducive to the children's intellectual, cultural, and spiritual development (this is *not* to suggest that those who don't homeschool aren't interested in those things). Before we got married, she made it clear she never aspired to run or work in a business, even after the kids left home.

On the face of it, you can easily see the potential for tension in the relationship, can't you? As a young writer, I didn't earn a tenth of the money Lisa would have needed to make her dreams a reality. As a stay-at-home spouse, Lisa didn't earn any money to help me build a self-supporting writing career.

I would be lying if I implied that this situation didn't cause a few heated discussions in our household. Looking back, these "irreconcilable differences" can be seen as complementary, provided that neither of us insisted that the other lose the debate. By respecting what God had called each of us to do, we were able to make progress—albeit more slowly than either of us would have preferred. Yet the seeming lack of speedy progress helped to build patience and more selflessness in each of us—two extraordinarily valuable spiritual qualities.

The point is that we think we know best—*God, why can't you allow things to work out the way I want?*—but it just may be that our assumptions are wildly off-kilter. What we want may have the potential to destroy us. If our eyes are so set on the summit of Everest that we forget about having to come back down while there is still time, we may very well impale ourselves on our own desires.

Ambition can seize our souls, leaving little left over for intimate relationship (and it now hits women and men with equal force). What we sacrifice everything to achieve can turn around and bury us even as it reaches its fulfillment. It just may be that God gives us the marriage relationship to moderate and redirect our dreams. Forced to compromise, we learn to reevaluate what's truly important. We are asked to reconsider our priorities and slow down long enough to look at someone else's opinions or needs.

The duties of marriage call us out of ourselves to help us remember that ours is not the only vision in the world. God is building an entire church, and *each* member is crucial. The eye, the hand, the foot, the mouth—all have a role to play (1 Corinthians 12:14–31). We are just one cog in the machine, and God can replace any one of us without hesitation. Humility helps us relax and breathe and enjoy life.

When I was in college, I was deeply saddened by the tragic death of Keith Green, a gifted Christian musician who was amazingly effective in reaching teens. How could God let such a strong leader die? I wondered. But neither Dietrich Bonhoeffer, the great German writer and teacher, nor Blaise Pascal, a brilliant thinker and Christian apologist, lived to the age of forty. Jesus himself didn't even live for forty years here on this earth.

This reality teaches me plainly that my faithfulness is important, but my service isn't essential. If God thought the church could carry on without Bonhoeffer or Pascal living very long, there's no question it can survive and thrive without me writing another book or speaking at another retreat.

I wish I could have given Lisa her dream house, and I know Lisa wishes I could have been a writer from the very beginning of our marriage. And both of us are probably weak enough that, if given the choice, we would go back and take the easy road. But I'm not sure that to do so would have ultimately been in our best interest. Achieving our early ambition might have destroyed us. Looking back, the way things have played out, all but forcing on us a selfless patience, has produced a life way more meaningful and impactful. If you are willing to walk this selfless road, I believe the same will be true in your life too.

LOOKING BEYOND MARRIAGE

The importance of service—looking beyond the marriage relationship—is necessary because marriage itself is not eternal. When God provides us with a mate, there is no guarantee this mate will be with us for life. We certainly hope this will be the case, but very few marriages end in a simultaneous death. Marriage is for this world, and this world is passing away—at different times for each one of us.

Otto Piper suggests that "the loss of a spouse is not simply a sad natural occurrence but ... it is a divine intervention by which a marriage is terminated so that the surviving partner may devote himself fully to the service of God in the Church."[14] Listen carefully to his conclusion: "Therefore, every stage of the individual's sexual development both depends on his being subject to the law of God and is also a partial execution of the divine plan of redemption."

> MARRIAGE IS FOR THIS WORLD, AND THIS WORLD IS PASSING AWAY—AT DIFFERENT TIMES FOR EACH ONE OF US.

When marriage is placed within the context of God's redemptive plan, we stay married, as far as it depends on us, as a means to express God's commitment to his people; when the marriage is ended by God's design — through death — our ultimate purpose hasn't changed. Now we are free to perhaps more actively serve God in bringing knowledge of his redemptive plan to others.

When marriage becomes our primary pursuit, our delight in the relationship will be crippled by fear, possessiveness, and self-centeredness. We were made to admire, respect, and love someone who has a purpose bigger than ourselves, a purpose centered on God's untiring work of calling his people home to his heart of love.

We allow marriage to point beyond itself when we accept two central missions: becoming the people God created us to be, and doing the work God has given us to do. If we embrace — not just accept, but actively embrace — these two missions, we will have a full life, a rich life, a meaningful life, and a successful life. The irony is, we will probably also have a happy marriage, but that will come as a blessed by-product of putting everything else in order.

Epilogue

THE HOLY COUPLE

In our marriage we tell the next generation what sex and marriage and fidelity look like to Christians. We are prophets, for better and for worse, of the future of Christian marriage. *Evelyn and James Whitehead*

Our marriages are the testing ground for God to win us to himself. Our marriages are basic training for the one Marriage that will not disappoint.
Dan Allender and Tremper Longman III

I was alone, traveling in my car (having been separated from my family for over a week due to business travel), when I heard a song that stopped me short. After realistically portraying a relational struggle, the singer lifts the listener up with this chorus: "Ain't nobody gonna say good-bye ... This time, Baby, I'm learning how to love you, love you. Ain't nobody ... ever really tried to love you like I love you."

The poor grammar notwithstanding, this is a profound statement. It is undeniably biblical—focusing on learning to love rather than anything else. It struck me that if I could succeed in loving Lisa like nobody ever has or ever will, I will have been a "good" husband. My goal is that at the end of her life Lisa will be able to say, "Gary had his rough edges, and there were some struggles he faced his entire life, but for all his faults, Gary loved me like no one else ever could or ever has."

Lisa's parents have five children, so they can't give Lisa the exclusive love I can give her. Our children have two parents, so they can't focus on Lisa like I can. It's my job, calling, and mission to walk through the travails and challenges of marriage and declare, "Hey, I'm never leaving, and furthermore (you can immediately see I lack the songwriter's poetic spirit; I can't imagine her using the word *furthermore* in a song), I'm going to love you like you have never been loved."

I'm getting better. After that disastrous birthday experience so many years ago, I've learned how to shop for Lisa. In fact, she is reluctant to give me ideas now, as she thinks I do a better job on my own—and she enjoys being surprised. Strolling through a store one holiday season, I immediately knew Lisa would love a Japanese buckwheat pillow for Christmas—even though she had never heard of one. The kids thought I was crazy, but I knew she would like it, and I knew it would demonstrate that I've studied her and that I know her better than anyone else.

I was right.

I've been wrong about so many things in my marriage. There have been moments of betrayal, apathy, unkindness, selfishness—but marriage is a long walk. We can start out a little slowly, even occasionally lose our way, and still salvage a most meaningful journey.

If we view the marriage relationship as an opportunity to excel in love, it doesn't matter how difficult the person is whom we are called to love; it doesn't even matter whether that love is ever returned. We can still excel at love. We can still say, "Like it or not, I'm going to love you like nobody ever has."

This mirrors Christ's own love, a love without compare, a love that is infinitely deeper than any human love we could ever know. It is a love pregnant with the opportunity for spiritual birth and rebirth. The Russian Orthodox priest Alexander Yelchaninov wrote that "a single vivid experience of love will advance us much farther, will far more surely protect our souls from evil, than the most arduous *struggle* against sin."[1]

We need to further explore the power of human love to feed our divine love. Rather than seeing marriage as a cosmic competitor with heaven, we can embrace it as a school of faith. Maximus the Confessor (580–662) observed that the love we have for God and the love we have for others are not two distinct loves, but rather two aspects of a single total love. Jesus suggested the same thing, when in response to a question about the greatest commandment he declared that there is not just one, but two—not only must we love God, but also our neighbors (Mark 12:30–31).

THE LOVE WE HAVE FOR GOD AND THE LOVE WE HAVE FOR OTHERS ARE NOT TWO DISTINCT LOVES, BUT RATHER TWO ASPECTS OF A SINGLE TOTAL LOVE.

This is a love that can be practiced by either partner in a marriage relationship. If your spouse isn't a willing participant, you can still learn to grow by loving him or her.

But there's another challenge when two believers are both committed to pursuing a deeper spiritual reality in marriage—the formidable task of working to become not just a holy spouse but a holy couple.

PIONEERS

My mission is to integrate Scripture, church history, and the Christian classics, and then to apply that wisdom to help people become closer to Christ and to others. I am not as interested in breaking new ground as I am in recapturing the contemporary relevance of old ground that has been forgotten.

While we may not be breaking new ground with the idea of marriage spirituality, we are certainly walking with the minority. I have watched, though, as God has used *Sacred Marriage* to launch many new conversations and debates. Fifteen years after *Sacred Marriage* was first written, however, it is still a frustration to see how, for the most part, Christian spirituality continues to be viewed as largely a solitary pursuit. Seminaries still, by and large, perhaps unwittingly imply this by rarely (if ever) talking about spiritual formation in the family context, by offering only spiritual practices that assume the leisure of extended solitude, and by not even imagining practices that would take advantage of family life. Since most of the church serves God within a family relationship, it stands to reason that much of the teaching regarding the spiritual life should be placed in a marital context, with family life as an avenue to spiritual growth rather than a dead end. More needs to be said—that much is clear. And if God is gracious enough to give me the time and lend me some of his wisdom, I hope to be a part of that future conversation.

Let's take this one step further: What if a few Christian couples took the challenge to become a "couple saint"? Their relationship is a significant aspect of their sanctity—building it, showcasing it, using it to bless the church and the world. No longer defining their relationship to God in solitary terms, but working together to present themselves as a holy unit, they resemble a pair of cherubim in the middle of whom God's presence is radically enlivened.

It is, at the very least, an interesting invitation. Is there anyone who will accept that invitation for today—for such a time as this?

For those of you who want to continue this conversation and even add to it, I invite you to join a new online community dedicated to the topic of marriage and Christian spirituality. This Sacred Marriage blog reaches out to singles, engaged couples, newlyweds, and longtime weds, and the focus is on the marital relationship: making a wise choice, living with our choice, honoring God with our choice.

Here's the vision:

- Dedicated to living out Matthew 6:33 (Seek first his kingdom and his righteousness) in our marriages
- Helping singles make wise marital choices

- Helping engaged couples prepare to enter a life of rich intimacy
- Encouraging newlyweds as they encounter the early challenges of marriage
- Inspiring "not so newlyweds" to keep going deeper in their marriages as an act of worship, so they can truly explore the depths of love from God and with each other revealed in this amazing relationship we call marriage— from the time we first pledge our vows to the time God separates us through death, never letting up but being fully married, pursuing each other every step of the way
- Exploring marital love and companionship sustained by God, in which God is made known in ways that few communities may have ever tried to explore

Is it possible that God wants to create a web community dedicated to the pursuit of the connection between our spiritual life and our marriage? I think of this as a type of religious community where we live all over the world and are connected not by a common roof but a common call. We want to explore the connection between our marriages and our worship. We want to see how God can use our marriages to build his kingdom while he's also building us. Can we inspire each other, counsel each other, pray for each other, and console each other as we honestly share the difficulties and joys, the frustrations and ecstasies, of married life?

CAN WE INSPIRE EACH OTHER, COUNSEL EACH OTHER, PRAY FOR EACH OTHER, AND CONSOLE EACH OTHER AS WE HONESTLY SHARE THE DIFFICULTIES AND JOYS, THE FRUSTRATIONS AND ECSTASIES, OF MARRIED LIFE?

I hope you'll join us. I hope you'll enlist some friends. We won't have a monastery or convent to retreat to as we pray for each other and counsel each other, but we can connect via this portal. You can find this new community on my website at www.garythomas.com. You're also welcome to join us on Twitter at @garyLthomas or on Facebook at www.facebook.com /authorgarythomas as we continue this discussion.

ACKNOWLEDGMENTS

I've been extremely well served by Zondervan in writing this book. John Sloan did a marvelous job keeping the book on focus and well structured. Dirk Buursma provided one of the most satisfying copyediting experiences I've ever had. His gift at directing me toward a more precise word and his determination to still preserve my voice were greatly appreciated. Karen Lee-Thorp stepped in to give this updated edition a welcomed boost. Thank you, Karen, for your insights here. And a special word of thanks as well goes out to Curtis Yates, my agent, for your support and encouragement.

I'd also like to thank the hundreds of churches that have invited me into their life and whose members have shared their stories and sought to live out the biblical call of a truly sacred marriage. What a joy it has been to work in this ministry with so many fine congregations.

For this second edition, I want to especially mention Brooks Powell, a young intern who, by the time this book makes its way into its second incarnation, may well be writing his own books. He offered many helpful comments on how to express this message to a younger generation.

Finally, this book has been lived out with a woman beyond compare. I have tested her and been tested by her; I have sinned against her and sought her forgiveness; I have laughed with her, cried with her, prayed with her, and conceived children with her. Lisa, I adore you more every day. I can't imagine life without you. Thank you for sharing this life with me. Your personality has put the celebration in our marriage; your faith has made it sacred. You are truly a treasure.

QUESTIONS FOR DISCUSSION AND REFLECTION

Chapter 1: The Greatest Challenge in the World

1. Why did you choose to get married? (Or if not married right now, why do you want to get married?) Is this a biblical reason?
2. How do you think most Christians would describe the purpose of marriage?
3. How do you react to the idea that God may have designed marriage to make us holy even more than to make us happy?

Chapter 2: Romanticism's Ruse

1. What do you think of Gary's critique of romantic love as the basis—or measurement of success—for marriage? How have your attitudes toward romantic love changed over time?
2. Were you encouraged or discouraged by the author's premise that marriage is a crucible in which we can learn more about ourselves and about God? What has been your personal experience in this regard?
3. Do you agree with Gary that, in one sense, moderns expect too much from marriage? If so, in what way?

4. What has your marriage revealed to you about your sinful attitudes, selfish behaviors, and other character flaws? Why do you think marriage brings so many character issues to the surface?
5. Gary says God is the One who ultimately fulfills us, not our mate. If this is so, what contribution does our mate make to our life?

Chapter 3: Finding God in Marriage

1. What aspect, event, or element of your marriage has taught you the most about how God loves us?
2. How can a discouraged spouse directly apply Gary's admonition to seek God in the midst of disappointments rather than to obsess over where the spouse falls short? What mental exercises would you suggest?
3. Can you think of any analogies that Gary doesn't mention about how marriage reveals God and his love to the world?
4. Gary contrasts a human-centered view of marriage (staying put as long as our desires and expectations are being met) and a God-centered view (preserving the marriage because it brings glory to God and points a sinful world to a reconciling Creator). What provides the greatest motivation for you to maintain and preserve your marital commitment?
5. In your own marital experience, are you motivated more by what makes you happy or by what pleases God? How can churches support and encourage this latter and higher motivation?
6. What aspect of God's character would you most like your marriage to reveal to the world? How can you accomplish this?

Chapter 4: Learning to Love

1. Compare and contrast what our culture usually means by the word *love* with how the Bible defines it.
2. Discuss some of the ways that marriage seems uniquely designed to train us in how to love.

3. If somebody tried to describe your love for God solely by how well you love your spouse, what would they conclude? What one or two things can you do to serve your spouse, strengthen your marriage, and please God?
4. How much time do you spend thinking about how to make your spouse happy compared to the amount of time you spend thinking about how well your spouse is pleasing you? Do you think your answer is about right, or do you need to do better in this area?
5. Discuss how marriage can reveal men's poor attitudes and prejudices about women, and how it can also illuminate women's critical thoughts about men. Is your marriage confronting these stereotypes, or is it suffering from them? What can you do to uncover and renounce such negative attitudes?
6. God loves us in spite of our flaws. How does marriage teach us to love our spouse in spite of their imperfections?
7. You and your spouse are different in many ways. Which differences have you grown to appreciate? Which ones still annoy you? Are these differences something you can learn from with better understanding? How so?

Chapter 5: Holy Honor

1. How is any lack of respect or active contempt for your spouse negatively affecting your own life and the lives of your children?
2. Are you more apt to look for "evidences of God's grace" in your spouse, or is it your pattern to be consumed with your mate's flaws? What practical steps can you take to choose respect over contempt?
3. What evidences of grace can you see in your mate when you take the time to look for them? What are personal qualities of your mate and contributions your mate makes to your life for which you should regularly thank God?

4. How many of your marital disagreements are rooted in gender differences as compared to personal disagreements? How can recognizing such distinctions improve the quality of your relationship?
5. How does trying to understand our spouses rather than judging them help us to fulfill the biblical command to respect them?
6. Discuss some of the ways you can actively honor your spouse.
7. How would your marriage benefit if you and your spouse became better at showing respect to each other?
8. Gary writes that "we're not married in a carefree garden of Eden; we're married in the midst of many responsibilities that compete for our energy." In light of this, do you believe you give your spouse sufficient leeway and understanding?

CHAPTER 6: THE SOUL'S EMBRACE

1. Do you know any married couples who seem unusually successful in prayer? If so, what stands out about their prayer habits?
2. Has your prayer life ever been hindered due to negative attitudes toward your spouse? Are there any negative attitudes hindering your prayer life today?
3. Gary writes, "We're told that we should improve our prayer lives if we want to have stronger marriages. But Peter tells us we should improve our marriages so we can have stronger prayer lives." How can you imagine having a stronger prayer life if your marriage can be closer to the way God intended it to be?
4. How would you say the quality and quantity of sexual activity in your marriage affect the way you pray? The way your spouse prays?
5. Gary writes, "Dissension is a major prayer killer. Looked at from this perspective, the institution of marriage is designed to force us to become reconcilers. That's the only way we'll

survive spiritually." How well do you and your spouse resolve disagreements in a timely manner? What happens to your praying when you are upset with your spouse?

6. What idea about sexual activity and prayer intrigued you the most? What other aspects of being married might contain hidden lessons about prayer? How has your marriage helped you grow in prayer?

CHAPTER 7: THE CLEANSING OF MARRIAGE

1. What most surprised you about your own sin during the first year or two of your marriage?
2. What is your overall reaction to the idea that God intends to use your marriage to expose your sin and help you grow out of it?
3. Is your marriage a safe place for your sin to be revealed? How can it become more nurturing in this regard?
4. How might Gary's comment, "Couples don't fall out of love so much as they fall out of repentance," help restore a troubled marriage?
5. Do you agrcc with Gary that "much of our marital dissatisfaction stems from self-hatred"? How can we avoid the flight mentality—running from what we've done or become—and instead use our marriage to fight the sin that's revealed?
6. Why do you think spouses are often afraid to confess their sins or admit their faults? What needs to happen in our marriages so that it's safe to be more transparent? (Or what is true of your marriage that has helped you become transparent?)
7. Identify the top two weaknesses in the way you relate to your mate. What are the positive virtues that are the moral/spiritual opposites of those two weaknesses (for example, harshness/gentleness; criticism/encouragement)? Which one will you work on this week?
8. Have you ever used your knowledge of a weakness in your mate to shame or punish him or her? How could

you have used that situation to build up your spouse and encourage spiritual growth?

Chapter 8: Sacred History

1. How can understanding Israel's history with God (times of celebration, anger, infidelity, and silence) help couples grow in all seasons of marriage? What lessons have you learned that will help you face the angry or silent seasons?
2. How can the church more effectively teach about the benefits of perseverance when addressing our culture?
3. What do you see as the relationship between perseverance and personal holiness? What messages of modern life are hostile to perseverance and holiness?
4. How can the concept of perseverance and persistence help you be patient with your spouse's growth in holiness?
5. What would you lose if the sacred history of your marriage were ended? What would your spouse lose? Your children? Your church?
6. Spend some time talking with your spouse about which stories should go into the sacred history of your marriage—to be told to your children, family, and friends.
7. Discuss how respecting and telling the sacred history of your marriage can foster community with other couples you know.
8. How can you make the idea of eternity and its rewards a practical motivation for perseverance in the daily grind of married life?
9. How do you want people to describe your marriage at your golden wedding anniversary?

Chapter 9: Sacred Struggle

1. Whom do you admire for the way they handled difficulties in their marriage? What do you admire most about these individuals?
2. What is the difference between productive, spiritually profitable marital struggle and debilitating marital

struggle? How can the difficulty in your marriage produce positive spiritual results?

3. How did you answer Gary's question, "Would I rather live a life of comfort and remain immature in Christ, or am I willing to be seasoned with suffering if by doing so I am conformed to the image of Christ?"
4. Gary says that a good marriage "takes struggle. You must crucify your selfishness. You must at times confront and at other times confess." Do you think this is overstated? Are there any exceptions? How might this belief provide perspective for couples going through difficult times?
5. How can sorrow "set us free," as Anne Morrow Lindbergh wrote? How can we encourage each other—as Anne urges—to add "understanding, patience, love, openness, and the willingness to remain vulnerable" to our disappointments and sorrow?
6. Do you think Abraham Lincoln and Anne Morrow Lindbergh would have accomplished what they did if both had been in relatively easy marriages? Why or why not?
7. How can the Christian belief in heaven encourage couples to persevere?
8. How do you think God can use the specific difficulties in your marriage to refine your character and prepare you for future ministry?
9. Why are difficulties and suffering inevitable in every marriage? What happens if we run from them? What happens if we face them head-on?
10. Do you and your mate face difficulties in your marriage differently? What can you learn from your spouse's approach? What can your spouse learn from your approach?

Chapter 10: Falling Forward

1. Donald Harvey argues that intimate relationships "are the result of planning. They are built. The sense of union that comes with genuine spiritual closeness will not just happen." Over the past year, how much

thought, prayer, and effort have you put into building genuine spiritual closeness?

2. What makes you feel like your spouse is falling forward toward you? What makes your spouse feel like you are falling forward toward them?
3. In which arena is it most difficult for you to grow toward your spouse: physical intimacy, emotional intimacy, or spiritual intimacy? Ask your spouse what you can do to improve in your weakest area.
4. What accommodation can you make in your marriage to foster deeper fellowship and intimacy?
5. Is there a file cabinet in your marriage's confessional? What do you have to do to forgive your spouse and get rid of the file cabinet?
6. Christian marriage expects you to give the gift of self to your mate. What are some ways in which you think your spouse truly wants to receive you? How can you give more of yourself in these ways?
7. Fellowship is fostered by three spiritual practices: learning not to run from conflict, learning how to compromise, and accepting your mate's weaknesses. Which of these disciplines is your strongest? Which is your weakest? What can you do to build on your strength and overcome your weakness?
8. Where do you fall on the spectrum of running from conflict to being brutally harsh during conflict? How can you work toward a healthier response?
9. Would you say that in the past you have been a falling-forward or a pulling-away spouse after you were offended? Based on the teaching here, what steps can you take to learn how to fall forward? What can you do to make it easier for your spouse to fall forward?

CHAPTER 11: MAKE ME A SERVANT

1. When is the last time you loved your spouse in such a way that it cost you something? What can you do for your spouse in the next few days that will fulfill this level of love?

2. Do you agree with Dietrich Bonhoeffer that "Christian marriage is marked by discipline and self-denial"? How does this view compare or contrast with the view you held before you got married?
3. Kathleen and Thomas Hart write of the "paschal mystery" of marriage—the process of dying and rising as a pattern of life for married people. What does your marriage call you to die to? What might it be calling you to rise to?
4. When you think back to why you decided to get married, were your motivations more selfish than selfless? In what way? How has this changed (or does it need to)?
5. Do you sometimes find it difficult to serve your spouse by letting them serve you? What can you do to grow in this area?
6. What are some of the world's messages to men that keep them from serving their wives? What are some of the world's messages to women that keep them from serving their husbands? How can we counteract these messages in our marriages?
7. When you think of your marriage, do you agree that "quarrels over money and time usually reflect a demand to 'own' our life rather than to serve the other with our wealth and existence"? How can you use your money and time to better serve your spouse?
8. Is your attitude toward the sexual relationship marked more by service or by the exercise of power? What can you do to grow in this area?
9. What do you think would be the greatest benefit for your marriage if you and your spouse became better servants of each other?

CHAPTER 12: SEXUAL SAINTS

1. In what ways has your past had a negative impact on your marriage's sexuality? How may seeking spiritual counsel help you deal with this past?
2. Were you shocked by Gary's assertion that "God doesn't

turn his eyes when a married couple goes to bed"? How does this make you feel? Consider praying with your spouse, specifically thanking God for the gift of sexual intimacy.

3. Has sex been more of a blessing or a burden in your marriage? Was it always this way? If not, what may have changed and why?
4. How well have you cultivated holy appetites? How may this be affecting your physical intimacy?
5. Has shame kept you from giving what you do have to your spouse? What is one small thing you can do to begin confronting this area of weakness?
6. How much do you think selfishness affects the average married couple with regard to their sex life? In what ways can an attitude of service transform the experience of marital sexuality?
7. How can gratitude for the marital sexual experience help a couple overcome guilt about previous sexual experience prior to marriage?
8. According to Gary, "Abstinence is not a cul-de-sac or dead end; it is a long on-ramp . . . I am not truly saying no, but rather, *wait*." What can you learn from the rhythm of abstaining and enjoyment inherent in married sexual expression? In other aspects of married life? In life in general?
9. How are you growing in the spiritual side of your sexuality (generosity and service)? What would you like to become increasingly true about you? What would you like to stop being true about you?
10. What one thing can you do in the next month to demonstrate to your spouse your desire to grow in the area of physical intimacy?

CHAPTER 13: SACRED PRESENCE

1. How can a husband and wife more consciously invite the presence of God into their marriage?
2. Are your spoken words inviting God's presence into your home, or are they pushing him away?

3. Have you ever experienced malicious silence in your marriage? How is this an offense to God?
4. How does listening invite God's presence into our homes?
5. How can marital dissatisfaction remind us of our need for fellowship with God?
6. Did you agree with Gary when he wrote, "I have discovered ... that my satisfaction or dissatisfaction with my marriage has far more to do with my relationship to God than it does with my relationship to [my wife]"? How so?
7. How does your spouse mirror a quality of God that you might be somewhat lacking in? What can you learn from this?
8. Gary suggests that if our pastor lived with us, we might treat our spouse differently in his presence—yet God is always present! How can we become more aware of God's presence, thereby creating a more nurturing and encouraging environment at home?
9. Gary warns, "There hasn't been a single marriage in all of human history that could fill a soul that has been emptied of purpose through noncreative living." Has life's busyness kept you from being fully engaged in creating a family together? What can you do to become more creative in your family?
10. Gary writes, "The family that will enjoy Jesus' presence as a customary part of their union is a family that is joined precisely because husband and wife want to invite Jesus into the deeper parts of their marriage." What are some of the deeper parts of your marriage that you've never thought about asking Jesus into? How would you go about inviting him there? What would be the implications of such a step?

Chapter 14: Sacred Mission

1. Before you got married, what did you sense God wanted to do with your life? What was your mate's life mission

before you got married? How has marriage affected these life missions? How do you feel about this?

2. Have you, in any way, committed what Gary calls spiritual fraud—agreeing to get married but then acting like a single man or woman after the wedding? What do you need to do to renounce this?
3. How can we find the right balance between faithfulness to our calling and faithfulness to our marital vows?
4. Do you believe that either your or your spouse's ambition may be suffocating your relationship? If so, discuss the best way to confront this.
5. Honestly consider how an early ambition, had it been fulfilled, might have harmed you and your marriage.
6. What ministries at church or in your community are you engaged in? What ministries is your spouse engaged in? Which do you share? How is your marriage healthier (or weaker) because you serve in contexts outside of your home?
7. Consider the effects these stages of family life can have on ministry:
   - newly married without children
   - married with toddlers
   - raising teenagers
   - empty nesters

   What are the advantages and challenges of each phase of life as it relates to living out your ministry calling?
8. What do you think would happen in a marriage if a couple focused only on their emotional satisfaction with each other to the exclusion of any involvement in or service to God's work?
9. How has being married shaped and strengthened the way you engage in ministry?

EPILOGUE: THE HOLY COUPLE

1. Will you commit to praying at least several times a week, "Lord, how can I love my spouse today like she [or he] has never been loved?"
2. What appeals to you about Gary's challenge to become a couple saint with your spouse? What concerns you about such a challenge?
3. As you consider everything you've read, what one or two areas will most help you begin remaking your marriage into a God-honoring one?

NOTES

Chapter 1: The Greatest Challenge in the World

1. Francis de Sales, *Thy Will Be Done: Letters to Persons in the World* (Manchester, NH: Sophia Institute, 1995), 42.

Chapter 2: Romanticism's Ruse

1. Derrick Sherwin Bailey, *The Mystery of Love and Marriage: A Study in the Theology of Sexual Relation* (New York: Harper, 1952), 4.
2. Eventually, however, Frieda did leave her husband and children for Lawrence. The account of this and several other literary marriages are explored in John Tytell's *Passionate Lives* (New York: Birch Lane, 1991).
3. Katherine Anne Porter, "The Necessary Enemy," in *The Collected Essays and Occasional Writings of Katherine Anne Porter* (New York: Delacorte, 1970), 185.
4. Ibid.
5. Ibid., 182–83.
6. Ibid., 185–86.
7. Ibid., 186.
8. C. S. Lewis, *The Screwtape Letters* (New York: Macmillan, 1951), 94–95.
9. I've since come to understand that in this verse Paul is probably repeating a phrase offered by the Corinthians—but this is not the place to go into the complexities of the Greek language or the sentence structure. Gordon Fee's commentary on 1 Corinthians (Grand Rapids: Eerdmans, 1994) contains the most thorough and well-reasoned explanation of this passage I've read.
10. Quoted in Evelyn Eaton Whitehead and James D. Whitehead, *A Sense of Sexuality: Christian Love and Intimacy* (New York: Doubleday, 1989), 100.
11. See Mary Anne McPherson Oliver, *Conjugal Spirituality: The Primacy of Mutual Love in Christian Tradition* (Kansas City: Sheed and Ward, 1994), 12.

12. Ibid.
13. Gary and Betsy Ricucci, *Love That Lasts: Making a Magnificent Marriage* (Gaithersburg, MD: PDI Communications, 1993), 95.

CHAPTER 3: FINDING GOD IN MARRIAGE

1. Belden C. Lane, "Rabbinical Stories: A Primer on Theological Method," *Christian Century*, December 16, 1981, 1307–08.
2. See Derrick Sherwin Bailey, *The Mystery of Love and Marriage* (New York: Harper, 1952), 101.
3. Philip E. Hughes, *The Second Epistle to the Corinthians*, New International Commentary on the New Testament (Grand Rapids: Eerdmans, 1982), 178.
4. C. K. Barrett, *A Commentary on the Second Epistle to the Corinthians*, Harper's New Testament Commentaries (New York: Harper, 1973), 175.

CHAPTER 4: LEARNING TO LOVE

1. Katherine Anne Porter, "The Necessary Enemy," in *The Collected Essays and Occasional Writings of Katherine Anne Porter* (New York: Delacorte, 1970), 184.
2. This excerpt and the following accounts are taken from the pamphlet *Do You Love Me?* by John Barger (Manchester, NH: Sophia Institute, 1987).

CHAPTER 5: HOLY HONOR

1. Quoted in Leon Morris, *The Gospel According to John*, New International Commentary on the New Testament (Grand Rapids: Eerdmans, 1971), 274.
2. Gary and Betsy Ricucci, *Love That Lasts* (Gaithersburg, MD: PDI Communications, 1993), 70.
3. John Owen, *Sin and Temptation*, ed. James Houston (Portland, OR: Multnomah, 1983), 29.
4. William Law, *A Serious Call to a Devout and Holy Life and the Spirit of Love* (New York: Paulist, 1978), 294.
5. Dan Allender and Tremper Longman III, *Intimate Allies* (Wheaton, IL: Tyndale House, 1995), 287.
6. Ibid., 281.

CHAPTER 6: THE SOUL'S EMBRACE

1. This quote and the next three quotes are taken from Terry Glaspey, *Pathway to the Heart of God* (Eugene, OR: Harvest House, 1998), 16, 24–25.
2. This quote and the following quotes are taken from Phyllis Alsdurf, "McCartney on the Rebound," *Christianity Today*, May 18, 1998.
3. Quoted in Philip Yancey, *What's So Amazing About Grace?* (Grand Rapids: Zondervan, 1997), 265.

4. Where you place the commas and emphasis in this sentence is crucial for a right exegesis. I'm following Dr. Gordon Fee's interpretation offered in his commentary on 1 Corinthians. Note that Exodus 21:10 in the Old Testament also addresses "marital rights"—even in the midst of a polygamous society.

CHAPTER 7: THE CLEANSING OF MARRIAGE

1. Pseudo-Athanasius, "The Life and Activity of the Holy and Blessed Teacher Syncletica," in *Ascetic Behavior in Greco-Roman Antiquity*, ed. Vincent Wimbush (Minneapolis: Fortress, 1990), 284.
2. Saint Ambrose, *Concerning Virgins*, book 1, chap. VI, para. 25–26.
3. C. S. Lewis, *The Four Loves* (New York: Harcourt Brace, 1971), 111.
4. Thomas N. Hart and Kathleen Fischer Hart, *The First Two Years of Marriage* (New York: Paulist, 1983), 50.
5. Dan Allender and Tremper Longman III, *Intimate Allies* (Wheaton, IL: Tyndale House, 1995), 278.
6. Ibid., 288.
7. François de Salignac de La Mothe Fénelon, *Christian Perfection* (Minneapolis: Bethany House, 1975), 205.
8. William Law, *A Serious Call to a Devout and Holy Life and the Spirit of Love* (New York: Paulist, 1978), 228.
9. Fénelon, *Christian Perfection*, 90.

CHAPTER 8: SACRED HISTORY

1. Thomas N. Hart and Kathleen Fischer Hart, *The First Two Years of Marriage* (New York: Paulist, 1983), 15.
2. Cited in Mary Anne McPherson Oliver, *Conjugal Spirituality* (Kansas City: Sheed and Ward, 1994), 26.
3. Ibid., 33.
4. Ibid., 34.
5. Anne Tyler, *A Patchwork Planet* (New York: Knopf, 1998), 218–19.
6. Jerry Jenkins, *Hedges: Loving Your Marriage Enough to Protect It* (Brentwood, TN: Wolgemuth and Hyatt, 1989), 142.

CHAPTER 9: SACRED STRUGGLE

1. Dietrich Bonhoeffer, *Discipleship* (Minneapolis: Fortress, 2003), 158.
2. William Law, *A Serious Call to a Devout and Holy Life* (New York: Paulist, 1978), 290.
3. Kieran Kavanaugh, ed., *John of the Cross: Selected Writings* (New York: Paulist, 1987), 97.
4. Gary and Betsy Ricucci, *Love That Lasts* (Gaithersburg, MD: PDI Communications, 1993), 50.
5. Thomas à Kempis, *Of the Imitation of Christ: Four Books*, ed. Thomas Keble (Oxford: J. Parker, 1866), 106.

6. Otto Piper, *The Biblical View of Sex and Marriage* (New York: Scribner's, 1960), 114–15.
7. Teresa of Avila, *The Interior Castle* (New York: Paulist, 1979), 168.
8. Kavanaugh, ed., *John of the Cross: Selected Writings*, 96.
9. Piper, *Biblical View of Sex and Marriage*, 134.
10. The Lincoln material was gleaned from several works: *Abraham Lincoln, Speeches and Writings, 1832–1858* (New York: Library of America, 1989); Frederick Owen, *Abraham Lincoln: The Man and His Faith* (Wheaton, IL: Tyndale House, 1976); Shelby Foote, *The Civil War: A Narrative, Volumes 1 and 2* (New York: Random House, 1958, 1963); and Dale Carnegie, *How to Win Friends and Influence People* (New York: Simon and Schuster, 1994).

    The Lindbergh material was gleaned from several works: Anne Morrow Lindbergh, *Bring Me a Unicorn* (New York: Harcourt Brace Jovanovich, 1971); Anne Morrow Lindbergh, *Hour of Gold, Hour of Lead* (New York: Harcourt Brace Jovanovich, 1973); Dorothy Herrmann, *Anne Morrow Lindbergh: A Gift for Life* (New York: Ticknor and Fields, 1993); Roxanne Chadwick, *Anne Morrow Lindbergh: Pilot and Poet* (Minneapolis: Lerner, 1987); and A. Scott Berg, *Lindbergh* (New York: Putnam, 1998).
11. Eugene Peterson, *Take and Read* (Grand Rapids: Eerdmans, 1996), 44.

CHAPTER 10: FALLING FORWARD

1. Quoted in Gary and Betsy Ricucci, *Love That Lasts* (Gaithersburg, MD: PDI Communications, 1993), 129.
2. I heard L'Engle recite this poem at a forum I attended in Bellingham, Washington, in 1998.
3. Thomas N. Hart and Kathleen Fischer Hart, *The First Two Years of Marriage* (New York: Paulist, 1983), 19.
4. Evelyn Eaton Whitehead and James D. Whitehead, *A Sense of Sexuality* (New York: Doubleday, 1989), 197.
5. Quoted in Ricucci, *Love That Lasts*, 124.
6. Philip Yancey, *What's So Amazing About Grace?* (Grand Rapids: Zondervan, 1997), 84.
7. Ibid., 280.
8. C. S. Lewis, *Mere Christianity* (New York: Macmillan, 1960), 105–6.

CHAPTER 11: MAKE ME A SERVANT

1. Otto Piper, *The Biblical View of Sex and Marriage* (New York: Scribner's, 1960), 153.
2. This and the following quotes are taken from Robert Draper, "Death Takes a Honeymoon," *GQ*, June 1998, 232–35.
3. Jack Friedman, "Winning at Home," *People*, January 11, 1999.

4. Elizabeth Gilbert, "Losing Is Not an Option," *GQ*, September 1999.
5. Dietrich Bonhoeffer, *The Cost of Discipleship*, rev. ed. (New York: Macmillan, 1963), 149.
6. Thomas N. Hart and Kathleen Fischer Hart, *The First Two Years of Marriage* (New York: Paulist, 1983), 123.
7. Piper, *Biblical View of Sex and Marriage*, 157.
8. Dan Allender and Tremper Longman III, *Intimate Allies* (Wheaton, IL: Tyndale House, 1995), 317–18.
9. See Richard Gillis, "A Lifelong Player: A Clinic with Gary Player," *Golf Today* online, www.golftoday.co.uk/golf_international_mag/features/gary_player_clinic.html (accessed July 31, 2014).
10. Quoted in Evelyn Eaton Whitehead and James D. Whitehead, *A Sense of Sexuality: Christian Love and Intimacy* (New York: Doubleday, 1989), 13.

CHAPTER 12: SEXUAL SAINTS

1. Dan Allender and Tremper Longman III, *Intimate Allies* (Wheaton, IL: Tyndale House, 1995), 228.
2. John Calvin discusses this in his *Institutes of the Christian Religion*, book IV, chap. 12, para. 26.
3. Edmund Leites, *The Puritan Conscience and Modern Sexuality* (New Haven, CT: Yale University Press, 1986), 12–13.
4. Otto Piper, *The Biblical View of Sex and Marriage* (New York: Scribner's, 1960), 79.
5. Nahmanides, *The Holy Letter: A Study in Medieval Jewish Sexual Morality*, trans. Seymour Cohen (New York: Ktav, 1976), 60.
6. Gary and Betsy Ricucci, *Love That Lasts* (Gaithersburg, MD: PDI Communications, 1993), 159.
7. Harold Best, *Music Through the Eyes of Faith* (San Francisco: HarperSanFrancisco, 1993), 40.
8. Thankfulness is a fundamental Christian virtue that is essential for a healthy soul. I discuss this more thoroughly in my book *The Glorious Pursuit* (Colorado Springs: NavPress, 1998).
9. Piper, *Biblical View of Sex and Marriage*, 215.
10. Ibid., 216.
11. Thomas N. Hart, *Living Happily Ever After: Toward a Theology of Christian Marriage* (New York: Paulist, 1979), 44.
12. C. S. Lewis, *The Screwtape Letters* (New York: Macmillan, 1951), 101.
13. Ibid., 102–3.
14. Evelyn Eaton Whitehead and James D. Whitehead, *A Sense of Sexuality* (New York: Doubleday, 1989), 75.
15. See the discussion in Whitehead and Whitehead, *Sense of Sexuality*, 150.

CHAPTER 13: SACRED PRESENCE

1. Evelyn Eaton Whitehead and James D. Whitehead, *Marrying Well: Stages on the Journey of Christian Marriage* (New York: Doubleday, 1983), 187.
2. François de Salignac de La Mothe Fénelon, *Christian Perfection* (Minneapolis: Bethany House, 1975), 4, emphasis added.
3. Brother Lawrence, *The Practice of the Presence of God*, trans. John J. Delaney (New York: Doubleday, 1977), First Conversation.
4. Ibid., Second Conversation.
5. Mary Anne McPherson Oliver, *Conjugal Spirituality* (Kansas City: Sheed and Ward, 1994), 61.
6. Dan Allender and Tremper Longman III, *Intimate Allies* (Wheaton, IL: Tyndale House, 1995), 89.
7. Ibid., 99.
8. Ibid., 101.
9. Ibid., 161.
10. Ibid., 78.

CHAPTER 14: SACRED MISSION

1. Dietrich Bonhoeffer, *Letters and Papers from Prison* (Minneapolis: Fortress, 2010), 460.
2. Francis de Sales, *Thy Will Be Done: Letters to Persons in the World* (Manchester, NH: Sophia Institute, 1995), 20.
3. Ibid., 43.
4. Ibid., 46.
5. Ibid., 60.
6. Ibid., 47.
7. Ibid.
8. Ibid.
9. Ibid., 48.
10. Ibid.
11. Ibid.
12. Count Helmuth James von Moltke, *A German of the Resistance: The Last Letters of Count Helmuth James von Moltke* (London: Oxford University Press, 1946), 51, emphasis added.
13. Quoted in Anatoli Boukreev and G. Weston DeWalt, *The Climb* (New York: St. Martin's, 1997), 142.
14. Otto Piper, *The Biblical View of Sex and Marriage* (New York: Scribner's, 1960), 78.

EPILOGUE: THE HOLY COUPLE

1. Alexander Yelchaninov, "Fragments of a Diary: 1881–1934," in *A Treasury of Russian Spirituality*, ed. G. P. Fedotov (Belmont, MA: Nordland, 1975), 461.

GARY THOMAS

Please understand that Gary is neither qualified nor able to provide counsel via e-mail.

For information about Gary's speaking schedule, visit his website (www.garythomas.com). You can follow him on Twitter (@garyLthomas) or connect with him on Facebook at www.facebook.com/authorgarythomas. To inquire about inviting Gary to your church, please e-mail laura@garythomas.com or fill out a request on his website.

Sacred Marriage Participant's Guide with DVD

What If God Designed Marriage to Make Us Holy More Than to Make Us Happy?

Gary Thomas with Kevin and Sherry Harney

In this six-session small group Bible study, writer and speaker Gary Thomas invites you to see how God can use marriage as a discipline and a motivation to reflect more of the character of Jesus.

Your marriage is much more than a union between you and your spouse; it is a spiritual discipline ideally suited to help you know God more fully and intimately. *Sacred Marriage* shifts the focus from marital enrichment to spiritual enrichment in ways that can help you love your mate more. Whether it is delightful or difficult, your marriage can become a doorway to a closer walk with God.

The DVD features ten- to fifteen-minute teaching vignettes from Gary Thomas. In addition to providing life-changing insights, the Participant's Guide offers discussion questions that will spark meaningful conversations in your group or between you and your spouse, or to simply ponder by yourself. You'll also find self-assessments, activities, and highlights that are created to help you engage deeply and prayerfully with the content of this study.

Sessions include:

1. God's Purpose for Marriage
2. The Refining Power of Marriage
3. The God-Centered Spouse
4. Sacred History
5. Sexual Saints
6. Marriage: The Love Laboratory

Available in stores and online!